The Instant Pot AIR FRYER LID Cookbook:

500 Healthy Instant Pot Air Fryer Lid Recipes for Beginners and Not Only

Tasha Martin

Copyright © 2020 Tasha Martin

All rights reserved

No part of this publication may be reproduced or distributed in any form or by any means, electronic or mechanical, scanning, photocopying, recording or otherwise, without prior written permission from the publisher.

Limit of Liability / Disclaimer of Warranty: The Publisher and the author are not a licensed physician, medical professional or practitioner and offers no medical counseling, treatments or diagnoses. The Publisher and the author make no warranties with respect to the completeness and accuracy of the contents of this work. The content presented herein, has not been evaluated by the U.S. Food and Drug Administration, and it is not intended to diagnose or cure any disease. This book isn't intended as a substitute for medical advice as physicians. Full medical clearance from a licensed physician should be obtained before beginning any diet. The advice and strategies contained herein may not be suitable for every situation. Neither the Publisher nor the author claims no responsibility to any person or entity for any liability, damage or loss caused directly or indirectly as a result of the use, application or interpretation of the information presented in this work.

Instant Pot is a registered trademark of Instant Brands Inc. All other trademarks are the property of their respective owners. The Publisher is not associated with any product or vendor mentioned in this book.

All the nutritional information contained in this book is provided for informational purposes only. The information is based on the specific brands, measurements and ingredients used to make the recipe. Therefore, the nutritional information in this work in no way is intended to be a guarantee of the actual nutritional value of the recipe made by the reader. The publisher and the author will not be responsible for any damages resulting in reliance of the reader on the nutritional information.

The Publisher publishes its books in a variety of electronic, audio and print formats. Some content that appears in print may not be available in electronic or audio books, and vice versa.

ISBN 9798557827232

Table of Contents

Breakfast Recipes 7
- Salmon Scramble 7
- Creamy Mango Mix 7
- Beef and Tomato Bowls 7
- Beef Bowls 7
- Creamy Muffins 7
- Tomato Eggs Mix 7
- Eggplant Frittata 7
- Sausage Bowls 8
- Greek Potato Mix 8
- Beef, Corn and Potato Mix 8
- Turmeric Hash 8
- Chorizo Eggs Mix 8
- Herbed Scramble 8
- Creamy Chives Frittata 8
- Cheddar Omelet 9
- Green Beans and Olives Mix 9
- Cod and Eggs Mix 9
- Pork Puffs 9
- Tuna, Spinach and Tomatoes Bowls 9
- Peas and Eggs Mix 9
- Almond Rice Mix 10
- Coconut Rice Bowls 10
- Rice Pudding 10
- Chili Zucchini Hash 10
- Cheddar Hash Mix 10
- Salmon and Spinach Wraps 10
- Kale and Pumpkin Eggs 10
- Almond Berry Pancakes 10
- Tomato and Quinoa Mix 11
- Avocado and Spinach Salad 11
- Hash Browns and Veggies Mix 11
- Greens and Potato Breakfast Salad 11
- Creamy Turmeric Broccoli Bowls 11
- Mushroom Eggs 11
- Tofu and Scallions Scramble 11
- Mozzarella Peppers and Tomatoes Bowls 12
- Salmon Salad 12
- Mozzarella Spinach Scramble 12
- Creamy Eggplant and Garlic Spread 12
- Olives and Tomato Salad 12
- Almond Pumpkin Rice 12
- Cinnamon Apple Spread 13
- Carrot Pudding 13
- Mint Berries Bowls 13
- Beans and Kale Bowls 13
- Butter Coconut Quinoa 13
- Cumin Avocado Scramble 13
- Cheesy Turkey and Olives Tortillas 13
- Turkey and Corn Bowls 14
- Potato, Carrots and Olives Casserole 14

Side Dish Recipes 15
- Italian Carrots 15
- Dill Carrots 15
- Lime Carrots and Beets 15
- Mushroom Sauté 15
- Chives Eggplants 15
- Curry Quinoa Mix 15
- Lemon Potatoes and Beets Mix 15
- Lime Carrots Mix 15
- Lime Mushrooms 16
- Rosemary Zucchinis Mix 16
- Mozzarella Mushrooms 16
- Rosemary Olives 16
- Masala Zucchinis 16
- Creamy Cabbage Mix 16
- Cilantro Rice Mix 16
- Turmeric Quinoa 16
- Rosemary Mushrooms and Leeks 17
- Spiced Chives Rice 17
- Paprika Sweet Potatoes Mix 17
- Fennel Rice 17
- Indian Rice 17
- Coriander Rice 17
- Lime Leeks and Artichokes Sauté 17
- Balsamic Beans Mix 18
- Chives Green Beans 18
- Mango Rice 18
- Lime Lentils and Chickpeas 18
- Balsamic Corn and Cauliflower 18
- Paprika Carrots Puree 18
- Butter Hot Zucchini Mix 18
- Spiced Butternut 18
- Turmeric Asparagus 19
- Chili Bulgur Mix 19
- Green Peas and Quinoa 19
- Paprika Peas 19
- Citrus Broccoli Mix 19
- Rosemary Beets 19
- Lemon Paprika Green Beans 19
- Balsamic Cabbage 20
- Cilantro Peppers 20
- Creamy Chard Mix 20
- Carrots and Spring Onions Mix 20
- Herbed Eggplant Sauté 20
- Sweet Potatoes and Celery Mix 20
- Chili Rice and Scallions 20
- Turmeric Lentils and Onion Mix 20
- Tomato Broccoli and Corn Mix 21
- Cumin and Parsley Beans Mix 21
- Ginger Chickpeas Mix 21
- Garlic Zucchini 21

Beans and Grains Recipes 22
- Parsley Wild Rice 22
- Nutmeg Quinoa Mix 22
- Chili Beans and Peas 22
- Paprika Bulgur Mix 22
- Coconut Millet 22
- Jalapeno Rice and Calamari 22
- Fennel Quinoa 22
- Curry Chives Rice 22
- Pesto Buttery Rice 23
- Lemon Quinoa 23
- Beans and Mushrooms Mix 23
- Tomato Beans Mix 23
- Beans and Quinoa 23
- Berries Rice 23
- Simple Beans Mix 23
- Chives Beans Mix 24
- Paprika Barley 24
- Quinoa Salad 24
- Spring Onions Beans 24
- Cracked What and Veggies Mix 24
- Turmeric Beans Mix 24
- Soy Bulgur Mix 24
- Ginger Bulgur 24
- Peanuts and Walnuts Rice 25
- Parsley Couscous Mix 25
- Indian Couscous 25
- Lemon Millet Mix 25
- Celery Quinoa Mix 25
- Curry Hot Beans 25
- Spinach Almond Quinoa 25
- Basil Chickpeas 26
- Lentils and Tomatoes Mix 26
- Cranberry Beans Mix 26
- Hot Lentils Mix 26
- Quinoa and Eggplant Tacos 26
- Lentils with Peppers and Zucchinis Mix 26
- Quinoa and Sauce 26
- Cilantro Lentils and Rice Mix 26
- Bok Choy Salad 27
- Chickpeas Salad 27
- Chickpeas and Kale Mix 27
- Chickpeas, Spinach and Bulgur 27

Basil Lime Chickpeas ... 27
Thyme Kidney Beans ... 27
Butter Quinoa Curry ... 27
Bulgur and Peppers Mix ... 28
Black Beans and Onion Mix ... 28
Rosemary Black Beans ... 28
Tomato Quinoa ... 28
Chives Salsa Lentils ... 28

Snacks and Appetizers Recipes ... 29

Cod Bites ... 29
Balsamic Chicken Wings ... 29
Mozzarella Balls ... 29
Mixed Salsa ... 29
Turmeric Cheese Dip ... 29
Minty Greek Dip ... 29
Shrimp Platter ... 29
Kale and Yogurt Dip ... 30
Potato Chips ... 30
Masala Shrimp Dip ... 30
Chives Broccoli Spread ... 30
Coated Broccoli Bites ... 30
Yogurt Dip ... 30
Tofu Bites ... 30
Balsamic Dip ... 31
Creamy Chickpeas Spread ... 31
Garlic Olives Dip ... 31
Tabasco Carrot Bites ... 31
Zucchini and Capers Dip ... 31
Tomato Salsa ... 31
Paprika Sausage Bites ... 31
Shrimp Bowls ... 31
Cauliflower Dip ... 32
Balsamic Mango and Corn Salsa ... 32
Shallots Dip ... 32
Apple Bites ... 32
Corn and Olives Salsa ... 32
Hot Ginger and Chili Dip ... 32
Turmeric Cream Dip ... 32
Cranberry and Tomato Salsa ... 33
Greek Cucumber and Onions Dip ... 33
Eggplant, Corn and Tomato Salsa ... 33
Chili Sprouts Bites ... 33
Cayenne Leeks Spread ... 33
Apple Salsa ... 33
Fennel Salsa ... 33
Corn Dip ... 34
Corn and Radish Salsa ... 34
Shallots and Olives Dip ... 34
Creamy Lime Dip ... 34
Chicken and Peppers Dip ... 34
Beet and Tomatoes Salsa ... 34
Carrot Chips ... 34
Zucchini and Spring Onions Cakes ... 35
Mushroom, Olives and Beets Bowls ... 35
Chili Mushroom Meatballs ... 35
Avocado and Cucumber Bowls ... 35
Wrapped Carrot Bites ... 35
Bacon Corn Dip ... 35
Corn and Avocado Spread ... 35
Avocado Balls ... 36
Shrimp and Avocado Salsa ... 36
Cashew and Lemon Dip ... 36
Salmon Salad ... 36
Salmon Balls ... 36
Chicken Meatballs ... 36
Ginger and Shallots Dip ... 37
Asparagus Salsa ... 37
Radish Bites ... 37
Olives and Yogurt Dip ... 37

Fish and Seafood Recipes ... 38

Herbed Cod ... 38
Orange Salmon ... 38
Coriander Salmon ... 38
Chives Citrus Shrimp ... 38
Lime Cod Mix ... 38
Dill Tilapia ... 38
Balsamic Salmon ... 38
Lime Shrimp ... 39
Fennel Salmon ... 39
Chili Salmon ... 39
Shrimp and Beets ... 39
Mustard Tuna ... 39
Salmon and Spring Onions Sauce ... 39
Chives Shrimp ... 39
Rosemary Salmon and Potatoes ... 39
Lime Cod and Fennel ... 40
Tuna Steaks and Lime Sauce ... 40
Cilantro Shrimp Mix ... 40
Balsamic Sea Bass Mix ... 40
Rosemary Shrimp and Beets ... 40
Paprika Lemon Sea Bass ... 40
Oregano Cod and Green Beans ... 40
Herbed Shrimp ... 41
Cod and Herbed Roasted Peppers ... 41
Paprika Shrimp and Radishes ... 41
Parmesan Lemon Shrimp ... 41
Black Cod and Veggies ... 41
Lime Cod and Zucchinis ... 41
Shrimp with Peppers and Spinach ... 41
Lime Salmon and Sprouts ... 42
Minty Shrimp and Pine Nuts Mix ... 42
Turmeric Cod and Asparagus ... 42
Rosemary Trout ... 42
Garlic Mackerel ... 42
Cilantro Trout Mix ... 42
Indian Sea Bass ... 42
Butter Shrimp and Rice ... 43
Creamy Trout and Okra ... 43
Cilantro Mussels ... 43
Cod with Eggplants and Tomato Sauce ... 43
Lemongrass and Orange Shrimp ... 43
Coconut Trout ... 43
Balsamic Tuna and Onions ... 43
Cod with Spring Onions and Mango ... 44
Thyme Sea Bass ... 44
Tuna and Rhubarb ... 44
Garlic Rosemary Cod Mix ... 44
Trout and Balsamic Mushrooms Mix ... 44
Parsley Trout ... 44
Smoked Shrimp Mix ... 44
Shrimp and Chives Sauce ... 45
Coriander Sea Bass and Broccoli ... 45
Orange Snapper ... 45
Cod with Caraway Chard ... 45
Cod and Bok Choy ... 45
Herbed Tuna ... 45
Tuna with Tomatoes and Pineapples ... 45
Basil Tuna ... 46
Mackerel and Radish ... 46
Sea Bass and Rosemary Tomatoes ... 46

Poultry Recipes ... 47

Cheesy Chicken Bake ... 47
Turkey and Herbed Green Beans ... 47
Chicken with Peppers and Sauce ... 47
Paprika Chicken ... 47
Garlic Chicken Thighs ... 47
Turmeric Chicken Wings ... 47
Creamy Oregano Turkey ... 47
Orange Turkey Mix ... 48
Lemon Chicken and Asparagus ... 48
Herbed Turkey and Olives ... 48
Chicken and Walnuts ... 48
Creamy Chicken ... 48
Lemon Chicken ... 48
Basil Turkey and Spinach ... 48
Cayenne Chicken Wings ... 49
Chicken with Soy Sauce ... 49

Balsamic Chili Chicken ... 49
Cinnamon Chicken ... 49
Masala Turkey and Okra ... 49
Cilantro Turkey Mix ... 49
Buttery Turkey ... 49
Coriander Turkey ... 50
Cumin Chicken ... 50
Turkey with Onion and Fennel ... 50
Chicken with Artichokes ... 50
Parsley Turkey Mix ... 50
Coconut Chicken and Almonds ... 50
Lime Chicken and Radishes ... 50
Chicken and Cilantro Tomatoes ... 51
Turmeric Lemon Turkey ... 51
Chicken and Butter Mushrooms ... 51
Rosemary Turkey and Corn ... 51
Turkey with Garlic Quinoa ... 51
Chicken and Veggies Mix ... 51
Chicken and Tomato Sprouts ... 52
Chicken and Wine Sauce ... 52
Turkey and Balsamic Broccoli ... 52
Chicken with Chili Kale and Sauce ... 52
Turkey with Peppers and Bok Choy ... 52
Italian Turkey Mix ... 52
Chicken and Rice ... 52
Salsa Chicken ... 53
Spiced Duck Mix ... 53
Creamy Turkey Mix ... 53
Rosemary Duck Mix ... 53
Cardamom Chives Chicken ... 53
Lime Duck with Rhubarb ... 53
Peppercorn and Coriander Chicken ... 53
Duck and Mushrooms Mix ... 54
Balsamic Duck and Peppers ... 54
Parsley Duck and Zucchini Mix ... 54
Curry Turkey ... 54
Turkey and Lemon Beans ... 54
Mint Buttery Duck ... 54
Chicken and Creamy Sauce ... 55
Chicken, Kale and Tomatoes Salad ... 55
Duck and Creamy Berries ... 55
Turkey with Lime Avocado ... 55
Garlic Lime Turkey Mix ... 55
Cumin Duck Mix ... 55
Chicken and Ginger Beets ... 55

Meat Recipes ... 57
Pork and Tomato Peppers ... 57
Dill Lamb Mix ... 57
Rosemary Pork Chops ... 57
Spiced Pork Chops ... 57
Paprika Pork Chops ... 57
Turmeric Pork ... 57
Hot Lamb ... 57
Creamy Lamb ... 57
Masala Pork Chops ... 58
Mustard Garlic Lamb ... 58
Balsamic Beef and Eggplant Mix ... 58
Herbed Lamb and Green Beans ... 58
Pork and Tomato Spinach Mix ... 58
Pork and Sauce ... 58
Pork with Tomato Radishes ... 58
Balsamic Pork and Cabbage ... 59
Italian Pork with Tomatoes and Peppers ... 59
Cocoa and Rosemary Lamb Chops ... 59
Pork and Red Wine Sauce ... 59
Ginger Pork Mix ... 59
Beef Stew ... 59
Lemon Beef Mix ... 59
Almond Beef Mix ... 60
Pork and Garlic Broccoli ... 60
Beef and Coconut Mushrooms ... 60
Beef and Onions Stew ... 60
Pork with Tomato and Fennel Mix ... 60
Beef with Scallions and Kale ... 60

Pork and Passata Mix ... 60
Butter Beef and Chili Potatoes ... 61
Lamb and Onion Stew ... 61
Herbed Beef with Tomatoes and Okra ... 61
Lamb with Tomatoes ... 61
Basil Lamb ... 61
Cilantro Beef Mix ... 61
Basil Lamb Stew ... 62
Parsley Beef and Carrots Stew ... 62
Lamb and Tomato Artichokes Stew ... 62
Curry Beef and Spinach ... 62
Cumin Beef and Garlic ... 62
Lemon Chili Lamb ... 62
Mint and Cilantro Lamb Chops ... 62
Lamb with Shallots Sauce ... 62
Lamb with Rosemary Apples ... 63
Beef and Tomato Olives Sauce ... 63
Lamb with Lime Endives ... 63
Mexican Lamb Mix ... 63
Green Curry Beef ... 63
Beef with Balsamic Sun-dried Tomatoes ... 63
Coriander Lamb Cutlets ... 64
Herbed Lamb Balls ... 64
Lime and Cumin Lamb Mix ... 64
Lamb with Spring Onions and Corn ... 64
Beef and Squash ... 64
Masala Beef Mix ... 64
Creamy Marjoram Pork ... 64
Creamy Spiced Lamb ... 65
Yogurt Beef Mix ... 65
Beef and Mustard Fennel ... 65
Lamb Meatloaf ... 65
Pork Chops with Corn ... 65
Beef and Paprika Broccoli ... 65
Cajun Chili Beef ... 65
Pork with Sprouts ... 66
Pork Chops with Turmeric Sauce ... 66
Lamb and Spinach Mix ... 66
Beef and Cucumber Mix ... 66
Nutmeg Pork and Sour Cream Mix ... 66
Nutmeg and Chili Beef ... 66
Lamb with Dill Asparagus ... 66

Vegetable Recipes ... 68
Masala Artichokes ... 68
Chili Beet ... 68
Yogurt Potatoes Mix ... 68
Chili Tomatoes ... 68
Garlic Potato Mix ... 68
Creamy Artichokes ... 68
Cayenne Beets ... 68
Mustard Broccoli ... 68
Butter Cauliflower ... 69
Coriander Broccoli and Beets ... 69
Paprika Asparagus ... 69
Parmesan Turmeric Potatoes ... 69
Garlic Broccoli Mix ... 69
Lime Carrots ... 69
Bell Peppers and Tomato Sauce ... 69
Masala Carrots ... 70
Beets and Cream Sauce ... 70
Chard Sauté ... 70
Rosemary Mushrooms Mix ... 70
Salsa Kale ... 70
Chives Brussels Sprouts ... 70
Lime Tomatoes ... 70
Coriander Zucchini ... 71
Balsamic and Garlic Green Beans ... 71
Lime Avocado Mix ... 71
Chili Black Beans ... 71
Simple Tomatoes and Peppers ... 71
Cilantro Sweet Potatoes ... 71
Parsley Sprouts ... 71
Coriander Tomatoes ... 72
Lime and Coriander Green Beans ... 72

Chili Tomato and Onions	72
Kale and Corn Salad	72
Garlic Paprika Carrots	72
Creamy Green Beans	72
Garlic and Lime Corn	72
Green Beans and Spinach Salad	73
Red Cabbage Sauté	73
Cabbage and Spring Onions Sauté	73
Butter Kale	73
Coriander and Butter Fennel	73
Oregano Kale	73
Almond Endives	73
Mozzarella Beets	74
Mushrooms with Potatoes and Sauce	74
Herbed Corn and Fennel	74
Greens Sauté	74
Chili Mustard Greens	74
Mint Fennel Mix	74
Nutmeg and Lemon Potatoes	74

Dessert Recipes 76

Cocoa Cupcakes	76
Avocado Vanilla Cookies	76
Creamy Ghee Bars	76
Lime Pineapple Bars	76
Squash Coconut Bread	76
Lemon Butter Cream	76
Almond Berry Cake	76
Almond Donuts	77
Coconut Cookies	77
Ginger Almond Cream	77
Butter Berry Muffins	77
Lemon Apple Jam	77
Vanilla Cream	77
Butter Cream	77
Blackberry Jam	78
Avocado and Blueberries Cream	78
Brownies	78
Cocoa Ghee Cream	78
Coconut Cream	78
Carrot Cream Cheese Bars	78
Pecan Almond Bars	78
Chocolate Cream	79
Walnut Bars	79
Yogurt Cream	79
Coconut Cream Cheese Pudding	79
Rhubarb Almond Cake	79
Mango Bowls	79
Rhubarb Coconut Cream	79
Lime Almond Cake	80
Apple Bowls	80
Mango Compote	80
Plums and Cocoa Cream	80
Cocoa Bombs	80
Coconut Berry Cake	80
Pineapple Coconut Pudding	80
Berry Compote	81
Lime Strawberry Compote	81
Pineapple and Coconut Cake	81
Chia Pudding	81
Plum and Coconut Cream	81
Pineapple Stew	81
Dates Bowls	81
Rice Bowls	81
Dates Butter Bars	82
Coconut Rice Pudding	82
Avocado Bowls	82
Cinnamon Apple Cake	82
Cinnamon Cream	82
Cheesy Mango Mix	82
Cherries and Mango Mix	82

Breakfast Recipes

Salmon Scramble

Prep time: 10 minutes | **Cooking:** 15 minutes | **Servings:** 4

Ingredients:

- 1 cup smoked salmon fillets, boneless and cubed
- 8 eggs, whisked
- 1 red onion, chopped
- Cooking spray
- ½ teaspoon sweet paprika
- ½ teaspoon turmeric powder
- ½ cup heavy cream
- 1 tablespoon chives, chopped
- Salt and black pepper to the taste

Directions:

1. Grease the multi level air fryer pan with cooking spray and combine all the ingredients inside.
2. Place the pan into the instant pot.
3. Seal the instant pot with the air fryer lid and cook on Bake mode at 380 degrees F for 15 minutes.
4. Divide between plates and serve for breakfast.

Nutrition:

calories 170, fat 2, fiber 2, carbs 12, protein 4

Creamy Mango Mix

Prep time: 5 minutes | **Cooking:** 10 minutes | **Servings:** 4

Ingredients:

- 1 cup mango, peeled and cubed
- 1 cup heavy cream
- 2 tablespoons sugar
- Juice of 1 lime
- 2 teaspoons vanilla extract

Directions:

1. Place all the ingredients in the multi level air fryer basket.
2. Place the basket in the instant pot.
3. Seal the instant pot with the air fryer lid, cook everything on Bake mode at 370 degrees F for 10 minutes, divide into bowls and serve for breakfast.

Nutrition:

calories 170, fat 6, fiber 5, carbs 11, protein 2

Beef and Tomato Bowls

Prep time: 5 minutes | **Cooking:** 20 minutes | **Servings:** 4

Ingredients:

- 1 pound beef stew meat, ground
- 1 red onion, chopped
- 1 teaspoon chili powder
- 8 eggs, whisked
- A drizzle of olive oil
- ½ cup canned tomatoes, crushed
- 1 red chili pepper, chopped
- 2 tablespoons parsley, chopped
- Salt and white pepper to the taste

Directions:

1. Place all the ingredients in the multi level air fryer's pan.
2. Place the pan in the instant pot.
3. Seal the instant pot with air fryer lid.
4. Cook on Air fry mode at 400 degrees F for 20 minutes.
5. Divide into bowls and serve for breakfast.

Nutrition:

calories 200, fat 6, fiber 1, carbs 11, protein 3

Beef Bowls

Prep time: 5 minutes | **Cooking:** 20 minutes | **Servings:** 4

Ingredients:

- 1 pound beef stew meat, ground
- 1 tablespoon olive oil
- ½ cup mushrooms, sliced
- 1 cup gold potatoes, cubed
- 1 red onion, chopped
- 1 garlic clove, minced
- ½ cup cherry tomatoes, halved
- 4 eggs, whisked
- Salt and black pepper to the taste

Directions:

1. Place the meat potatoes, onion and mushrooms in the multi level air fryer's pan.
2. Place the pan in the instant pot.
3. Seal the instant pot with air fryer lid and cook on Air Fry mode for 5 minutes.
4. Add the other ingredients, cook for 15 minutes more, divide between plates and serve for breakfast.

Nutrition:

calories 160, fat 2, fiber 5, carbs 12, protein 9

Creamy Muffins

Prep time: 5 minutes | **Cooking:** 20 minutes | **Servings:** 4

Ingredients:

- 3 eggs, whisked
- 1 tablespoon butter, melted
- 1 cup carrots, peeled and grated
- 1 cup heavy cream
- ½ cup almond flour
- 1 cup almond milk
- Cooking spray
- 1 tablespoon baking powder

Directions:

1. In a bowl, combine the eggs with the butter, carrots and the other ingredients except the cooking spray, and whisk well.
2. Grease a muffin pan that fits the multi level air fryer with the cooking spray and divide the carrots mix inside.
3. Put the pan in the instant pot and seal with the air fryer lid.
4. Cook on Bake mode at 392 degrees F for 20 minutes.
5. Serve the muffins for breakfast.

Nutrition:

calories 190, fat 12, fiber 2, carbs 11, protein 5

Tomato Eggs Mix

Prep time: 5 minutes | **Cooking:** 20 minutes | **Servings:** 4

Ingredients:

- 8 eggs, whisked
- 1 cup cherry tomatoes, halved
- ½ teaspoon sweet paprika
- ½ cup cheddar cheese, shredded
- 1 tablespoon chives, chopped
- A pinch of salt and black pepper
- ¼ cup coconut milk
- 1 tablespoon parsley, chopped

Directions:

1. In a bowl, combine the eggs with the tomatoes, paprika and the other ingredients and whisk well.
2. Pour this into the multi level air fryer pan, introduce the pan in the instant pot and seal with the air fryer lid.
3. Cook on Air fry mode at 350 degrees F for 20 minutes.
4. Divide the mix into bowls and serve for breakfast.

Nutrition:

calories 210, fat 4, fiber 2, carbs 12, protein 9

Eggplant Frittata

Prep time: 10 minutes | **Cooking:** 20 minutes | **Servings:** 4

Ingredients:

- 1 pound eggplant, cubed
- 1 cup heavy cream
- 8 eggs, whisked
- ½ teaspoon turmeric powder
- ½ teaspoon coriander, ground
- ½ teaspoon nutmeg, ground
- 1 tablespoon chives, chopped
- Salt and black pepper to the taste
- ½ teaspoon garlic powder

Breakfast Recipes | 7

- ½ teaspoon Italian seasoning

Directions:
1. Place all the ingredients in the multi level air fryer's pan.
2. Put the pan in the instant pot and seal with the air fryer lid
3. Cook on Bake mode at 400 degrees F for 20 minutes.
4. Divide between plates and serve.

Nutrition:
calories 251, fat 11, fiber 4, carbs 8, protein 7

Sausage Bowls

Prep time: 10 minutes | **Cooking:** 25 minutes | **Servings:** 4

Ingredients:
- 1 tablespoon olive oil
- 2 cups corn
- 1 cup sausages, sliced
- 1 red onion, chopped
- 8 eggs, whisked
- 1 teaspoon chili powder
- ½ cup green bell pepper, chopped
- 1 tablespoon chives, chopped
- 1 tablespoon dill, chopped
- 1 teaspoon thyme, chopped
- Salt and black pepper to the taste
- ½ cup heavy cream

Directions:
1. Put the sausages and onion in the multi level air fryer's basket.
2. Put the basket into the instant pot and seal the instant pot with the air fryer lid.
3. Cook on Air fry mode at 350 degrees F for 5 minutes.
4. Add the corn, eggs and the other ingredients, toss, cook on Bake mode for 20 minutes more.
5. Divide into bowls and serve for breakfast.

Nutrition:
calories 251, fat 6, fiber 9, carbs 14, protein 7

Greek Potato Mix

Prep time: 5 minutes | **Cooking:** 20 minutes | **Servings:** 4

Ingredients:
- 1 pound gold potatoes, peeled cubed
- 4 eggs, whisked
- ½ teaspoon turmeric powder
- 1 tablespoon rosemary, chopped
- 1 tablespoon olive oil
- Salt and black pepper to the taste
- 1 cup Greek yogurt

Directions:
1. Put the potatoes in the multi level air fryer's basket.
2. Put the basket in the instant pot and seal with the air fryer lid.
3. Cook on Air fry mode at 360 degrees F for 5 minutes.
4. Add the eggs mixed with the other ingredients, seal with the air fryer lid again and cook for 15 minutes more.
5. Divide into bowls and serve for breakfast.

Nutrition:
calories 251, fat 7, fiber 4, carbs 14, protein 7

Beef, Corn and Potato Mix

Prep time: 10 minutes | **Cooking:** 20 minutes | **Servings:** 4

Ingredients:
- 1 pound beef stew meat, ground
- 1 tablespoon olive oil
- 1 cup corn
- 1 red onion, chopped
- 2 eggs, whisked
- ½ teaspoon chili powder
- ½ teaspoon sweet paprika
- 1 cup canned tomatoes, crushed
- Salt and black pepper to the taste

Directions:
1. Put the beef and onions in the multi level air fryer's pan.
2. Put the pan in the instant pot and seal with the air fryer lid.
3. Cook on Air fry mode at 400 degrees F for 10 minutes.
4. Add the other ingredients, seal with air fryer lid again and cook on Bake mode for another 10 minutes.
5. Serve for breakfast.

Nutrition:
calories 181, fat 11, fiber 1, carbs 14, protein 4

Turmeric Hash

Prep time: 5 minutes | **Cooking:** 20 minutes | **Servings:** 4

Ingredients:
- 1 pound hash browns
- 1 cup pearl onions, peeled and halved
- 8 eggs, whisked
- 1 tablespoon butter, melted
- 1 teaspoon turmeric powder
- A pinch of salt and black pepper
- 1 cup buttermilk

Directions:
1. Put all the ingredients in the multi level air fryer's pan and mix them.
2. Put the pan in the instant pot and seal with the air fryer lid.
3. Cook on Bake mode at 400 degrees F for 20 minutes and serve.

Nutrition:
calories 202, fat 11, fiber 9, carbs 14, protein 7

Chorizo Eggs Mix

Prep time: 5 minutes | **Cooking:** 20 minutes | **Servings:** 4

Ingredients:
- 4 eggs, whisked
- 1 cup chorizo, chopped
- 1 cup broccoli florets
- 1 teaspoon sweet paprika
- 1 tablespoon olive oil
- 1 tablespoon cilantro, chopped
- ½ cup mozzarella cheese, shredded
- Salt and black pepper to the taste

Directions:
1. Put the chorizo in the multi level air fryer's pan.
2. Put the pan in the instant pot and seal with the air fryer lid.
3. Cook on Air fry mode at 400 degrees F for 5 minutes.
4. Add the other ingredients, toss, cook for 15 minutes more, divide into bowls and serve.

Nutrition:
calories 270, fat 6, fiber 9, carbs 12, protein 7

Herbed Scramble

Prep time: 5 minutes | **Cooking:** 15 minutes | **Servings:** 4

Ingredients:
- 1 tablespoon avocado oil
- 8 eggs, whisked
- 1 teaspoon coriander, ground
- 1 tablespoon oregano, chopped
- ½ teaspoon chili powder
- Salt and black pepper to the taste

Directions:
1. Grease the multi level air fryer's pan with the oil and combine all the ingredients inside.
2. Put the pan in the instant pot and seal with the air fryer lid.
3. Cook on Bake mode at 350 degrees F for 15 minutes and serve.

Nutrition:
calories 216, fat 11, fiber 6, carbs 9, protein 4

Creamy Chives Frittata

Prep time: 5 minutes | **Cooking:** 20 minutes | **Servings:** 4

Ingredients:
- 8 eggs, whisked
- 1 tablespoon avocado oil

- 1 cup red onion, chopped
- 1 teaspoon chili powder
- 1 red bell pepper, chopped
- Salt and black pepper to the taste
- ½ cup heavy cream
- 1 tablespoon chives, chopped

Directions:
1. In a bowl, combine the eggs with the chili, pepper, salt, pepper, cream and chives and whisk well.
2. Put the onions in the multi level air fryer 's pan, put the pan in the instant pot and seal with the air fryer lid.
3. Cook on Air fry mode at 350 degrees F for 5 minutes.
4. Add the eggs mixture, spread and cook for 15 minutes more.
5. Divide between plates and serve for breakfast.

Nutrition:
calories 271, fat 11, fiber 7, carbs 14, protein 6

Cheddar Omelet
Prep time: 5 minutes | **Cooking:** 15 minutes | **Servings:** 4

Ingredients:
- 1 tablespoon butter, melted
- 8 eggs, whisked
- 1 teaspoon turmeric powder
- 1 cup cheddar cheese, shredded
- Salt and black pepper to the taste

Directions:
1. Grease the multi level air fryer's pan with the butter and combine all the ingredients inside.
2. Put the pan in the instant pot and seal with the air fryer lid.
3. Cook on Bake mode at 370 degrees F for 15 minutes and serve for breakfast.

Nutrition:
calories 200, fat 3, fiber 5, carbs 12, protein 4

Green Beans and Olives Mix
Prep time: 10 minutes | **Cooking:** 15 minutes | **Servings:** 4

Ingredients:
- 4 eggs, whisked
- 1 tablespoon avocado oil
- ½ pound green beans, trimmed and halved
- 1 red onion, chopped
- 1 cup black olives, pitted and halved
- Salt and black pepper to the taste

Directions:
1. Grease the multi level air fryer's pan with the oil and combine all the ingredients inside.
2. Put the pan in the instant pot and seal with the air fryer lid.
3. Cook on Broil mode at 320 degrees F for 15 minutes, divide into bowls and serve for breakfast.

Nutrition:
calories 212, fat 8, fiber 6, carbs 8, protein 6

Cod and Eggs Mix
Prep time: 5 minutes | **Cooking:** 20 minutes | **Servings:** 4

Ingredients:
- 1 tablespoon olive oil
- 1 red onion, chopped
- 8 eggs, whisked
- 1 green bell pepper, chopped
- 1 red onion, chopped
- 1 cup cod fillets, boneless and cubed
- 1 tablespoon chives, chopped
- A pinch of salt and black pepper

Directions:
1. Combine all the ingredients in the multi level air fryer's pan and put the pan in the instant pot.
2. Seal with the air fryer lid and cook everything on Bake mode at 350 degrees F for 20 minutes.
3. Divide between plates and serve.

Nutrition:
calories 230, fat 12, fiber 7, carbs 14, protein 5

Pork Puffs
Prep time: 5 minutes | **Cooking:** 20 minutes | **Servings:** 4

Ingredients:
- 1 puff pastry sheet
- ½ pound pork stew meat, ground and browned
- 1 tablespoon chives, chopped
- 1 egg, whisked
- ½ cup mozzarella, shredded
- A pinch of salt and black pepper
- Cooking spray

Directions:
1. Roll out puff pastry on a working surface, cut it in squares, divide the meat combined with the other ingredients except the cooking spray on half of them, top with the other halves and seal the edges.
2. Place the puffs in the multi level air fryer's basket.
3. Put the basket in the instant pot and seal with the air fryer lid.
4. Cook on Air fry mode at 370 degrees F for 20 minutes.
5. Divide the patties between plates and serve for breakfast.

Nutrition:
calories 212, fat 12, fiber 7, carbs 14, protein 8

Tuna, Spinach and Tomatoes Bowls
Prep time: 10 minutes | **Cooking:** 10 minutes | **Servings:** 4

Ingredients:
- 2 cups canned tuna, drained and flaked
- 1 red onion, chopped
- 1 cup baby spinach
- 1 cup cherry tomatoes, halved
- 1 cup corn
- 1 cup black olives, pitted and halved
- 1 tablespoon chives, chopped
- 1 tablespoons lime juice
- A pinch of salt and black pepper

Directions:
1. Combine all the ingredients in the multi level air fryer's pan.
2. Put the pan in the instant pot and seal with the air fryer lid.
3. Cook on Air fry mode at 350 degrees F for 10 minutes, divide into bowls and serve.

Nutrition:
calories 212, fat 8, fiber 7, carbs 8, protein 6

Peas and Eggs Mix
Prep time: 5 minutes | **Cooking:** 15 minutes | **Servings:** 4

Ingredients:
- ½ pound baby peas
- 1 cup cherry tomatoes, halved
- 8 eggs, whisked
- 1 tablespoon olive oil
- 1 red onion, chopped
- 1 teaspoon chili powder
- ½ cup heavy cream
- 1 tablespoon chives, chopped
- Salt and black pepper to the taste

Directions:
1. Heat up a pan with the oil over medium heat, add the onion and chili powder and cook for 5 minutes.
2. Transfer this to the multi level air fryer's pan and combine with the other ingredients.
3. Put the pan in the instant pot and seal with the air fryer lid.
4. Cook on Bake mode at 350 degrees F for 10 minutes.
5. Divide into bowls and serve for breakfast.

Nutrition:
calories 212, fat 9, fiber 4, carbs 13, protein 7

Almond Rice Mix

Prep time: 10 minutes | **Cooking:** 20 minutes | **Servings:** 4

Ingredients:

- 1 cup cauliflower rice
- 2 cups almond milk
- 1 teaspoon vanilla extract
- ½ teaspoon nutmeg, ground
- ½ cup raisins

Directions:

1. Put all the ingredients in the multi level air fryer's pan.
2. Put the pan in the instant pot and seal with the air fryer lid.
3. Cook on Bake mode at 360 degrees F for 20 minutes.
4. Divide into bowls and serve for breakfast.

Nutrition:

calories 161, fat 7, fiber 6, carbs 9, protein 6

Coconut Rice Bowls

Prep time: 5 minutes | **Cooking:** 20 minutes | **Servings:** 4

Ingredients:

- 1 cup white rice
- 1 cup pears, cored and cubed
- 2 cups coconut milk
- 2 tablespoons sugar
- 1 tablespoon butter, soft
- ½ teaspoon cinnamon powder

Directions:

1. Put all the ingredients in the multi level air fryer's pan.
2. Put the pan in the instant pot and seal with the air fryer lid.
3. Cook on Bake mode at 370 degrees F for 20 minutes.
4. Divide into bowls and serve.

Nutrition:

calories 210, fat 9, fiber 11, carbs 12, protein 5

Rice Pudding

Prep time: 5 minutes | **Cooking:** 20 minutes | **Servings:** 4

Ingredients:

- 1 cup white rice
- 2 cups coconut milk
- 1 cup blackberries
- 2 tablespoons sugar
- 1 teaspoon vanilla extract

Directions:

1. Put all the ingredients in the multi level air fryer's pan.
2. Put the pan in the instant pot and seal with the air fryer lid.
3. Cook on Bake mode at 360 degrees F for 20 minutes.
4. Divide into bowls and serve for breakfast.

Nutrition:

calories 201, fat 6, fiber 8, carbs 19, protein 6

Chili Zucchini Hash

Prep time: 5 minutes | **Cooking:** 20 minutes | **Servings:** 4

Ingredients:

- 1 red onion, chopped
- 1 pound hash browns
- 1 cup zucchinis, cubed
- 8 eggs, whisked
- 1 teaspoon chili powder
- 1 teaspoon turmeric powder
- 1 tablespoon olive oil
- ½ cup mozzarella, shredded

Directions:

1. Put all the ingredients in the multi level air fryer's pan.
2. Put the pan in the instant pot and seal with the air fryer lid.
3. Cook on Air fry mode at 360 degrees F for 20 minutes.
4. Divide the mix between plates and serve for breakfast.

Nutrition:

calories 202, fat 12, fiber 4, carbs 7, protein 2

Cheddar Hash Mix

Prep time: 6 minutes | **Cooking:** 20 minutes | **Servings:** 4

Ingredients:

- 8 eggs, whisked
- ½ pound hash browns
- 1 teaspoon chili powder
- ½ teaspoon sweet paprika
- ½ cup cheddar cheese, shredded
- 1 tablespoon tarragon, chopped
- Salt and black pepper to the taste
- ¼ cup heavy cream

Directions:

1. Put all the ingredients in the multi level air fryer's pan.
2. Put the pan in the instant pot and seal with the air fryer lid.
3. Cook on Air Fry mode at 370 degrees F for 20 minutes.
4. Divide between plates and serve for breakfast.

Nutrition:

calories 251, fat 8, fiber 4, carbs 15, protein 4

Salmon and Spinach Wraps

Prep time: 5 minutes | **Cooking:** 10 minutes | **Servings:** 4

Ingredients:

- 4 corn tortillas
- 2 cups smoked salmon, boneless and cut into strips
- 1 cup black olives, pitted and halved
- 1 cup baby spinach
- 1 cup cherry tomatoes, halved
- 4 tablespoons mayonnaise
- 2 tablespoons mustard

Directions:

1. Spread the mayonnaise and the mustard on each tortilla, place them in your multi level air fryers' basket.
2. Put the basket in the instant pot and seal with the air fryer lid.
3. Heat them up on Air fry mode at 400 degrees F for 5 minutes.
4. Divide the salmon, spinach and the rest of the ingredients on the tortillas, roll them, place in the multi level air fryer basket again and cook them on Air fry mode at 400 degrees F for 5 minutes more.
5. Divide everything between plates and serve for breakfast right away.

Nutrition:

calories 212, fat 8, fiber 8, carbs 9, protein 4

Kale and Pumpkin Eggs

Prep time: 5 minutes | **Cooking:** 15 minutes | **Servings:** 4

Ingredients:

- 1 tablespoon olive oil
- 8 eggs, whisked
- ½ teaspoon coriander, ground
- 1 teaspoon chili powder
- 2 cups kale, torn
- A pinch of salt and black pepper
- 2 tablespoons pumpkin seeds
- 1 tablespoon chives, chopped

Directions:

1. Put all the ingredients in the multi level air fryer's pan.
2. Put the pan in the instant pot and seal with the air fryer lid.
3. Cook on Air fry mode at 360 degrees F for 15 minutes.
4. Divide between plates and serve for breakfast.

Nutrition:

calories 162, fat 4, fiber 7, carbs 9, protein 4

Almond Berry Pancakes

Prep time: 10 minutes | **Cooking:** 15 minutes | **Servings:** 4

Ingredients:

- 2 cups almond flour
- 1 cup almond milk
- 2 tablespoons sugar
- 2 teaspoons baking soda
- ¼ teaspoon vanilla extract
- 2 eggs, whisked

- 1 cup strawberries, chopped
- Cooking spray

Directions:
1. In a bowl, combine the flour with the milk and the other ingredients except the cooking spray and whisk well.
2. Grease your multi level air fryer's pan with the cooking spray, pour ¼ of the batter and spread.
3. Put the pan in the instant pot and seal with the air fryer lid.
4. Cook on Air fry mode at 360 degrees F for 3 minutes on each side and transfer to a plate.
5. Repeat with the rest of the batter and serve the pancakes for breakfast.

Nutrition:
calories 172, fat 4, fiber 4, carbs 8, protein 3

Tomato and Quinoa Mix

Prep time: 5 minutes | **Cooking:** 15 minutes | **Servings:** 4

Ingredients:
- 1 tablespoon olive oil
- 1 cup quinoa
- 2 cups veggie stock
- ½ cup corn
- 1 tablespoon chives, chopped
- 1 cup cherry tomatoes, halved
- ½ cup kalamata olives, pitted and halved
- 2 tablespoons lime juice
- 1 cup baby spinach

Directions:
1. Put all the ingredients in the multi level air fryer's pan.
2. Put the pan in the instant pot and seal with the air fryer lid.
3. Cook on Air fry mode at 370 degrees F for 15 minutes.
4. Divide into bowls and serve.

Nutrition:
calories 209, fat 7, fiber 6, carbs 8, protein 4

Avocado and Spinach Salad

Prep time: 10 minutes | **Cooking:** 10 minutes | **Servings:** 4

Ingredients:
- 2 cups avocado, peeled, pitted and cubed
- 1 cup black olives, pitted and halved
- 1 cup cherry tomatoes, halved
- ½ teaspoon sweet paprika
- 1 cup baby spinach
- Juice of 1 lime
- A drizzle of olive oil
- Salt and black pepper to the taste

Directions:
1. Combine all the ingredients in the multi level air fryer's pan.
2. Put the pan in the instant pot and seal with the air fryer lid.
3. Cook on Air fry mode at 330 degrees F for 10 minutes, divide into bowls and serve.

Nutrition:
calories 189, fat 3, fiber 7, carbs 12, protein 5

Hash Browns and Veggies Mix

Prep time: 10 minutes | **Cooking:** 20 minutes | **Servings:** 4

Ingredients:
- 1 red onion, chopped
- 1 tablespoon olive oil
- 1 cup green beans, trimmed and halved
- 1 cup cherry tomatoes, halved
- 1 cup black olives, pitted and halved
- 1 cup mushrooms, sliced
- 1 cup zucchinis, cubed
- ½ pound hash browns
- 8 eggs, whisked
- ½ teaspoon sweet paprika
- Salt and black pepper to the taste
- 1 teaspoon oregano, dried
- ½ teaspoon cumin, ground
- 1 tablespoon chives, chopped

Directions:
1. Combine all the ingredients in the multi level air fryer's pan.
2. Put the pan in the instant pot and seal with the air fryer lid.
3. Cook on Air fry mode at 350 degrees F for 20 minutes, divide into bowls and serve.

Nutrition:
calories 230, fat 11, fiber 7, carbs 14, protein 5

Greens and Potato Breakfast Salad

Prep time: 5 minutes | **Cooking:** 20 minutes | **Servings:** 4

Ingredients:
- ½ pound sweet potatoes, peeled and cut into wedges
- 1 cup cherry tomatoes, halved
- 1 cup baby spinach
- ½ cup baby kale
- ½ cup baby spinach
- 1 cup mild salsa
- A pinch of salt and black pepper
- ½ teaspoon chili powder
- Cooking spray

Directions:
1. Combine all the ingredients in the multi level air fryer's pan.
2. Put the pan in the instant pot and seal with the air fryer lid.
3. Cook on Air fry mode at 380 degrees F for 20 minutes, divide into bowls and serve.

Nutrition:
calories 251, fat 11, fiber 7, carbs 9, protein 5

Creamy Turmeric Broccoli Bowls

Prep time: 10 minutes | **Cooking:** 20 minutes | **Servings:** 4

Ingredients:
- 1 pound broccoli florets
- 4 eggs, whisked
- Salt and black pepper to the taste
- 1 cup sour cream
- ¼ cup Greek yogurt
- 1 teaspoon turmeric powder

Directions:
1. Combine all the ingredients in the multi level air fryer's pan.
2. Put the pan in the instant pot and seal with the air fryer lid.
3. Cook on Air fry mode at 360 degrees F for 20 minutes, divide into bowls and serve.

Nutrition:
calories 150, fat 3, fiber 2, carbs 10, protein 3

Mushroom Eggs

Prep time: 10 minutes | **Cooking:** 20 minutes | **Servings:** 4

Ingredients:
- ½ pound gold potatoes, peeled and cubed
- 1 cup white mushrooms, sliced
- 8 eggs, whisked
- 1 red onion, chopped
- Salt and black pepper to the taste
- ¼ teaspoon sweet paprika
- 1 tablespoon olive oil
- ½ cup heavy cream
- 1 tablespoon cilantro, chopped

Directions:
1. Combine the potatoes, mushrooms and the other ingredients in the multi level air fryer's pan.
2. Put the pan in the instant pot and seal with the air fryer lid.
3. Cook on Air fry mode at 380 degrees F for 20 minutes.
4. Divide between plates and serve for breakfast.

Nutrition:
calories 202, fat 8, fiber 1, carbs 11, protein 6

Tofu and Scallions Scramble

Prep time: 10 minutes | **Cooking:** 15 minutes | **Servings:** 4

Ingredients:
- 4 scallions, chopped
- 8 eggs, whisked
- ½ teaspoon turmeric powder
- ½ teaspoon garam masala
- Salt and black pepper to the taste
- 3 ounces firm tofu, crumbled
- 1 tablespoon chives, chopped

Directions:
1. Combine the scallions mixed with the eggs and the other ingredients in the multi level air fryer's pan.
2. Put the pan in the instant pot and seal with the air fryer lid.
3. Cook on Air fry mode at 400 degrees F for 15 minutes, divide into bowls and serve.

Nutrition:
calories 135, fat 2, fiber 2, carbs 8, protein 3

Mozzarella Peppers and Tomatoes Bowls
Prep time: 4 minutes | **Cooking:** 20 minutes | **Servings:** 4

Ingredients:
- 1 red bell pepper, cut into strips
- 1 green bell pepper, cut into strips
- 1 orange bell pepper, cut into strips
- 1 cup cherry tomatoes, halved
- 1 cup kalamata olives, pitted and halved
- 1 cup heavy cream
- 1 cup corn
- 1 tablespoon avocado oil
- Salt and black pepper to the taste
- 1 cup mozzarella, shredded

Directions:
1. In the multi level air fryer's pan, mix the peppers with the tomatoes and the other ingredients.
2. Put the pan in the instant pot and seal with the air fryer lid.
3. Cook on Bake mode at 380 degrees f for 20 minutes, divide into bowls and serve.

Nutrition:
calories 210, fat 2, fiber 1, carbs 6, protein 5

Salmon Salad
Prep time: 5 minutes | **Cooking:** 10 minutes | **Servings:** 4

Ingredients:
- 1 red onion, chopped
- 1 cup baby kale
- ½ cup kalamata olives, pitted and halved
- 1 cup smoked salmon, boneless and cut into strips
- Salt and black pepper to the taste
- 3 tablespoons mayonnaise
- 2 tablespoons olive oil
- Juice of 1 lime

Directions:
1. In the multi level air fryer's pan, mix the salmon with the kale and the other ingredients.
2. Put the pan in the instant pot and seal with the air fryer lid.
3. Cook on Bake mode at 360 degrees f for 10 minutes, divide into bowls and serve.

Nutrition:
calories 200, fat 5, fiber 3, carbs 7, protein 6

Mozzarella Spinach Scramble
Prep time: 5 minutes ı **Cooking:** 15 minutes | **Servings:** 4

Ingredients:
- 1 cup baby spinach
- 8 eggs, whisked
- 1 tablespoon olive oil
- ½ cup coconut cream
- ½ cup mozzarella, crumbled
- Salt and black pepper to the taste
- 1 tablespoon chives, chopped

Directions:
1. In a bowl, mix the eggs with the spinach and the other ingredients except the oil and whisk.
2. Grease the multi level air fryer's pan with the oil and pour the mix inside.
3. Put the pan in the instant pot and seal with the air fryer lid.
4. Cook on Bake mode at 360 degrees F for 15 minutes and serve.

Nutrition:
calories 200, fat 12, fiber 2, carbs 13, protein 5

Creamy Eggplant and Garlic Spread
Prep time: 10 minutes | **Cooking:** 20 minutes | **Servings:** 4

Ingredients:
- 1 pound eggplants, cubed
- 1 tablespoon olive oil
- 2 tablespoons tahini paste
- ½ teaspoon sweet paprika
- 1 cup heavy cream
- 2 garlic cloves, minced
- 1 red onion, chopped
- 1 tablespoon chives, chopped
- Salt and black pepper to the taste

Directions:
1. In the multi level air fryer's pan, mix the eggplants with the other ingredients and toss.
2. Put the pan in the instant pot and seal with the air fryer lid.
3. Cook on Bake mode at 300 degrees f for 20 minutes, blend using an immersion blender and serve for breakfast.

Nutrition:
calories 210, fat 1, fiber 3, carbs 14, protein 6

Olives and Tomato Salad
Prep time: 5 minutes | **Cooking:** 10 minutes | **Servings:** 4

Ingredients:
- 1 cup cherry tomatoes, halved
- 1 cup black olives, pitted and halved
- 1 cup kalamata olives, pitted and halved
- 1 cup corn
- 1 cup avocado, peeled, pitted and cubed
- A drizzle of olive oil
- Salt and black pepper to the taste
- 1 tablespoon basil, chopped
- 1 tablespoon oregano, chopped
- 1 tablespoon sage, chopped
- 1 tablespoon chives, chopped

Directions:
1. In the multi level air fryer's pan, mix the tomatoes with the olives and the other ingredients and toss.
2. Put the pan in the instant pot and seal with the air fryer lid.
3. Cook on Bake mode at 330 degrees f for 10 minutes, divide into bowls and serve.

Nutrition:
calories 140, fat 2, fiber 3, carbs 8, protein 4

Almond Pumpkin Rice
Prep time: 10 minutes | **Cooking:** 20 minutes | **Servings:** 4

Ingredients:
- 1 cup white rice
- 2 cups almond milk
- ½ cup pumpkin puree
- 3 tablespoons sugar
- ½ teaspoon cinnamon powder

Directions:
1. In the multi level air fryer's pan, mix rice with the other ingredients and toss well.
2. Put the pan in the instant pot and seal with the air fryer lid.
3. Cook on Bake mode at 360 degrees f for 20 minutes, divide into bowls and serve for breakfast.

Nutrition:
calories 141, fat 4, fiber 7, carbs 8, protein 5

Cinnamon Apple Spread

Prep time: 10 minutes | **Cooking:** 15 minutes | **Servings:** 6

Ingredients:

- 1 cup apples, cored, peeled and chopped
- 1 cup coconut cream
- ½ cup heavy cream
- ½ teaspoon cinnamon powder
- ¼ teaspoon nutmeg, ground
- ½ teaspoon vanilla extract
- 2 tablespoons sugar

Directions:

1. , In the multi level air fryer's pan, mix the apples with the cream and the other ingredients.
2. Put the pan in the instant pot and seal with the air fryer lid.
3. Cook on Air Fry mode at 360 degrees f for 15 minutes.
4. Blend using an immersion blender, divide into bowls and serve for breakfast.

Nutrition:

calories 212, fat 5, fiber 7, carbs 14, protein 5

Carrot Pudding

Prep time: 5 minutes | **Cooking:** 20 minutes | **Ingredients:** 4

Ingredients:

- 2 cups almond milk
- 1 cup white rice
- 1 cup carrots, peeled and grated
- 1 teaspoon cinnamon powder
- 2 tablespoons sugar
- Cooking spray

Directions:

1. In the multi level air fryer's pan, mix the rice with carrots and the other ingredients.
2. Put the pan in the instant pot and seal with air fryer lid.
3. Cook on Bake mode at 370 degrees F for 20 minutes and serve.

Nutrition:

calories 172, fat 7, fiber 4, carbs 14, protein 5

Mint Berries Bowls

Prep time: 10 minutes | **Cooking:** 15 minutes | **Servings:** 4

Ingredients:

- 1 cup strawberries
- 1 cup blackberries
- 1 cup blueberries
- Juice of 1 lime
- 1 cup heavy cream
- 2 tablespoons sugar
- 1 tablespoon mint, chopped
- ½ teaspoon vanilla extract
- Cooking spray

Directions:

1. In the multi level air fryer's pan, mix the berries with lime juice and the other ingredients.
2. Put the pan in the instant pot and seal with the air fryer lid.
3. Cook on Air fry mode at 380 degrees f for 20 minutes, divide into bowls and serve.

Nutrition:

calories 172, fat 6, fiber 8, carbs 11, protein 5

Beans and Kale Bowls

Prep time: 10 minutes | **Cooking:** 15 minutes | **Servings:** 4

Ingredients:

- 1 cup canned black beans, drained and rinsed
- 1 cup canned red kidney beans, drain and rinsed
- 1 cup canned white beans, drained and rinsed
- 1 cup baby spinach
- 1 cup baby kale
- ½ cup heavy cream
- 1 cup cherry tomatoes, halved
- 1 tablespoon chives, chopped
- Salt and black pepper to the taste
- ¼ teaspoon rosemary, dried

Directions:

1. In the multi level air fryer's pan, mix the beans with the spinach and the other ingredients.
2. Put the pan in the instant pot and seal with the air fryer lid.
3. Cook on Air Fry mode at 370 degrees F for 15 minutes, divide into bowls and serve.

Nutrition:

calories 203, fat 4, fiber 6, carbs 12, protein 4

Butter Coconut Quinoa

Prep time: 5 minutes | **Cooking:** 20 minutes | **Servings:** 4

Ingredients:

- 1 cup quinoa
- 2 cups coconut milk
- 1 cup apples, cored, peeled and roughly chopped
- 3 tablespoons maple syrup
- 2 tablespoons butter, melted
- 1 teaspoon nutmeg, ground

Directions:

1. In the multi level air fryer's pan, mix the quinoa with the coconut milk and the other ingredients.
2. Put the pan in the instant pot and seal with the air fryer lid.
3. Cook on Bake mode at 370 degrees f for 20 minutes, divide into bowls and serve.

Nutrition:

calories 208, fat 6, fiber 9, carbs 14, protein 3

Cumin Avocado Scramble

Prep time: 5 minutes | **Cooking:** 15 minutes | **Servings:** 4

Ingredients:

- 1 tablespoon avocado oil
- 1 cup avocado, peeled, pitted and mashed
- 8 eggs, whisked
- ½ teaspoon cumin, ground
- ½ teaspoon smoked paprika
- Salt and black pepper to the taste
- 1 tablespoon cilantro, chopped

Directions:

1. In the multi level air fryer's pan, mix the eggs with the avocado and the other ingredients and toss well.
2. Put the pan in the instant pot and seal with the air fryer lid.
3. Cook on Bake mode at 360 degrees f for 15 minutes, divide between plates and serve.

Nutrition:

calories 220, fat 11, fiber 3, carbs 4, protein 6

Cheesy Turkey and Olives Tortillas

Prep time: 5 minutes | **Cooking:** 14 minutes | **Servings:** 4

Ingredients:

- 1 pound turkey breast, skinless, boneless, ground and browned
- 4 corn tortillas
- Cooking spray
- 1 cup cherry tomatoes, halved
- 1 cup kalamata olives, pitted and halved
- 1 cup corn
- 1 cup baby spinach
- 1 cup cheddar cheese, shredded
- Salt and black pepper to the taste

Directions:

1. Divide the meat, tomatoes and the other ingredients except the cooking spray on each tortilla, roll and grease them with the cooking spray
2. Put the tortillas in the multi level air fryer's basket.
3. Put the basket in the instant pot and seal with the air fryer lid.
4. Cook on Air fry mode at 350 degrees F for 7 minutes on each side and serve for breakfast.

Nutrition:

calories 244, fat 11, fiber 4, carbs 5, protein 7

Turkey and Corn Bowls

Prep time: 5 minutes | **Cooking:** 20 minutes | **Servings:** 4

Ingredients:

- 1 red bell pepper, cut into strips
- 1 pound turkey breast, skinless, boneless, ground
- 4 eggs, whisked
- Salt and black pepper to the taste
- 1 cup corn
- 1 cup black olives, pitted and halved
- 1 cup mild salsa
- Cooking spray

Directions:

1. In the multi level air fryer's pan, mix the turkey with the corn and the other ingredients and toss.
2. Put the pan in the instant pot and seal with the air fryer lid.
3. Cook on Air fry mode at 350 degrees f for 20 minutes, divide into bowls and serve.

Nutrition:

calories 229, fat 13, fiber 3, carbs 4, protein 7

Potato, Carrots and Olives Casserole

Prep time: 5 minutes | **Cooking:** 20 minutes | **Servings:** 4

Ingredients:

- 1 pound gold potatoes, peeled and cubed
- 4 eggs, whisked
- 1 teaspoon chili powder
- 1 cup carrots, peeled and sliced
- 1 cup black olives, pitted and halved
- 1 cup mozzarella, shredded
- 2 tablespoons butter, melted
- A pinch of salt and black pepper

Directions:

1. In the multi level air fryer's pan, mix the potatoes with the eggs and the other ingredients except the cheese and toss.
2. Sprinkle the mozzarella on top.
3. Put the pan in the instant pot and seal with the air fryer lid.
4. Cook on Bake mode at 350 degrees f for 20 minutes, divide between plates and serve

Nutrition:

calories 240, fat 9, fiber 2, carbs 4, protein 8

Side Dish Recipes

Italian Carrots

Prep time: 5 minutes | **Cooking:** 20 minutes | **Servings:** 4

Ingredients:
- 1 pound baby carrots, peeled
- 2 teaspoons olive oil
- 1 cup heavy cream
- 1 teaspoon Italian seasoning
- Salt and black pepper to the taste
- 1 tablespoon lemon juice

Directions:
1. In the multi level air fryer's pan, mix the carrots and the other ingredients.
2. Put the pan in the instant pot and seal with the air fryer lid.
3. Cook on Bake mode at 350 degrees F for 20 minutes and serve as a side dish.

Nutrition:
calories 132, fat 4, fiber 3, carbs 11, protein 4

Dill Carrots

Prep time: 5 minutes | **Cooking:** 20 minutes | **Servings:** 4

Ingredients:
- 1 pound baby carrots, peeled
- A pinch of salt and black pepper
- 2 tablespoons maple syrup
- 1 tablespoon dill, chopped
- 1 tablespoon avocado oil

Directions:
1. 1. In the multi level air fryer's pan, combine all the ingredients and toss.
2. 2. Put the pan in the instant pot and seal with the air fryer lid.
3. 3. Cook on Bake mode at 360 degrees F for 20 minutes and serve as a side dish.

Nutrition:
calories 174, fat 5, fiber 3, carbs 11, protein 4

Lime Carrots and Beets

Prep time: 10 minutes | **Cooking:** 30 minutes | **Servings:** 4

Ingredients:
- 2 beets, peeled and cubed
- 1 pound baby carrots, peeled
- 1 tablespoon lime juice
- 1 teaspoon sweet paprika
- ½ teaspoon chili powder
- 1 tablespoon olive oil

Directions:
1. 1. In the multi level air fryer's pan, mix the beets with the carrots and eth other ingredients.
2. 2. Put the pan in the instant pot and seal with the air fryer lid.
3. 3. Cook on Bake mode at 370 degrees f for 30 minutes, divide between plates and serve.

Nutrition:
calories 171, fat 4, fiber 2, carbs 13, protein 3

Mushroom Sauté

Prep time: 10 minutes | **Cooking:** 20 minutes | **Servings:** 4

Ingredients:
- 1 tablespoon olive oil
- 1 cup white mushrooms, halved
- 1 cup corn
- ½ cup heavy cream
- 3 garlic cloves, minced
- 1 tablespoon chives, chopped
- Juice of 1 lime
- A pinch of salt and black pepper

Directions:
1. In the multi level air fryer's pan, combine the mushrooms with the other ingredients.
2. Put the pan in the instant pot and seal with the air fryer lid.
3. Cook on Bake mode at 360 degrees F for 20 minutes.
4. Divide between plates and serve.

Nutrition:
calories 182, fat 3, fiber 2, carbs 8, protein 4

Chives Eggplants

Prep time: 10 minutes | **Cooking:** 20 minutes | **Servings:** 4

Ingredients:
- 2 pounds eggplant, cubed
- 1 tablespoon olive oil
- 1 teaspoon chili powder
- 1 tablespoon red curry paste
- ½ cup coconut cream
- 1 tablespoon chives, chopped

Directions:
1. In the multi level air fryer's pan, mix the eggplants with the chili powder and the other ingredients and toss.
2. Put the pan in the instant pot and seal with the air fryer lid.
3. Cook on Bake mode at 370 degrees f for 20 minutes, divide between plates and serve as a side dish.

Nutrition:
calories 182, fat 4, fiber 7, carbs 12, protein 4

Curry Quinoa Mix

Prep time: 10 minutes | **Cooking:** 20 minutes | **Servings:** 4

Ingredients:
- 1 teaspoon olive oil
- 1 cup cauliflower florets
- 1 cup quinoa
- 2 cups veggie stock
- 1 teaspoon curry powder
- ½ teaspoon turmeric powder
- 3 garlic cloves, minced
- Juice of 1 lime

Directions:
1. In the multi level air fryer's pan, mix the quinoa with the cauliflower and the other ingredients and toss.
2. Put the pan in the instant pot and seal with the air fryer lid.
3. Cook on Bake mode at 370 degrees F for 20 minutes, divide between plates and serve.

Nutrition:
calories 182, fat 4, fiber 3, carbs 11, protein 4

Lemon Potatoes and Beets Mix

Prep time: 10 minutes | **Cooking:** 30 minutes | **Servings:** 4

Ingredients:
- 2 sweet potatoes, peeled and cut into wedges
- 2 beets, peeled and cubed
- 1 tablespoon olive oil
- Juice of 1 lemon
- Salt and black pepper the taste
- 1 tablespoon chives, chopped

Directions:
1. In the multi level air fryer's basket combine the potatoes with the other ingredients and toss.
2. Put the basket in the instant pot and seal with the air fryer lid.
3. Cook on Air fry mode at 380 degrees F for 30 minutes and serve.

Nutrition:
calories 190, fat 4, fiber 4, carbs 14, protein 4

Lime Carrots Mix

Prep time: 10 minutes | **Cooking:** 20 minutes | **Servings:** 4

Ingredients:
- 1 pound baby carrots, peeled
- 1 cup radishes, halved
- Juice of 1 lime
- Salt and black pepper to the taste
- 1 tablespoon olive oil

Directions:

1. In the multi level air fryer's basket combine the carrots with the other ingredients and toss.
2. Put the basket in the instant pot and seal with the air fryer lid.
3. Cook on Air fry mode at 370 degrees F for 20 minutes and serve.

Nutrition:
calories 160, fat 3, fiber 4, carbs 7, protein 3

Lime Mushrooms

Prep time: 5 minutes | **Cooking:** 20 minutes | **Servings:** 4

Ingredients:
- 2 pounds mushrooms, halved
- 1 teaspoon allspice, ground
- 1 tablespoon avocado oil
- Juice of 1 lime
- 1 red onion, chopped
- Salt and black pepper to the taste
- 1 tablespoon chives, chopped

Directions:
1. In the multi level air fryer's basket combine the mushrooms with allspice and the other ingredients and toss.
2. Put the basket in the instant pot and seal with the air fryer lid.
3. Cook on Air fry mode at 380 degrees F for 20 minutes and serve.

Nutrition:
calories 202, fat 6, fiber 1, carbs 16, protein 4

Rosemary Zucchinis Mix

Prep time: 10 minutes | **Cooking:** 20 minutes | **Servings:** 4

Ingredients:
- 2 teaspoons olive oil
- 1 pound zucchinis, sliced
- 1 cup radishes, halved
- ½ teaspoon rosemary, dried
- Salt and black pepper to the taste
- 1 tablespoon chives, chopped

Directions:
1. In the multi level air fryer's basket combine the zucchinis with the radishes and the other ingredients and toss.
2. Put the basket in the instant pot and seal with the air fryer lid.
3. Cook on Air fry mode at 400 degrees F for 20 minutes and serve as a side dish.

Nutrition:
calories 200, fat 4, fiber 1, carbs 15, protein 4

Mozzarella Mushrooms

Prep time: 10 minutes | **Cooking:** 20 minutes | **Servings:** 4

Ingredients:
- 1 pound mushrooms, halved
- 1 tablespoon yellow curry paste
- ½ teaspoon curry powder
- 1 tablespoon mozzarella cheese, grated
- 2 teaspoons olive oil
- 1 tablespoon chives, chopped
- Salt and black pepper to the taste

Directions:
1. In the multi level air fryer's pan, combine the mushrooms with the curry paste and the other ingredients and toss.
2. Put the pan in the instant pot and seal with the air fryer lid.
3. Cook on Bake mode at 380 degrees F for 20 minutes and serve.

Nutrition:
calories 161, fat 7, fiber 1, carbs 12, protein 6

Rosemary Olives

Prep time: 10 minutes | **Cooking:** 15 minutes | **Servings:** 4

Ingredients:
- 2 cups kalamata olives, pitted and halved
- 1 cup black olives, pitted and halved
- Salt and black pepper to the taste
- 2 teaspoons olive oil
- Juice of 1 lime
- ½ teaspoon rosemary, dried

Directions:
1. In the multi level air fryer's pan, combine the olives with the rosemary and the other ingredients and toss.
2. Put the pan in the instant pot and seal with the air fryer lid.
3. Cook on Air fry mode at 400 degrees F for 15 minutes and serve

Nutrition:
calories 180, fat 7, fiber 2, carbs 12, protein 6

Masala Zucchinis

Prep time: 10 minutes | **Cooking:** 20 minutes | **Servings:** 4

Ingredients:
- 1 pound zucchinis, roughly cubed
- 4 garlic cloves, minced
- 2 teaspoons olive oil
- ½ teaspoon turmeric powder
- ½ teaspoon garam masala
- Salt and black pepper to the taste
- 1 tablespoon dill, chopped

Directions:
1. In the multi level air fryer's pan, combine the zucchinis with the garlic and the other ingredients and toss.
2. Put the pan in the instant pot and seal with the air fryer lid.
3. Cook on Bake mode at 400 degrees F for 20 minutes and serve.

Nutrition:
calories 173, fat 3, fiber 2, carbs 16, protein 4

Creamy Cabbage Mix

Prep time: 10 minutes | **Cooking:** 20 minute I **Servings:** 4

Ingredients:
- 1 pound red cabbage, shredded
- 1 cup bacon, chopped
- 3 spring onions, chopped
- 2 teaspoons olive oil
- 1 yellow onion, chopped
- Salt and black pepper to the taste
- 1 cup heavy cream

Directions:
1. In the multi level air fryer's pan, combine the cabbage with the bacon and the other ingredients.
2. Put the pan in the instant pot and seal with the air fryer lid.
3. Cook on Bake mode at 400 degrees F for 20 minutes and serve.

Nutrition:
calories 208, fat 10, fiber 4, carbs 12, protein 4

Cilantro Rice Mix

Prep time: 10 minutes | **Cooking:** 30 minutes | **Servings:** 4

Ingredients:
- 1 red onion, chopped
- 1 cup white rice
- 2 cups veggie stock
- ½ cup peanuts, chopped
- 1 teaspoon olive oil
- Salt and black pepper to the taste
- 1 tablespoon cilantro, chopped

Directions:
1. In the multi level air fryer's pan, combine the rice with the stock and the other ingredients and toss.
2. Put the pan in the instant pot and seal with the air fryer lid.
3. Cook on Air fry mode at 380 degrees F for 30 minutes and serve.

Nutrition:
calories 200, fat 4, fiber 6, carbs 16, protein 4

Turmeric Quinoa

Prep time: 10 minutes | **Cooking:** 20 minutes | **Servings:** 4

Ingredients:
- 1 cup quinoa
- 2 cups veggie stock
- ½ cup walnuts, chopped
- 3 spring onions, chopped
- ½ teaspoon turmeric powder
- 1 tablespoon olive oil
- Salt and black pepper to the taste

Directions:
1. In the multi level air fryer's pan, combine the quinoa with the stock, walnuts and the other ingredients and toss.
2. Put the pan in the instant pot and seal with the air fryer lid.
3. Cook on Bake mode at 380 degrees F for 20 minutes and serve.

Nutrition:
calories 171, fat 4, fiber 8, carbs 16, protein 7

Rosemary Mushrooms and Leeks

Prep time: 10 minutes | **Cooking:** 20 minutes | **Servings:** 4

Ingredients:
- 2 leeks, sliced
- 1 pound white mushrooms, halved
- 2 teaspoons olive oil
- ½ teaspoon rosemary, dried
- 2 garlic cloves, minced
- A pinch of salt and black pepper
- 1 tablespoon cilantro, chopped

Directions:
1. In the multi level air fryer's pan, combine the leeks with mushrooms and the other ingredients and toss.
2. Put the pan in the instant pot and seal with the air fryer lid.
3. Cook on Bake mode at 360 degrees F for 20 minutes and serve.

Nutrition:
calories 261, fat 5, fiber 8, carbs 15, protein 5

Spiced Chives Rice

Prep time: 5 minutes | **Cooking:** 25 minutes | **Servings:** 4

Ingredients:
- 2 teaspoons olive oil
- 1 cup white rice
- 2 cups chicken stock
- ½ cup heavy cream
- ½ teaspoon turmeric powder
- ½ teaspoon nutmeg, ground
- 1 tablespoon chives, chopped

Directions:
1. In the multi level air fryer's pan, combine the rice with cream, stock and the other ingredients and toss.
2. Put the pan in the instant pot and seal with the air fryer lid.
3. Cook on Bake mode at 360 degrees F for 25 minutes and serve.

Nutrition:
calories 251, fat 6, fiber 8, carbs 16, protein 6

Paprika Sweet Potatoes Mix

Prep time: 5 minutes | **Cooking:** 25 minutes | **Servings:** 4

Ingredients:
- 2 pounds sweet potatoes, peeled and cut into wedges
- 3 leeks, sliced
- 2 teaspoons avocado oil
- 1 teaspoon sweet paprika
- ½ teaspoon chili powder
- Salt and black pepper to the taste
- ½ teaspoon rosemary, dried
- 1 tablespoon dill, chopped

Directions:
1. In the multi level air fryer's pan, combine the potatoes with the leeks and the other ingredients and toss.
2. Put the pan in the instant pot and seal with the air fryer lid.
3. Cook on Bake mode at 360 degrees F for 25 minutes and serve.

Nutrition:
calories 251, fat 6, fiber 5, carbs 16, protein 6

Fennel Rice

Prep time: 10 minutes | **Cooking:** 20 minutes | **Servings:** 4

Ingredients:
- 2 teaspoons olive oil
- 1 cup wild rice
- ½ cup almonds, chopped
- 1 fennel bulb, sliced
- 2 cups veggie stock
- ½ teaspoon sweet paprika
- Salt and black pepper to the taste
- 1 tablespoon chives, chopped

Directions:
1. In the multi level air fryer's pan, combine the rice with the fennel
2. Put the pan in the instant pot and seal with the air fryer lid.
3. Cook on Bake mode at 400 degrees F for 20 minutes and serve.

Nutrition:
calories 251, fat 4, fiber 3, carbs 13, protein 6

Indian Rice

Prep time: 10 minutes | **Cooking:** 20 minutes | **Servings:** 4

Ingredients:
- 2 teaspoons avocado oil
- 1 cup white rice
- 2 cups veggie stock
- 1 tablespoon mint, chopped
- ½ teaspoon garam masala
- Salt and black pepper to the taste
- ¼ cup green onions, chopped

Directions:
1. In the multi level air fryer's pan, combine the rice with the masala and the other ingredients and toss.
2. Put the pan in the instant pot and seal with the air fryer lid.
3. Cook on Bake mode at 370 degrees F for 20 minutes and serve as a side dish.

Nutrition:
calories 200, fat 5, fiber 5, carbs 9, protein 5

Coriander Rice

Prep time: 10 minutes | **Cooking:** 25 minutes | **Servings:** 4

Ingredients:
- 2 tablespoons butter, melted
- 1 cup wild rice
- 2 cups veggie stock
- ½ teaspoon sweet paprika
- ½ teaspoon coriander, ground
- Salt and black pepper to the taste
- 2 tablespoons parsley, chopped
- ½ teaspoon cumin, ground

Directions:
1. In the multi level air fryer's pan, combine the rice with the paprika, butter and the other ingredients and toss.
2. Put the pan in the instant pot and seal with the air fryer lid.
3. Cook on Bake mode at 370 degrees F for 25 minutes and serve.

Nutrition:
calories 200, fat 6, fiber 5, carbs 15, protein 5

Lime Leeks and Artichokes Sauté

Prep time: 10 minutes | **Cooking:** 20 minutes | **Servings:** 4

Ingredients:
- 1 tablespoon avocado oil
- 1 cup canned artichoke hearts, drained
- 1 tablespoon thyme, chopped
- 2 leeks, sliced
- ½ teaspoon cumin, ground
- Juice of 1 lime
- 2 garlic cloves, minced
- Salt and black pepper to the taste

Directions:
1. In the multi level air fryer's pan, combine the artichokes with the

Side Dish Recipes | 17

thyme and the other ingredients and toss.
2. Put the pan in the instant pot and seal with the air fryer lid.
3. Cook on Bake mode at 370 degrees F for 20 minutes and serve as a side dish.

Nutrition:

calories 215, fat 4, fiber 6, carbs 14, protein 4

Balsamic Beans Mix

Prep time: 10 minutes | **Cooking:** 20 minutes | **Servings:** 4

Ingredients:

- 2 cups canned black beans, drained and rinsed
- 2 spring onions, chopped
- 1 garlic clove, minced
- 2 tablespoons balsamic vinegar
- 1 tablespoon dill, chopped
- 4 tablespoons olive oil
- Salt and black pepper to the taste

Directions:

1. In the multi level air fryer's pan, combine the beans with spring onions, garlic and the other ingredients and toss.
2. Put the pan in the instant pot and seal with the air fryer lid.
3. Cook on Bake mode at 380 degrees F for 20 minutes and serve.

Nutrition:

calories 231, fat 4, fiber 6, carbs 14, protein 6

Chives Green Beans

Prep time: 5 minutes | **Cooking:** 20 minutes | **Servings:** 4

Ingredients:

- 1 pound green beans, trimmed and halved
- 1 teaspoon cumin, ground
- Juice of 1 lime
- ½ teaspoon sweet paprika
- Salt and black pepper to the taste
- 1 tablespoon chives, chopped

Directions:

1. In the multi level air fryer's pan, combine the green beans with lime juice and the other ingredients and toss.
2. Put the pan in the instant pot and seal with the air fryer lid.
3. Cook on Bake mode at 370 degrees F for 20 minutes and serve.

Nutrition:

calories 265, fat 6, fiber 7, carbs 14, protein 6

Mango Rice

Prep time: 10 minutes | **Cooking:** 20 minutes | **Servings:** 4

Ingredients:

- 1 cup wild rice
- ½ cup mango, peeled and cubed
- ¼ cup cherries, pitted and halved
- 1 tablespoon avocado oil
- ½ teaspoon sweet paprika
- Salt and black pepper to the taste
- 1 tablespoon chives, chopped

Directions:

1. In the multi level air fryer's pan, combine the rice with mango, cherries and the other ingredients and toss.
2. Put the pan in the instant pot and seal with the air fryer lid.
3. Cook on Bake mode at 370 degrees F for 20 minutes and serve as a side dish.

Nutrition:

calories 200, fat 4, fiber 5, carbs 11, protein 4

Lime Lentils and Chickpeas

Prep time: 10 minutes | **Cooking:** 20 minutes | **Servings:** 4

Ingredients:

- 1 cup canned lentils, drained
- 1 cup canned chickpeas, drained
- 1 tablespoon olive oil
- Juice of 1 lime
- Salt and black pepper to the taste
- 1 yellow onion, chopped
- 1 green bell pepper, chopped
- 1 tablespoon chives, chopped

Directions:

1. In the multi level air fryer's pan, combine the lentils with chickpeas and the other ingredients and toss.
2. Put the pan in the instant pot and seal with the air fryer lid.
3. Cook on Bake mode at 370 degrees F for 20 minutes and serve.

Nutrition:

calories 161, fat 4, fiber 6, carbs 15, protein 6

Balsamic Corn and Cauliflower

Prep time: 5 minutes | **Cooking:** 20 minutes | **Servings:** 4

Ingredients:

- 1 pound cauliflower florets
- ½ pound baby carrots, peeled
- 1 cup corn
- 1 tablespoon olive oil
- 1 tablespoon balsamic vinegar
- Salt and black pepper to the taste
- ½ teaspoon turmeric powder

Directions:

1. In the multi level air fryer's pan, combine the cauliflower with the carrots and the other ingredients and toss,.
2. Put the pan in the instant pot and seal with the air fryer lid.
3. Cook on Bake mode at 360 degrees F for 20 minutes and serve.

Nutrition:

calories 140, fat 2, fiber 6, carbs 15, protein 4

Paprika Carrots Puree

Prep time: 10 minutes | **Cooking:** 20 minutes | **Servings:** 4

Ingredients:

- 1 pound carrots, peeled
- 1 teaspoon sweet paprika
- 1 teaspoon turmeric powder
- Salt and black pepper to the taste
- ¼ cup sour cream
- ½ cup chicken stock

Directions:

1. In the multi level air fryer's pan, combine the carrots with the paprika and the other ingredients except the sour cream and toss.
2. Put the pan in the instant pot and seal with the air fryer lid.
3. Cook on Bake mode at 370 degrees F for 20 minutes, add the sour cream, mash everything and serve.

Nutrition:

calories 151, fat 3, fiber 6, carbs 11, protein 4

Butter Hot Zucchini Mix

Prep time: 5 minutes | **Cooking:** 20 minutes | **Servings:** 4

Ingredients:

- 2 pounds zucchinis, roughly cubed
- 1 tablespoon maple syrup
- ½ teaspoon sweet paprika
- ½ teaspoon chili powder
- 1 tablespoon butter, soft
- Salt and black pepper to the taste

Directions:

1. In the multi level air fryer's pan, combine the zucchinis with the maple syrup and the other ingredients and toss.
2. Put the pan in the instant pot and seal with the air fryer lid.
3. Cook on Bake mode at 370 degrees F for 20 minutes and serve.

Nutrition:

calories 100, fat 3, fiber 3, carbs 7, protein 6

Spiced Butternut

Prep time: 10 minutes | **Cooking:** 20 minutes | **Servings:** 4

Ingredients:
- 1 pound butternut squash, peeled and cut into medium chunks
- 2 tablespoons butter, melted
- ½ teaspoon nutmeg, ground
- ½ teaspoon allspice, ground
- 2 tablespoons honey
- 1 tablespoon avocado oil
- Salt and black pepper to the taste

Directions:
1. In the multi level air fryer's pan, combine the squash with the butter and the other ingredients and toss.
2. Put the pan in the instant pot and seal with the air fryer lid.
3. Cook on Bake mode at 370 degrees F for 20 minutes and serve.

Nutrition:
calories 200, fat 6, fiber 7, carbs 15, protein 5

Turmeric Asparagus

Prep time: 5 minutes | **Cooking:** 12 minutes | **Servings:** 4

Ingredients:
- 1 pound asparagus, trimmed
- 3 tablespoons butter, melted
- A pinch of salt and black pepper
- ½ teaspoon turmeric powder
- ½ teaspoon coriander, ground

Directions:
1. In the multi level air fryer's basket, combine the asparagus with the rest of the ingredients and toss.
2. Put the basket in the instant pot and seal with the air fryer lid.
3. Cook on Air fry mode at 380 degrees F for 12 minutes and serve.

Nutrition:
calories 141, fat 4, fiber 4, carbs 8, protein 3

Chili Bulgur Mix

Prep time: 5 minutes | **Cooking:** 20 minutes | **Servings:** 4

Ingredients:
- 1 fennel bulb, sliced
- 1 cup bulgur
- 1 cup veggie stock
- ½ teaspoon chili powder
- ½ teaspoon nutmeg, ground
- Salt and black pepper to the taste

Directions:
1. In the multi level air fryer's pan, combine the bulgur with the fennel and the other ingredients and toss.
2. Put the pan in the instant pot and seal with the air fryer lid.
3. Cook on Bake mode at 370 degrees F for 20 minutes and serve.

Nutrition:
calories 151, fat 3, fiber 6, carbs 8, protein 3

Green Peas and Quinoa

Prep time: 10 minutes | **Cooking:** 20 minutes | **Servings:** 4

Ingredients:
- 1 cup green peas
- 1 cup quinoa
- 2 cups veggie stock
- 1 tablespoon chives, chopped
- 1 teaspoon sweet paprika
- Salt and black pepper to the taste

Directions:
1. In the multi level air fryer's pan, combine quinoa with green peas and the other ingredients and toss.
2. Put the pan in the instant pot and seal with the air fryer lid.
3. Cook on Bake mode at 370 degrees F for 20 minutes and serve.

Nutrition:
calories 151, fat 2, fiber 6, carbs 9, protein 5

Paprika Peas

Prep time: 10 minutes | **Cooking:** 15 minutes | **Servings:** 4

Ingredients:
- ½ pound green peas
- ½ teaspoon sweet paprika
- Juice of ½ lime
- A drizzle of olive oil
- Salt and black pepper to the taste

Directions:
1. In the multi level air fryer's pan, combine the peas with the paprika and the other ingredients and toss.
2. Put the pan in the instant pot and seal with the air fryer lid.
3. Cook on Bake mode at 370 degrees F for 15 minutes and serve.

Nutrition:
calories 151, fat 3, fiber 7, carbs 8, protein 4

Citrus Broccoli Mix

Prep time: 5 minutes | **Cooking:** 20 minutes | **Servings:** 4

Ingredients:
- 1 pound broccoli florets
- 1 cup oranges, peeled and cut into segments
- ½ tablespoon avocado oil
- Juice of 1 orange
- ½ teaspoon hot paprika
- Salt and black pepper to the taste
- 1 tablespoon chives, chopped

Directions:
1. In the multi level air fryer's pan, combine the broccoli with the oranges and the other ingredients and toss.
2. Put the pan in the instant pot and seal with the air fryer lid.
3. Cook on Bake mode at 380 degrees F for 20 minutes and serve.

Nutrition:
calories 151, fat 7, fiber 4, carbs 9, protein 4

Rosemary Beets

Prep time: 10 minutes | **Cooking:** 20 minutes | **Servings:** 4

Ingredients:
- 1 pound beets, trimmed, peeled and cut into wedges
- 1 tablespoon avocado oil
- Juice of 1 orange
- Salt and black pepper to the taste
- 1 tablespoon rosemary, chopped

Directions:
1. In the multi level air fryer's pan, combine the beets with the orange juice and the other ingredients and toss.
2. Put the pan in the instant pot and seal with the air fryer lid.
3. Cook on Bake mode at 400 degrees F for 20 minutes and serve.

Nutrition:
calories 121, fat 3, fiber 5, carbs 12, protein 4

Lemon Paprika Green Beans

Prep time: 10 minutes | **Cooking:** 20 minutes | **Servings:** 4

Ingredients:
- 1 pound green beans, trimmed and halved
- 1 tablespoon parsley, chopped
- Juice of ½ lemon
- 1 teaspoon olive oil
- Salt and black pepper to the taste
- ½ teaspoon sweet paprika

Directions:
1. In the multi level air fryer's pan, combine the green beans with the parsley and the other ingredients and toss.
2. Put the pan in the instant pot and seal with the air fryer lid.
3. Cook on Bake mode at 380 degrees F for 20 minutes and serve.

Nutrition:
calories 141, fat 3, fiber 2, carbs 12, protein 3

Balsamic Cabbage

Prep time: 10 minutes | **Cooking:** 20 minutes | **Servings:** 4

Ingredients:

- 1 red onion, chopped
- 1 tablespoon olive oil
- 1 pound red cabbage, shredded
- 1 tablespoon balsamic vinegar
- Salt and black pepper to the taste

Directions:

1. In the multi level air fryer's pan, combine the cabbage with the vinegar and the other ingredients and toss.
2. Put the pan in the instant pot and seal with the air fryer lid.
3. Cook on Bake mode at 380 degrees F for 20 minutes and serve.

Nutrition:

calories 151, fat 4, fiber 4, carbs 12, protein 3

Cilantro Peppers

Prep time: 10 minutes | **Cooking:** 20 minutes | **Servings:** 4

Ingredients:

- 1 tablespoon lemon juice
- 1 tablespoon lemon zest, grated
- 1 pound red bell peppers, cut into strips
- 1 teaspoon sweet paprika
- Salt and black pepper to the taste
- 1 tablespoon cilantro, chopped

Directions:

1. In the multi level air fryer's pan, combine the peppers with the paprika and the other ingredients and toss.
2. Put the pan in the instant pot and seal with the air fryer lid.
3. Cook on Bake mode at 400 degrees F for 20 minutes and serve.

Nutrition:

calories 150, fat 1, fiber 3, carbs 3, protein 2

Creamy Chard Mix

Prep time: 10 minutes | **Cooking:** 20 minutes | **Servings:** 4

Ingredients:

- 1 pound red chard, torn
- 1 teaspoon sweet paprika
- 1 tablespoon olive oil
- ½ cup heavy cream
- Salt and black pepper to the taste
- 1 tablespoon chives, chopped
- ½ teaspoon coriander, ground

Directions:

1. In the multi level air fryer's pan, combine the chard with the cream and the other ingredients and toss.
2. Put the pan in the instant pot and seal with the air fryer lid.
3. Cook on Bake mode at 380 degrees F for 20 minutes and serve.

Nutrition:

calories 180, fat 4, fiber 2, carbs 13, protein 4

Carrots and Spring Onions Mix

Prep time: 10 minutes | **Cooking:** 20 minutes | **Servings:** 4

Ingredients:

- 1 pound carrots, peeled and cut in chunks
- 2 teaspoons avocado oil
- ½ cup oranges, peeled and cut into wedges
- 2 tablespoons orange zest, grated
- ½ cup spring onions, chopped
- A pinch of salt and black pepper

Directions:

1. In the multi level air fryer's pan, combine the carrots with the oranges and the other ingredients and toss.
2. Put the pan in the instant pot and seal with the air fryer lid.
3. Cook on Bake mode at 380 degrees F for 20 minutes and serve as a side dish.

Nutrition:

calories 180, fat 4, fiber 8, carbs 12, protein 4

Herbed Eggplant Sauté

Prep time: 10 minutes | **Cooking:** 20 minutes | **Servings:** 4

Ingredients:

- 1 pound eggplants, cut into chunks
- 1 teaspoon basil, chopped
- 1 teaspoon chives, chopped
- 1 teaspoon thyme, chopped
- 1 teaspoon curry powder
- Salt and black pepper to the taste
- 2 tablespoons avocado oil

Directions:

1. In the multi level air fryer's pan, combine the eggplant chunks with the other ingredients and toss.
2. Put the pan in the instant pot and seal with the air fryer lid.
3. Cook on Bake mode at 370 degrees F for 20 minutes and serve as a side dish.

Nutrition:

calories 160, fat 2, fiber 3, carbs 13, protein 4

Sweet Potatoes and Celery Mix

Prep time: 5 minutes | **Cooking:** 30 minutes | **Servings:** 4

Ingredients:

- 2 pounds sweet potatoes, peeled and cut into wedges
- 1 teaspoon hot paprika
- ½ teaspoon red pepper flakes, crushed
- 1 yellow onion, chopped
- 2 celery ribs, chopped
- 1 tablespoon olive oil
- Salt and black pepper to the taste

Directions:

1. In the multi level air fryer's basket, combine the sweet potatoes with the celery and the other ingredients.
2. Put the basket in the instant pot and seal with the air fryer lid.
3. Cook on Air Fry mode at 370 degrees F for 30 minutes and serve.

Nutrition:

calories 190, fat 4, fiber 4, carbs 9, protein 6

Chili Rice and Scallions

Prep time: 5 minutes | **Cooking:** 20 minutes | **Servings:** 4

Ingredients:

- 3 scallions, chopped
- 1 teaspoon olive oil
- 1 cup white rice
- 2 cups veggie stock
- 1 red chili, minced
- ½ teaspoon chili powder
- Salt and black pepper to the taste

Directions:

1. In the multi level air fryer's pan, combine the rice with the scallions and the other ingredients and toss.
2. Put the pan in the instant pot and seal with the air fryer lid.
3. Cook on Bake mode at 370 degrees F for 20 minutes and serve.

Nutrition:

calories 200, fat 7, fiber 4, carbs 9, protein 5

Turmeric Lentils and Onion Mix

Prep time: 5 minutes | **Cooking:** 20 minutes | **Servings:** 4

Ingredients:

- 1 tablespoon avocado oil
- 2 cups canned lentils, drained
- 1 teaspoon turmeric powder
- 1 red onion, chopped
- ¼ cup veggie stock
- Salt and black pepper to the taste
- 4 tablespoons tomato sauce

Directions:
1. In the multi level air fryer's pan, combine the lentils with the turmeric and the other ingredients and toss.
2. Put the pan in the instant pot and seal with the air fryer lid.
3. Cook on Bake mode at 365 degrees F for 20 minutes and serve.

Nutrition:
calories 188, fat 3, fiber 4, carbs 9, protein 7

Tomato Broccoli and Corn Mix

Prep time: 5 minutes | **Cooking:** 20 minutes | **Servings:** 4

Ingredients:
- 1 cup corn
- 1 pound broccoli florets
- 2 teaspoons olive oil
- Juice of 1 lime
- 1 tablespoon tomato sauce
- 1 tablespoon cilantro, chopped
- Salt and black pepper to the taste

Directions:
1. In the multi level air fryer's pan, combine the broccoli with corn and the other ingredients and toss.
2. Put the pan in the instant pot and seal with the air fryer lid.
3. Cook on Bake mode at 370 degrees F for 20 minutes and serve.

Nutrition:
calories 199, fat 6, fiber 6, carbs 9, protein 6

Cumin and Parsley Beans Mix

Prep time: 6 minutes | **Cooking:** 25 minutes | **Servings:** 4

Ingredients:
- 1 cup canned white beans, drained and rinsed
- 1 cup canned red kidney beans, drained and rinsed
- 1 cup green beans, trimmed and halved
- 1 tablespoon olive oil
- ½ teaspoon cumin seeds
- ½ teaspoon coriander, ground
- ½ teaspoon garam masala
- Salt and black pepper to the taste
- 1 tablespoon lemon juice
- 1 tablespoon parsley, chopped

Directions:
1. In the multi level air fryer's pan, combine the beans with the cumin, coriander and the other ingredients and toss.
2. Put the pan in the instant pot and seal with the air fryer lid.
3. Cook on Bake mode at 37 degrees F for 25 minutes and serve.

Nutrition:
calories 199, fat 6, fiber 4, carbs 12 protein 6

Ginger Chickpeas Mix

Prep time: 10 minutes | **Cooking:** 20 minutes | **Servings:** 4

Ingredients:
- 2 cups canned chickpeas, drained
- 2 teaspoons avocado oil
- 1 teaspoon cinnamon powder
- 4 garlic cloves, minced
- 1 teaspoon ginger, grated
- ¼ teaspoon cardamom powder
- Salt and black pepper to the taste
- Juice of 1 lime

Directions:
1. In the multi level air fryer's pan, combine the chickpeas with the cinnamon and the other ingredients and toss.
2. Put the pan in the instant pot and seal with the air fryer lid.
3. Cook on Bake mode at 370 degrees F for 20 minutes and serve.

Nutrition:
calories 188, fat 4, fiber 8, carbs 15, protein 7

Garlic Zucchini

Prep time: 10 minutes | **Cooking:** 20 minutes | **Servings:** 4

Ingredients:
- 2 pounds zucchinis, roughly cubed
- 1 teaspoon garam masala
- 1 teaspoon fennel seeds, crushed
- ½ teaspoon mustard seeds
- 1 teaspoon garlic powder
- ¼ cup veggie stock
- Juice of ½ lime
- Salt and black pepper to the taste

Directions:
1. In the multi level air fryer's pan, combine the zucchinis with the masala and the other ingredients and toss.
2. Put the pan in the instant pot and seal with the air fryer lid.
3. Cook on Bake mode at 370 degrees F for 20 minutes and serve.

Nutrition:
calories 199, fat 4, fiber 7, carbs 12, protein 6

Beans and Grains Recipes

Parsley Wild Rice

Prep time: 10 minutes | **Cooking:** 25 minutes | **Servings:** 4

Ingredients:

- 1 cup wild rice
- 2 cups chicken stock
- ½ cup shallots, chopped
- ½ teaspoon sweet paprika
- ½ teaspoon cumin, ground
- A pinch of salt and black pepper
- A drizzle of olive oil
- 1 tablespoon parsley, chopped

Directions:

1. In the multi level air fryer's pan, combine the rice with the stock, shallots and the other ingredients and toss.
2. Put the pan in the instant pot and seal with the air fryer lid.
3. Cook on Bake mode at 350 degrees F for 25 minutes and serve.

Nutrition:

calories 142, fat 4, fiber 4, carbs 16, protein 4

Nutmeg Quinoa Mix

Prep time: 5 minutes | **Cooking:** 30 minutes | **Servings:** 4

Ingredients:

- 2 teaspoons avocado oil
- 1 red onion, chopped
- 1 cup quinoa
- ½ cup butternut squash, peeled and cubed
- 1 cup chicken stock
- 2 garlic cloves, minced
- ½ teaspoon nutmeg, ground
- A pinch of salt and black pepper

Directions:

1. In the multi level air fryer's pan, combine the rice with the quinoa with the squash and the other ingredients and toss.
2. Put the pan in the instant pot and seal with the air fryer lid.
3. Cook on Bake mode at 350 degrees F for 30 minutes and serve.

Nutrition:

calories 261, fat 6, fiber 7, carbs 29, protein 4

Chili Beans and Peas

Prep time: 10 minutes | **Cooking:** 25 minutes | **Servings:** 4

Ingredients:

- 2 cups canned black beans, drained
- 1 cup green peas
- 1 cup mild salsa
- ½ teaspoon cumin, ground
- ½ teaspoon chili powder
- ½ teaspoon green chili, minced
- ½ teaspoon ginger, grated
- A pinch of salt and black pepper

Directions:

1. In the multi level air fryer's pan, combine the beans with the peas and the other ingredients and toss.
2. Put the pan in the instant pot and seal with the air fryer lid.
3. Cook on Bake mode at 370 degrees F for 25 minutes and serve.

Nutrition:

calories 283, fat 4, fiber 8, carbs 34, protein 14

Paprika Bulgur Mix

Prep time: 10 minutes | **Cooking:** 25 minutes | **Servings:** 4

Ingredients:

- 1 cup bulgur
- 1 cup veggie stock
- ½ cup green peas
- 1 teaspoon sweet paprika
- 1 teaspoon coriander, ground
- Salt and black pepper to the taste
- 2 teaspoons olive oil
- ¼ cup parsley, chopped

Directions:

1. In the multi level air fryer's pan, combine the bulgur with the peas and the other ingredients and toss.
2. Put the pan in the instant pot and seal with the air fryer lid.
3. Cook on Bake mode at 360 degrees F for 25 minutes and serve.

Nutrition:

calories 313, fat 12, fiber 14, carbs 27, protein 44

Coconut Millet

Prep time: 10 minutes | **Cooking:** 20 minutes | **Servings:** 4

Ingredients:

- 3 cups coconut milk
- ½ teaspoon nutmeg, ground
- ½ teaspoon cinnamon powder
- 1 tablespoon honey
- 1 cup millet
- ¼ cup raisins

Directions:

1. In the multi level air fryer's pan, combine the millet with the coconut milk and the other ingredients and toss.
2. Put the pan in the instant pot and seal with the air fryer lid.
3. Cook on Bake mode at 380 degrees F for 20 minutes and serve.

Nutrition:

calories 231, fat 6, fiber 6, carbs 18, protein 6

Jalapeno Rice and Calamari

Prep time: 10 minutes | **Cooking:** 25 minutes | **Servings:** 4

Ingredients:

- 1 cup wild rice
- 2 cups fish stock
- ½ cup calamari rings
- ½ teaspoon sweet paprika
- ½ teaspoon curry powder
- 1 tablespoon olive oil
- 1 jalapeno pepper, chopped
- A pinch of salt and black pepper
- 1 tablespoon parsley, chopped

Directions:

1. In the multi level air fryer's pan, combine the rice with calamari and the other ingredients and toss.
2. Put the pan in the instant pot and seal with the air fryer lid.
3. Cook on Bake mode at 350 degrees F for 25 minutes and serve.

Nutrition:

calories 394, fat 5, fiber 8, carbs 18, protein 4

Fennel Quinoa

Prep time: 10 minutes | **Cooking:** 25 minutes | **Servings:** 4

Ingredients:

- 1 cup quinoa
- 1 cup veggie stock
- 1 fennel bulb, sliced
- ½ cup peas
- 2 teaspoons avocado oil
- 2 scallions, chopped
- 2 garlic cloves, minced
- 1 tablespoon basil, chopped
- Salt and black pepper to the taste

Directions:

1. In the multi level air fryer's pan, combine the quinoa with the fennel and the other ingredients and toss.
2. Put the pan in the instant pot and seal with the air fryer lid.
3. Cook on Bake mode at 370 degrees F for 25 minutes and serve.

Nutrition:

calories 264, fat 6, fiber 8, carbs 10, protein 5

Curry Chives Rice

Prep time: 10 minutes | **Cooking:** 25 minutes | **Servings:** 4

Ingredients:

- 1 cup wild rice
- 2 tablespoons green curry paste
- 2 cups chicken stock

- Salt and black pepper to the taste
- ½ teaspoon curry powder
- 1 tablespoon chives, chopped

Directions:
1. In the multi level air fryer's pan, combine the rice with curry paste and the other ingredients and toss.
2. Put the pan in the instant pot and seal with the air fryer lid.
3. Cook on Bake mode at 360 degrees F for 25 minutes and serve.

Nutrition:
calories 182, fat 1.6, fiber 2, carbs 37.5, protein 4.3

Pesto Buttery Rice

Prep time: 10 minutes | **Cooking:** 20 minutes | **Servings:** 4

Ingredients:
- 2 tablespoons butter, melted
- 1 cup white rice
- 2 cups veggie stock
- 2 tablespoons basil pesto
- ½ teaspoon chili powder
- ½ teaspoon turmeric powder
- Salt and black pepper to the taste

Directions:
1. In the multi level air fryer's pan, combine the rice with melted butter and the other ingredients and toss.
2. Put the pan in the instant pot and seal with the air fryer lid.
3. Cook on Air fry mode at 380 degrees F for 20 minutes and serve.

Nutrition:
calories 251, fat 4, fiber 3, carbs 13, protein 6

Lemon Quinoa

Prep time: 10 minutes | **Cooking:** 25 minutes | **Servings:** 4

Ingredients:
- 1 cup quinoa
- ¼ cup pine nuts, toasted
- 1 tablespoon basil pesto
- 2 cups veggie stock
- 1 tablespoon lemon juice
- 1 teaspoon garlic powder

Directions:
1. In the multi level air fryer's pan, combine the quinoa with pine nuts and the other ingredients and toss.
2. Put the pan in the instant pot and seal with the air fryer lid.
3. Cook on Bake mode at 350 degrees F for 25 minutes and serve.

Nutrition:
calories 200, fat 4, fiber 4, carbs 16, protein 4

Beans and Mushrooms Mix

Prep time: 5 minutes | **Cooking:** 25 minutes | **Servings:** 4

Ingredients:
- 2 teaspoons olive oil
- 2 spring onions, chopped
- 1 cup canned red kidney beans, drained
- 1 cup canned white beans, drained
- 2 tablespoons lime juice
- 1 cup mushrooms, halved
- 1 cup zucchinis, cubed
- 1 cup cherry tomatoes, cubed
- 1 red bell pepper, chopped
- 1 tablespoon tomato paste

Directions:
1. In the multi level air fryer's pan, combine the beans with the mushrooms and the other ingredients and toss.
2. Put the pan in the instant pot and seal with the air fryer lid.
3. Cook on Bake mode at 370 degrees F for 25 minutes and serve.

Nutrition:
calories 309, fat 11.7, fiber 4.6, carbs 8, protein 3.4

Tomato Beans Mix

Prep time: 10 minutes | **Cooking:** 25 minutes | **Servings:** 4

Ingredients:
- 1 yellow onion, chopped
- 1 cup canned black beans, drained
- 1 cup white beans, drained
- ¼ cup tomato sauce
- 1 tablespoon avocado oil
- 1 teaspoon cumin, ground
- Salt and black pepper to the taste
- 2 tablespoons parsley, chopped

Directions:
1. In the multi level air fryer's pan, combine the beans with tomato sauce and the other ingredients and toss.
2. Put the pan in the instant pot and seal with the air fryer lid.
3. Cook on Bake mode at 360 degrees F for 25 minutes and serve.

Nutrition:
calories 200, fat 6.4, fiber 6, carbs 16, protein 4

Beans and Quinoa

Prep time: 10 minutes | **Cooking:** 25 minutes | **Servings:** 4

Ingredients:
- 1 cup quinoa
- 1 cup canned black beans, drained
- 1 red chili pepper, chopped
- 1 teaspoon chili powder
- 1 cup veggie stock
- 2 teaspoons olive oil
- Salt and black pepper to the taste
- ½ teaspoon turmeric powder
- 1 tablespoon chives, chopped

Directions:
1. In the multi level air fryer's pan, combine the beans with the quinoa and the other ingredients and toss.
2. Put the pan in the instant pot and seal with the air fryer lid.
3. Cook on Air fry mode at 360 degrees F for 25 minutes and serve.

Nutrition:
calories 171, fat 4, fiber 8, carbs 16, protein 7

Berries Rice

Prep time: 10 minutes | **Cooking:** 20 minutes | **Servings:** 4

Ingredients:
- 1 cup white rice
- 2 cups coconut milk
- ½ cup mango, peeled and cubed
- ½ cup black berries, cubed
- 1 tablespoon sugar

Directions:
1. In the multi level air fryer's pan, combine the rice with berries and the other ingredients and toss.
2. Put the pan in the instant pot and seal with the air fryer lid.
3. Cook on Bake mode at 360 degrees F for 20 minutes and serve.

Nutrition:
calories 200, fat 4, fiber 5, carbs 11, protein 4

Simple Beans Mix

Prep time: 10 minutes | **Cooking:** 20 minutes | **Servings:** 4

Ingredients:
- 1 cup canned red kidney beans, drained
- 1 cup canned white beans, drained
- 1 teaspoon olive oil
- 1 tablespoon thyme, chopped
- ¼ cup tomato sauce
- Salt and black pepper to the taste

Directions:
1. In the multi level air fryer's pan, combine the beans with the thyme and the other ingredients and toss.
2. Put the pan in the instant pot and seal with the air fryer lid.
3. Cook on Bake mode at 350 degrees F for 20 minutes and serve.

Nutrition:
calories 161, fat 4, fiber 6, carbs 15, protein 6

Chives Beans Mix

Prep time: 10 minutes | **Cooking:** 25 minutes | **Servings:** 4

Ingredients:

- 1 cup canned red kidney beans, drained
- ½ pound baby kale
- ½ cup mild salsa
- 1 tablespoon olive oil
- ½ teaspoon sweet paprika
- Salt and black pepper to the taste
- ¼ cup chives, chopped

Directions:

1. In the multi level air fryer's pan, combine the beans with the kale and the other ingredients and toss.
2. Put the pan in the instant pot and seal with the air fryer lid.
3. Cook on Bake mode at 370 degrees F for 25 minutes and serve.

Nutrition:

calories 200, fat 12.2, fiber 3.4, carbs 7, protein 6

Paprika Barley

Prep time: 10 minutes | **Cooking:** 25 minutes | **Servings:** 4

Ingredients:

- 1 tablespoon olive oil
- 3 garlic cloves, minced
- 2 cups pearl barley, rinsed
- 2 cups veggie stock
- 1 teaspoon sweet paprika
- Salt and black pepper to the taste
- 1 tablespoon parsley, chopped

Directions:

1. In the multi level air fryer's pan, combine the barley with the garlic and the other ingredients and toss.
2. Put the pan in the instant pot and seal with the air fryer lid.
3. Cook on Bake mode at 370 degrees F for 25 minutes and serve.

Nutrition:

calories 232, fat 5, fiber 3.4, carbs 12, protein 4

Quinoa Salad

Prep time: 10 minutes | **Cooking:** 20 minutes | **Servings:** 4

Ingredients:

- 1 cup quinoa
- 2 cups veggie stock
- ½ cup broccoli florets
- 1 cup carrots, peeled and grated
- ¼ cup celery, chopped
- Salt and black pepper to the taste

Directions:

1. In the multi level air fryer's pan, combine the quinoa with the broccoli and the other ingredients and toss.
2. Put the pan in the instant pot and seal with the air fryer lid.
3. Cook on Air fry mode at 370 degrees F for 20 minutes and serve.

Nutrition:

calories 200, fat 4, fiber 2.3, carbs 12, protein 5

Spring Onions Beans

Prep time: 10 minutes | **Cooking:** 25 minutes | **Servings:** 4

Ingredients:

- 1 cup green beans, trimmed and halved
- 1 cup canned red kidney beans, drained
- 1 tablespoon olive oil
- ½ cup spring onions, chopped
- ½ cup cherry tomatoes, halved
- Salt and black pepper to the taste
- 1 tablespoon balsamic vinegar
- ½ cup kalamata olives, pitted and chopped

Directions:

1. In the multi level air fryer's pan, combine the beans with the spring onions and the other ingredients and toss.
2. Put the pan in the instant pot and seal with the air fryer lid.
3. Cook on Bake mode at 370 degrees F for 25 minutes and serve.

Nutrition:

calories 200, fat 2, fiber 2.3, carbs 4.5, protein 3.4

Cracked What and Veggies Mix

Prep time: 10 minutes | **Cooking:** 20 minutes | **Servings:** 4

Ingredients:

- ½ cup cracked whole wheat
- 1 cup veggie stock
- 1 cup white mushrooms, sliced
- ½ cup carrots, peeled and grated
- 1 cup cherry tomatoes, halved
- Salt and black pepper to the taste
- ¼ teaspoon cumin, ground
- 1 teaspoon curry powder
- 1 tablespoon cilantro, chopped

Directions:

1. In the multi level air fryer's pan, combine the wheat with the stock and the other ingredients and toss.
2. Put the pan in the instant pot and seal with the air fryer lid.
3. Cook on Bake mode at 380 degrees F for 20 minutes and serve.

Nutrition:

calories 200, fat 12, fiber 3, carbs 4.4, protein 3.4

Turmeric Beans Mix

Prep time: 5 minutes | **Cooking:** 25 minutes | **Servings:** 4

Ingredients:

- 2 cups canned white beans, drained
- 1 cup heavy cream
- ½ teaspoon turmeric powder
- 1 teaspoon fennel seeds
- ½ teaspoon garam masala
- A pinch of salt and black pepper

Directions:

1. In the multi level air fryer's pan, combine the beans with the cream and the other ingredients and toss.
2. Put the pan in the instant pot and seal with the air fryer lid.
3. Cook on Bake mode at 380 degrees F for 25 minutes and serve.

Nutrition:

calories 200, fat 12, fiber 2.3, carbs 5.5, protein 4.3

Soy Bulgur Mix

Prep time: 5 minutes | **Cooking:** 25 minutes | **Servings:** 4

Ingredients:

- 1 cup bulgur
- 2 teaspoons olive oil
- ½ cup walnuts, chopped
- 2 garlic cloves, minced
- 1 cup veggie stock
- 1 tablespoon soy sauce
- Salt and black pepper to the taste
- 1 tablespoon chives, chopped

Directions:

1. In the multi level air fryer's pan, combine the bulgur with the walnuts and the other ingredients and toss.
2. Put the pan in the instant pot and seal with the air fryer lid.
3. Cook on Bake mode at 370 degrees F for 25 minutes and serve.

Nutrition:

calories 233, fat 3, fiber 3.4, carbs 12, protein 4

Ginger Bulgur

Prep time: 5 minutes | **Cooking:** 25 minutes | **Servings:** 4

Ingredients:

- 1 red onion, chopped
- 1 cup bulgur
- 1 cup veggie stock
- 1 tablespoon mint, chopped
- Salt and black pepper to the taste
- ½ teaspoon ginger, grated
- 2 garlic clove, minced

- 1 tablespoon lemon juice
- ½ cup walnuts, toasted and chopped

Directions:
1. In the multi level air fryer's pan, combine the bulgur with the mint and the other ingredients and toss.
2. Put the pan in the instant pot and seal with the air fryer lid.
3. Cook on Bake mode at 370 degrees F for 25 minutes and serve.

Nutrition:
calories 263, fat 12, fiber 4, carbs 8.9, protein 4

Peanuts and Walnuts Rice

Prep time: 10 minutes | **Cooking:** 25 minutes | **Servings:** 4

Ingredients:
- 1 cup wild rice
- ½ cup peanuts, chopped
- ½ cup walnuts, chopped
- ½ cup spring onions, chopped
- 2 cups veggie stock
- A pinch of salt and black pepper

Directions:
1. In the multi level air fryer's pan, combine the rice with the peanuts and the other ingredients and toss.
2. Put the pan in the instant pot and seal with the air fryer lid.
3. Cook on Bake mode at 380 degrees F for 25 minutes and serve.

Nutrition:
calories 233, fat 12, fiber 4, carbs 4.5, protein 12

Parsley Couscous Mix

Prep time: 10 minutes | **Cooking:** 20 minutes | **Servings:** 4

Ingredients:
- 1 cup couscous, cooked
- 1 red bell pepper, chopped
- 1 red onion, chopped
- ½ cup mushrooms, halved
- ½ cup eggplants, cubed
- ½ teaspoon chili powder
- ½ cup chicken stock
- A handful parsley, chopped

Directions:
1. In the multi level air fryer's pan, combine the couscous with the pepper and the other ingredients and toss.
2. Put the pan in the instant pot and seal with the air fryer lid.
3. Cook on Bake mode at 370 degrees F for 20 minutes and serve.

Nutrition:
calories 300, fat 12, fiber 3, carbs 12, protein 4.5

Indian Couscous

Prep time: 10 minutes | **Cooking:** 20 minutes | **Servings:** 4

Ingredients:
- 2 spring onions, chopped
- 2 teaspoons olive oil
- 1 cup couscous, rinsed
- 2 cups veggie stock
- ½ teaspoon garam masala
- ¼ teaspoon coriander, ground
- Salt and black pepper to the taste
- 1 tablespoon chives, chopped

Directions:
1. In the multi level air fryer's pan, combine the couscous with the stock and the other ingredients and toss.
2. Put the pan in the instant pot and seal with the air fryer lid.
3. Cook on Bake mode at 360 degrees F for 20 minutes and serve.

Nutrition:
calories 200, fat 4, fiber 2.3, carbs 12, protein 6

Lemon Millet Mix

Prep time: 10 minutes | **Cooking:** 20 minutes | **Servings:** 4

Ingredients:
- 1 cup millet
- 2 cups veggie stock
- 1 cup baby kale, torn
- ½ teaspoon chili powder
- ½ teaspoon smoked paprika
- ¼ cup parsley, chopped
- 1 tablespoon lemon zest, grated
- 1 tablespoon lemon juice
- Salt and black pepper to the taste

Directions:
1. In the multi level air fryer's pan, combine the millet with the kale and the other ingredients and toss.
2. Put the pan in the instant pot and seal with the air fryer lid.
3. Cook on Bake mode at 370 degrees F for 20 minutes and serve.

Nutrition:
calories 200, fat 4, fiber 2.3, carbs 12, protein 6

Celery Quinoa Mix

Prep time: 10 minutes | **Cooking:** 20 minutes | **Servings:** 4

Ingredients:
- 1 cup quinoa
- 1 cup celery, chopped
- 4 cardamom pods, crushed
- 1 cup veggie stock
- 1 teaspoon coriander, ground
- 1 tablespoon lime juice
- ¼ cup cilantro, chopped
- ½ teaspoon cumin seeds, ground
- Salt and black pepper to the tasted

Directions:
1. In the multi level air fryer's pan, combine the quinoa with the celery, cardamom and the other ingredients and toss.
2. Put the pan in the instant pot and seal with the air fryer lid.
3. Cook on Bake mode at 380 degrees F for 20 minutes and serve.

Nutrition:
calories 232, fat 1, fiber 4.3, carbs 12, protein 5

Curry Hot Beans

Prep time: 10 minutes | **Cooking:** 20 minutes | **Servings:** 4

Ingredients:
- 1 cup canned black beans, drained and rinsed
- 1 cup canned red kidney beans, drained and rinsed
- 2 Thai chilies, chopped
- 1 tablespoon soy sauce
- 1 carrot, peeled and grated
- 1 tablespoon ginger, grated
- 2 curry leaves, crushed
- ¼ teaspoon mustard seeds
- A pinch of salt and black pepper

Directions:
1. In the multi level air fryer's pan, combine the beans with chilies and the other ingredients and toss.
2. Put the pan in the instant pot and seal with the air fryer lid.
3. Cook on Bake mode at 370 degrees F for 20 minutes and serve.

Nutrition:
calories 233, fat 12, fiber 3, carbs 7, protein 4

Spinach Almond Quinoa

Prep time: 10 minutes | **Cooking:** 20 minutes | **Servings:** 4

Ingredients:
- 2 cups quinoa
- 1 cup veggie stock
- 1 cup baby spinach, torn
- A pinch of salt and black pepper
- 2 teaspoons avocado oil
- 2 tomatoes, chopped
- ¼ cup almonds, sliced

Directions:
1. In the multi level air fryer's pan, combine the quinoa with the spinach and the other ingredients and toss.
2. Put the pan in the instant pot and seal with the air fryer lid.
3. Cook on Bake mode at 370 degrees F for 20 minutes and serve.

Nutrition: calories 253, fat 6, fiber 3.4, carbs 14, protein 7.5

Basil Chickpeas

Prep time: 10 minutes | **Cooking:** 20 minutes | **Servings:** 4

Ingredients:
- 2 cups canned chickpeas, drained
- 3 spring onions, chopped
- 1 tablespoon olive oil
- 1 teaspoon chili powder
- 1 teaspoon basil, dried
- Salt and black pepper to the taste
- ¼ cup tomato sauce

Directions:
1. In the multi level air fryer's pan, combine the chickpeas with the spring onions and the other ingredients and toss.
2. Put the pan in the instant pot and seal with the air fryer lid.
3. Cook on Bake mode at 376 degrees F for 20 minutes and serve.

Nutrition: calories 232, fat 12, fiber 4, carbs 8.5, protein 4

Lentils and Tomatoes Mix

Prep time: 10 minutes | **Cooking:** 20 minutes | **Servings:** 4

Ingredients:
- 1 cup canned lentils, drained
- 1 cup zucchinis, roughly cubed
- 2 teaspoons avocado oil
- Juice of 1 lime
- ½ cup tomato passata
- 2 celery ribs, chopped
- ¼ teaspoon red pepper flakes, crushed
- 1 cup tomatoes, cubed
- ½ teaspoon sweet paprika
- Salt and black pepper to the taste

Directions:
1. In the multi level air fryer's pan, combine the lentils with the zucchinis and the other ingredients and toss.
2. Put the pan in the instant pot and seal with the air fryer lid.
3. Cook on Bake mode at 370 degrees F for 20 minutes and serve.

Nutrition: calories 273, fat 12, fiber 5, carbs 12, protein 5

Cranberry Beans Mix

Prep time: 10 minutes | **Cooking:** 20 minutes | **Servings:** 4

Ingredients:
- 1 cup cranberry beans, soaked for 8 hours and drained
- 1 cup veggie stock
- ½ teaspoon sweet paprika
- Salt and black pepper to the taste
- 1 cup kale, chopped
- 2 teaspoons avocado oil
- ½ teaspoon garlic powder

Directions:
1. In the multi level air fryer's pan, combine the beans with the stock and the other ingredients and toss.
2. Put the pan in the instant pot and seal with the air fryer lid.
3. Cook on Air fry mode at 370 degrees F for 20 minutes and serve.

Nutrition: calories 223, fat 6, fiber 6, carbs 12, protein 8

Hot Lentils Mix

Prep time: 10 minutes | **Cooking:** 20 minutes | **Servings:** 4

Ingredients:
- 2 cups canned lentils, drained and rinsed
- 1 cup canned tomatoes and green chilies, chopped
- 1 cup veggie stock
- ½ teaspoon cumin, ground
- 2 tablespoons tomato paste
- 1 teaspoon chili powder
- ½ teaspoon hot paprika
- Salt and black pepper to the taste

Directions:
1. In the multi level air fryer's pan, combine the lentils with tomatoes and chilies and the other ingredients and toss.
2. Put the pan in the instant pot and seal with the air fryer lid.
3. Cook on Bake mode at 370 degrees F for 20 minutes and serve.

Nutrition: calories 232, fat 12, fiber 5, carbs 7, protein 3.5

Quinoa and Eggplant Tacos

Prep time: 10 minutes | **Cooking:** 20 minutes | **Servings:** 4

Ingredients:
- 2 cups quinoa
- ½ cup tomato sauce
- ½ teaspoon chili powder
- 1 teaspoon garlic powder
- 1 cup eggplant, cubed
- Taco shells for serving

Directions:
1. In the multi level air fryer's pan, combine the quinoa with tomato sauce and the other ingredients except the taco shells.
2. Put the pan in the instant pot and seal with the air fryer lid.
3. Cook on Bake mode at 370 degrees F for 20 minutes and serve.
4. Divide the mix into taco shells and serve.

Nutrition: calories 252, fat 12, fiber 5, carbs 12.1, protein 4.3

Lentils with Peppers and Zucchinis Mix

Prep time: 10 minutes | **Cooking:** 25 minutes | **Servings:** 4

Ingredients:
- 2 cups canned green lentils
- 2 cups chicken stock
- 3 spring onions, chopped
- 1 cup red bell pepper, chopped
- ½ cup zucchinis, cubed
- 1 tablespoon chives, chopped
- Salt and black pepper to the taste
- ½ teaspoon Italian seasoning

Directions:
1. In the multi level air fryer's pan, combine the lentils with pepper, zucchinis and the other ingredients and toss.
2. Put the pan in the instant pot and seal with the air fryer lid.
3. Cook on Bake mode at 370 degrees F for 25 minutes and serve.

Nutrition: calories 232, fat 12, fiber 3, carbs 8, protein 3.4

Quinoa and Sauce

Prep time: 10 minutes | **Cooking:** 20 minutes | **Servings:** 4

Ingredients:
- 1 tablespoon olive oil
- 1 cup quinoa
- 1 cup tomato sauce
- 1 yellow onion, chopped
- 1 celery stalk, chopped
- ½ teaspoon coriander, ground
- ½ teaspoon cumin, ground
- Salt and black pepper to the taste
- 1 teaspoon curry powder

Directions:
1. In the multi level air fryer's pan, combine the quinoa with tomato sauce and the other ingredients and toss.
2. Put the pan in the instant pot and seal with the air fryer lid.
3. Cook on Bake mode at 370 degrees F for 20 minutes and serve.

Nutrition: calories 182, fat 5, fiber 2.3, carbs 12, protein 7.4

Cilantro Lentils and Rice Mix

Prep time: 10 minutes | **Cooking:** 20 minutes | **Servings:** 4

Ingredients:
- 2 teaspoons olive oil
- 1 cup canned red lentils, drained
- 1 cup wild rice
- 2 cups veggie stock
- 1 yellow onion, chopped
- ¼ teaspoon garlic powder
- Salt and black pepper to the taste
- 1 tablespoon cilantro, chopped

Directions:
1. In the multi level air fryer's pan, combine the lentils with the rice and the other ingredients and toss.
2. Put the pan in the instant pot and seal with the air fryer lid.
3. Cook on Bake mode at 380 degrees F for 20 minutes and serve.

Nutrition:
calories 162, fat 11, fiber 4.4, carbs 25, protein 10.2

Bok Choy Salad

Prep time: 10 minutes | **Cooking:** 20 minutes | **Servings:** 4

Ingredients:
- 1 cup bok choy, torn
- 1 cup canned lentils, drained
- 1 cup veggie stock
- ½ cup spring onions, chopped
- 1 cup corn
- 1 cup black olives, pitted and halved
- ¼ cup red bell pepper, chopped
- 2 teaspoons olive oil
- Juice of 1 lemon
- 2 tablespoons parsley, chopped
- Salt and black pepper to the taste

Directions:
1. In the multi level air fryer's pan, combine the bok choy with the spring onions and the other ingredients and toss.
2. Put the pan in the instant pot and seal with the air fryer lid.
3. Cook on Bake mode at 380 degrees F for 20 minutes and serve.

Nutrition:
calories 172, fat 5, fiber 2.4, carbs 11, protein 7

Chickpeas Salad

Prep time: 10 minutes | **Cooking:** 20 minutes | **Servings:** 4

Ingredients:
- 2 cups canned chickpeas, drained and rinsed
- 1 cup corn
- 1 cup black olives, pitted and halved
- 1 cup baby spinach
- 1 cup cherry tomatoes, halved
- 2 teaspoons olive oil
- 2 teaspoons garam masala
- Salt and black pepper to the taste
- 1 tablespoon cilantro, chopped

Directions:
1. In the multi level air fryer's pan, combine the chickpeas with the corn and the other ingredients and toss.
2. Put the pan in the instant pot and seal with the air fryer lid.
3. Cook on Bake mode at 380 degrees F for 20 minutes and serve.

Nutrition:
calories 263, fat 8.3, fiber 2.3, carbs 14, protein 11.2

Chickpeas and Kale Mix

Prep time: 10 minutes | **Cooking:** 25 minutes | **Servings:** 4

Ingredients:
- 1 red onion, chopped
- ½ pound gold potatoes, peeled and cubed
- 2 cups canned chickpeas, drained and rinsed
- 1 cup cherry tomatoes, halved
- ½ cup avocado, peeled, pitted and cubed
- 1 tablespoon olive oil
- 1 cup baby kale
- 2 garlic cloves, minced
- Salt and black pepper to the taste
- 1 tablespoon parsley, chopped

Directions:
1. In the multi level air fryer's pan, combine the potatoes with chickpeas, kale and the other ingredients.
2. Put the pan in the instant pot and seal with the air fryer lid.
3. Cook on Bake mode at 370 degrees F for 25 minutes and serve.

Nutrition:
calories 300, fat 8, fiber 2.3, carbs 14, protein 11

Chickpeas, Spinach and Bulgur

Prep time: 10 minutes | **Cooking:** 25 minutes | **Servings:** 4

Ingredients:
- 2 cups canned chickpeas, drained and rinsed
- 1 cup bulgur
- 1 cup veggie stock
- 1 cup baby spinach
- 1 cup kalamata olives, pitted and halved
- 2 tomatoes, cubed
- 2 teaspoons olive oil
- 1 tablespoon chives, chopped
- Salt and black pepper to the taste

Directions:
1. In the multi level air fryer's pan, combine the chickpeas with the bulgur and the other ingredients and toss.
2. Put the pan in the instant pot and seal with the air fryer lid.
3. Cook on Bake mode at 380 degrees F for 25 minutes and serve.

Nutrition:
calories 232, fat 11, fiber 5.4, carbs 12, protein 7

Basil Lime Chickpeas

Prep time: 10 minutes | **Cooking:** 20 minutes | **Servings:** 4

Ingredients:
- 2 tablespoons basil pesto
- 2 cups canned chickpeas, drained
- 1 yellow onion, chopped
- 1 tablespoon avocado oil
- Juice of 1 lime
- ½ cup tomato sauce
- A pinch of salt and black pepper

Directions:
1. In the multi level air fryer's pan, combine the chickpeas with the spring onions and the other ingredients and toss.
2. Put the pan in the instant pot and seal with the air fryer lid.
3. Cook on Bake mode at 376 degrees F for 20 minutes and serve.

Nutrition:
calories 253, fat 4.4, fiber 2.3, carbs 12, protein 5

Thyme Kidney Beans

Prep time: 10 minutes | **Cooking:** 25 minutes | **Servings:** 4

Ingredients:
- 1 tablespoon avocado oil
- 2 cups canned red kidney beans, drained and rinsed
- ½ teaspoon thyme, dried
- ½ teaspoon cumin, ground
- 1 cup veggie stock
- 2 tablespoons tomato paste
- 1 teaspoon cayenne pepper
- Salt and black pepper to the taste

Directions:
1. In the multi level air fryer's pan, combine the beans with the thyme and the other ingredients and toss.
2. Put the pan in the instant pot and seal with the air fryer lid.
3. Cook on Bake mode at 380 degrees F for 25 minutes and serve.

Nutrition:
calories 200, fat 6, fiber 2, carbs 14, protein 11.2

Butter Quinoa Curry

Prep time: 10 minutes | **Cooking:** 20 minutes | **Servings:** 4

Ingredients:

- 2 cups quinoa
- 1 cup veggie stock
- 1 red onion, chopped
- 1 cup coconut cream
- 4 garlic cloves, chopped
- 1 tablespoon butter, melted
- 1 red chili pepper, chopped
- Salt and black pepper to the taste
- 1 teaspoon turmeric powder
- 2 teaspoons garam masala
- ¼ cup cilantro, chopped

Directions:

1. In the multi level air fryer's pan, combine the quinoa with the onion, coconut cream and the other ingredients and toss.
2. Put the pan in the instant pot and seal with the air fryer lid.
3. Cook on Bake mode at 380 degrees F for 20 minutes and serve.

Nutrition:

calories 252, fat 5, fiber 4, carbs 12, protein 5

Bulgur and Peppers Mix

Prep time: 10 minutes | **Cooking:** 20 minutes | **Servings:** 4

Ingredients:

- 1 cup bulgur
- 1 teaspoon Cajun seasoning
- 1 teaspoon coriander, ground
- 2 teaspoons olive oil
- 1 cup tomato paste
- 1 red bell pepper, chopped
- 1 green bell pepper, chopped
- A pinch of salt and black pepper
- 1 tablespoon chives, chopped

Directions:

1. In the multi level air fryer's pan, combine the bulgur with seasoning and the other ingredients and toss.
2. Put the pan in the instant pot and seal with the air fryer lid.
3. Cook on Bake mode at 380 degrees F for 20 minutes and serve.

Nutrition:

calories 232, fat 4, fiber 5, carbs 12, protein 6

Black Beans and Onion Mix

Prep time: 10 minutes | **Cooking:** 25 minutes | **Servings:** 4

Ingredients:

- 1 tablespoon avocado oil
- 2 cups canned black beans, drained and rinsed
- 1 cup bacon, chopped
- 1 red onion, chopped
- 1 cup tomato sauce
- A pinch of salt and black pepper
- 1 tablespoon chives, chopped

Directions:

1. In the multi level air fryer's pan, combine the beans with the bacon and the other ingredients and toss.
2. Put the pan in the instant pot and seal with the air fryer lid.
3. Cook on Bake mode at 370 degrees F for 25 minutes and serve.

Nutrition:

calories 262, fat 6, fiber 2.3, carbs 12, protein 6

Rosemary Black Beans

Prep time: 10 minutes | **Cooking:** 30 minutes | **Servings:** 4

Ingredients:

- 1 cup canned black beans, drained and rinsed
- 1 cup cherry tomatoes, halved
- 1 tablespoon olive oil
- 1 cup tomato sauce
- 1 yellow onion, chopped
- ½ teaspoon rosemary, dried
- 2 garlic cloves, minced
- 1 tablespoon chives, chopped
- Salt and black pepper to the taste

Directions:

1. In the multi level air fryer's pan, combine the beans with tomatoes and the other ingredients and toss.
2. Put the pan in the instant pot and seal with the air fryer lid.
3. Cook on Bake mode at 370 degrees F for 30 minutes and serve.

Nutrition:

calories 263, fat 7, fiber 2, carbs 12, protein 15

Tomato Quinoa

Prep time: 10 minutes | **Cooking:** 25 minutes | **Servings:** 4

Ingredients:

- 2 cups quinoa
- 1 cup veggie stock
- 4 garlic cloves, minced
- 2 teaspoons cumin, ground
- 1 teaspoon chipotle powder
- 2 tablespoons tomato paste
- ½ teaspoon coriander, ground
- Salt and black pepper to the taste

Directions:

1. In the multi level air fryer's pan, combine the quinoa with the stock and the other ingredients and toss.
2. Put the pan in the instant pot and seal with the air fryer lid.
3. Cook on Bake mode at 380 degrees F for 25 minutes and serve.

Nutrition:

calories 262, fat 12, fiber 3, carbs 12, protein 5

Chives Salsa Lentils

Prep time: 10 minutes | **Cooking:** 25 minutes | **Servings:** 4

Ingredients:

- 2 cups canned lentils, drained and rinsed
- 1 cup mild salsa
- Juice of 1 lime
- 2 teaspoons avocado oil
- Salt and black pepper to the taste
- 1 teaspoon sweet paprika
- 1 tablespoon chives, chopped

Directions:

1. In the multi level air fryer's pan, combine the lentils with salsa and the other ingredients and toss.
2. Put the pan in the instant pot and seal with the air fryer lid.
3. Cook on Bake mode at 370 degrees F for 20 minutes and serve.

Nutrition:

calories 252, fat 8, fiber 2.3, carbs 12, protein 6

Snacks and Appetizers Recipes

Cod Bites

Prep time: 10 minutes | **Cooking:** 20 minutes | **Servings:** 4

Ingredients:

- 1 pound cod fillets, boneless and cubed
- 2 eggs, whisked
- 2 cups coconut flesh, shredded
- 1 teaspoon turmeric powder
- ½ teaspoon rosemary, dried
- Salt and black pepper to the taste

Directions:

1. Put the coconut in a bowl and whisk the eggs with the other ingredients except the fish in another one.
2. Dredge the cod bites in eggs and then in coconut, and place them in the multi level air fryer's basket.
3. Put the basket in the instant pot and seal with the air fryer lid.
4. Cook on Air fry mode at 360 degrees F for 20 minutes.
5. Divide the mix into bowls and serve as a snack.

Nutrition:

calories 150, fat 4, fiber 3, carbs 13, protein 4

Balsamic Chicken Wings

Prep time: 10 minutes | **Cooking:** 25 minutes | **Servings:** 4

Ingredients:

- 1 pound chicken wings
- 2 tablespoons balsamic vinegar
- 2 tablespoons honey
- ½ teaspoon sweet paprika
- ½ teaspoon chili powder
- Salt and black pepper to the taste
- ½ tablespoon olive oil

Directions:

1. In a bowl, mix the chicken wings with the vinegar and the other ingredients, toss, place them in your multi level air fryer's basket and place the basket in the instant pot.
2. Seal with the air fryer lid and cook on Air fry mode at 400 degrees F for 25 minutes.
3. Serve as an appetizer.

Nutrition:

calories 181, fat 4, fiber 7, carbs 15, protein 18

Mozzarella Balls

Prep time: 10 minutes | **Cooking:** 14 minutes | **Servings:** 8

Ingredients:

- 3 zucchinis, grated
- Salt and black pepper to the taste
- 1 tablespoon almond flour
- 2 tablespoons mozzarella, shredded
- 2 tablespoons cheddar cheese, shredded
- ½ tablespoon lemon juice
- 1 tablespoon dill, chopped

Directions:

1. In a bowl, mix the zucchinis with the flour and the other ingredients, toss, and shape medium balls out of this mix.
2. Place the balls in the multi level air fryer's basket.
3. Put the basket in the instant pot and seal with the air fryer lid.
4. Cook on Air fry mode at 400 degrees F for 14 minutes and serve.

Nutrition:

calories 194, fat 9, fiber 2, carbs 11, protein 15

Mixed Salsa

Prep time: 4 minutes | **Cooking:** 12 minutes | **Servings:** 2

Ingredients:

- 1 yellow bell pepper, cut into strips
- 1 orange bell pepper, cut into strips
- 1 red bell pepper, cut into strips
- 1 cup cherry tomatoes, cubed
- 1 cup black olives, pitted and sliced
- 2 tablespoons balsamic vinegar
- Salt and black pepper to the taste
- 1 green onion, chopped
- 1 tablespoon chives, chopped

Directions:

1. In the multi level air fryer's pan, combine the peppers with the tomatoes and the other ingredients and toss.
2. Put the pan in the instant pot and seal with the air fryer lid.
3. Cook on Bake mode at 400 degrees F for 12 minutes and serve.

Nutrition:

calories 150, fat 1, fiber 2, carbs 7, protein 5

Turmeric Cheese Dip

Prep time: 4 minutes | **Cooking:** 10 minutes | **Servings:** 6

Ingredients:

- 2 cups cream cheese, soft
- 1 cup heavy cream
- ½ teaspoon turmeric powder
- Salt and black pepper to the taste
- 1 tablespoon chives, chopped
- 1 tablespoons basil, chopped

Directions:

1. In the multi level air fryer's pan, combine the cream cheese with the cream and the other ingredients and toss,
2. Put the pan in the instant pot and seal with the air fryer lid.
3. Cook on Bake mode at 360 degrees F for 10 minutes and serve as a snack

Nutrition:

calories 140, fat 1, fiber 4, carbs 8, protein 3

Minty Greek Dip

Prep time: 10 minutes | **Cooking:** 12 minutes | **Servings:** 6

Ingredients:

- 1 cup mozzarella, shredded
- 1 cup cheddar cheese, shredded
- 1 cup heavy cream
- ½ cup Greek yogurt
- 1 tablespoons mint, chopped

Directions:

1. In the multi level air fryer's pan, combine the mozzarella with the yogurt and the other ingredients and toss.
2. Put the pan in the instant pot and seal with the air fryer lid.
3. Cook on Bake mode at 390 degrees F for 12 minutes, divide into bowls and serve.

Nutrition:

calories 194, fat 4, fiber 2, carbs 12, protein 7

Shrimp Platter

Prep time: 5 minutes | **Cooking:** 12 minutes | **Servings:** 4

Ingredients:

- 1 pound shrimp, peeled and deveined
- 1 tablespoon Italian seasoning
- ½ teaspoon cumin, ground
- ½ teaspoon mustard seeds, crushed
- 2 tablespoons lemon juice
- Salt and black pepper to the taste
- A drizzle of olive oil

Directions:

1. In the multi level air fryer's basket, mix the shrimp with the seasoning and the other ingredients and toss.

2. Put the basket in the instant pot and seal with the air fryer lid.
3. Cook on Air fry mode at 390 degrees F for 20 minutes.
4. Arrange the shrimp on a platter and serve as an appetizer.

Nutrition:

calories 200, fat 5, fiber 3, carbs 13, protein 4

Kale and Yogurt Dip

Prep time: 10 minutes | **Cooking:** 15 minutes | **Servings:** 4

Ingredients:

- 2 cups baby kale
- 1 cup heavy cream
- 1 cup Greek Yogurt
- 4 garlic cloves, minced
- 1 avocado, peeled, pitted and cubed

Directions:

1. In a blender, mix the kale with the cream and the other ingredients, pulse well, and transfer this to the multi level air fryer's pan.
2. Put the pan in the instant pot and seal with the air fryer lid.
3. Cook on Bake mode at 380 degrees F for 15 minutes and serve cold as a party dip..

Nutrition:

calories 153, fat 1, fiber 2, carbs 11, protein 5

Potato Chips

Prep time: 10 minutes | **Cooking:** 20 minutes | **Servings:** 4

Ingredients:

- 2 sweet potatoes, thinly sliced
- 1 teaspoon sweet paprika
- 1 teaspoon chili powder
- Salt and black pepper to the taste
- 1 tablespoon olive oil

Directions:

1. In the multi level air fryer's basket, combine the potato chips with the other ingredients and toss.
2. Put the basket in the instant pot and seal with the air fryer lid.
3. Cook on Air fry mode at 400 degrees F for 20 minutes and serve.

Nutrition:

calories 143, fat 4, fiber 1.5, carbs 10, protein 5

Masala Shrimp Dip

Prep time: 5 minutes | **Cooking:** 12 minutes | **Servings:** 4

Ingredients:

- 1 pound shrimp, peeled, deveined and chopped
- 1 cup heavy cream
- 1 teaspoon garam masala
- 2 green onions, chopped
- 2 teaspoons olive oil
- Salt and black pepper to the taste

Directions:

1. In the multi level air fryer's pan, combine the shrimp with the cream and the other ingredients and toss well.
2. Put the pan in the instant pot and seal with the air fryer lid.
3. Cook on Bake mode at 350 degrees F for 12 minutes and serve as a party dip.

Nutrition:

calories 100, fat 3, fiber 3, carbs 12, protein 5

Chives Broccoli Spread

Prep time: 4 minutes | **Cooking:** 15 minutes | **Servings:** 4

Ingredients:

- 1 pound broccoli florets, chopped
- 1 cup heavy cream
- 1 teaspoon sweet paprika
- Salt and black pepper to the taste
- 1 teaspoon olive oil
- 2 teaspoons garlic powder
- 1 tablespoon chives, chopped

Directions:

1. In a blender, mix the broccoli with the cream and the other ingredients and pulse well.
2. Transfer to the multi level air fryer's pan, put the pan in the instant pot and seal with the air fryer lid.
3. Cook on Bake mode at 400 degrees F for 15 minutes.
4. Divide into bowls and serve as a party spread.

Nutrition:

calories 138, fat 2, fiber 2, carbs 11, protein 2

Coated Broccoli Bites

Prep time: 5 minutes | **Cooking:** 15 minutes | **Servings:** 4

Ingredients:

- 1 pound broccoli florets
- 2 eggs, whisked
- A drizzle of olive oil
- Salt and black pepper to the taste
- 3 tablespoons breadcrumbs

Directions:

1. In a bowl, mix the broccoli with the eggs and the other ingredients and toss.
2. Place them in your multi level air fryer's basket.
3. Put the basket in the instant pot, seal with the air fryer lid and cook on Air Fry mode at 360 degrees F for 15 minutes.
4. Divide into bowls and serve.

Nutrition:

calories 200, fat 7, fiber 1, carbs 13, protein 9

Yogurt Dip

Prep time: 10 minutes | **Cooking:** 15 minutes | **Servings:** 4

Ingredients:

- 1 cup heavy cream
- Juice and zest of 1 lemon
- ½ teaspoon turmeric powder
- Salt and black pepper to the taste
- ½ cup yogurt
- 1 teaspoon garlic powder

Directions:

1. In a bowl, mix the cream with the lemon juice, zest and the other ingredients, whisk and transfer to a ramekin.
2. Place the ramekin in the multi level air fryer's basket.
3. Put the basket in the instant pot and seal with the air fryer lid.
4. Cook on Bake mode at 360 degrees F for 15 minutes and serve as a party dip.

Nutrition:

calories 179, fat 6, fiber 12, carbs 11, protein 4

Tofu Bites

Prep time: 10 minutes | **Cooking:** 20 minutes | **Servings:** 4

Ingredients:

- 1 pound tofu, cubed
- A drizzle of avocado oil
- 1 tablespoon oregano, chopped
- 2 tablespoons balsamic vinegar
- A pinch of salt and black pepper

Directions:

1. In a bowl, mix the tofu with the oil and the other ingredients and toss.
2. Transfer the tofu bites to your multi level air fryer's basket.
3. Put the basket in the instant pot and seal with the air fryer lid.
4. Cook on Air fry mode at 370 degrees F for 20 minutes and serve

as a snack.

Nutrition:
calories 100, fat 4, fiber 1, carbs 11, protein 1

Balsamic Dip

Prep time: 10 minutes | **Cooking:** 30 minutes | **Servings:** 4

Ingredients:
- 1 pound cherry tomatoes, cubed
- 1 cup tomato sauce
- 1 red onion, chopped
- 1 tablespoon olive oil
- 2 tablespoons balsamic vinegar
- 3 garlic cloves, minced
- Salt and black pepper to the taste

Directions:
1. In the multi level air fryer's pan, combine the tomatoes with the other ingredients and toss.
2. Put the pan in the instant pot and seal with the air fryer lid.
3. Cook on Bake mode at 380 degrees F for 25 minutes and serve.

Nutrition:
calories 251, fat 14, fiber 5, carbs 23, protein 17

Creamy Chickpeas Spread

Prep time: 10 minutes | **Cooking:** 20 minutes | **Servings:** 4

Ingredients:
- 1 cup canned chickpeas, drained
- Juice of 1 lime
- 1 cup heavy cream
- 1 teaspoon coriander, ground
- Salt and black pepper to the taste
- 1 tablespoon chives, chopped

Directions:
1. In a blender, mix the chickpeas with the lime juice and the other ingredients and pulse.
2. Transfer to the multi level air fryer's pan.
3. Put the pan in the instant pot, seal with air fryer lid and cook on Bake mode at 370 degrees F for 20 minutes.
4. Divide into bowls and serve.

Nutrition:
calories 171, fat 6, fiber 4, carbs 12, protein 5

Garlic Olives Dip

Prep time: 10 minutes | **Cooking:** 15 minutes | **Servings:** 4

Ingredients:
- 4 garlic cloves, minced
- 1 cup Greek yogurt
- ½ cup black olives, pitted and chopped
- Salt and black pepper to the taste
- ½ teaspoon oregano, dried

Directions:
1. In the multi level air fryer's pan, combine the yogurt with the garlic and the other ingredients and toss.
2. Put the pan in the instant pot and seal with the air fryer lid.
3. Cook on Bake mode at 380 degrees F for 15 minutes and serve.

Nutrition:
calories 72, fat 1, fiber 0, carbs 2, protein 3

Tabasco Carrot Bites

Prep time: 10 minutes | **Cooking:** 20 minutes | **Servings:** 4

Ingredients:
- 1 tablespoon olive oil
- 1 pound baby carrots, peeled
- 2 tablespoons honey
- 1 tablespoon sweet paprika
- 1 teaspoon Tabasco sauce

Directions:
1. In the multi level air fryer's pan, combine the carrots with the other ingredients and toss.
2. Put the pan in the instant pot and seal with the air fryer lid.
3. Cook on Bake mode at 370 degrees F for 20 minutes and serve as a snack.

Nutrition:
calories 72, fat 1, fiber 3, carbs 7, protein 4

Zucchini and Capers Dip

Prep time: 10 minutes | **Cooking:** 15 minutes | **Servings:** 4

Ingredients:
- 4 spring onions, chopped
- 1 pound zucchinis, grated
- 2 tablespoons capers, drained
- 1 cup heavy cream
- Salt and white pepper to the taste
- 2 garlic cloves, minced

Directions:
1. In the multi level air fryer's pan, combine the zucchinis with the cream and the other ingredients.
2. Put the pan in the instant pot and seal with the air fryer lid.
3. Cook on Bake mode at 380 degrees F for 15 minutes.
4. Blend using an immersion blender and serve.

Nutrition:
calories 87, fat 6, fiber 2, carbs 5, protein 2

Tomato Salsa

Prep time: 10 minutes | **Cooking:** 15 minutes | **Servings:** 4

Ingredients:
- 4 spring onions, chopped
- 1 cup cherry tomatoes, halved
- 2 tablespoons basil, chopped
- 1 cup black olives, pitted and halved
- 1 cup kalamata olives, pitted and halved
- 2 tablespoons olive oil
- Juice of 1 lime
- Salt and black pepper to the taste

Directions:
1. In the multi level air fryer's pan, combine the tomatoes with the olives and the other ingredients.
2. Put the pan in the instant pot and seal with the air fryer lid.
3. Cook on Bake mode at 380 degrees F for 15 minutes, divide into bowls and serve.

Nutrition:
calories 141, fat 4, fiber 3, carbs 11, protein 4

Paprika Sausage Bites

Prep time: 5 minutes | **Cooking:** 15 minutes | **Servings:** 4

Ingredients:
- 2 cups pork sausage, sliced
- 2 tablespoons olive oil
- ½ teaspoon chili powder
- ½ teaspoon sweet paprika

Directions:
1. In the multi level air fryer's basket, combine the sausage with the other ingredients and toss.
2. Put the basket in the instant pot and seal with the air fryer lid.
3. Cook on Air fry mode at 370 degrees F for 15 minutes and serve as a snack.

Nutrition:
calories 151, fat 8, fiber 4, carbs 16, protein 5

Shrimp Bowls

Prep time: 10 minutes | **Cooking:** 20 minutes | **Servings:** 4

Ingredients:

- 1 pound white mushrooms, halved
- ½ pound shrimp, peeled and deveined
- Salt and black pepper to the taste
- 1 cup corn
- 1 cup baby spinach
- ¼ cup coconut cream
- 1 tablespoon chives, chopped
- 1 tablespoons parsley, minced

Directions:

1. In the multi level air fryer's pan, combine the shrimp with the mushrooms and the other ingredients and toss.
2. Put the pan in the instant pot and seal with the air fryer lid.
3. Cook on Bake mode at 350 degrees F for 20 minutes and serve as an appetizer.

Nutrition:

calories 200, fat 5, fiber 6, carbs 15, protein 5

Cauliflower Dip

Prep time: 5 minutes | **Cooking:** 20 minutes | **Servings:** 4

Ingredients:

- 2 tablespoons butter, melted
- 1 pound cauliflower florets
- 1 cup heavy cream
- Juice of 1 lime
- 1 tablespoon mint, chopped
- Salt and black pepper to the taste

Directions:

1. In the multi level air fryer's pan, combine the cauliflower with the butter and the other ingredients.
2. Put the pan in the instant pot and seal with the air fryer lid.
3. Cook on Bake mode at 370 degrees F for 20 minutes.
4. Blend using an immersion blender, divide into bowls and serve.

Nutrition:

calories 161, fat 5, fiber 9, carbs 14, protein 6

Balsamic Mango and Corn Salsa

Prep time: 10 minutes | **Cooking:** 10 minutes | **Servings:** 4

Ingredients:

- 2 cups mango, peeled and cubed
- 1 cup corn
- 1 cup cherry tomatoes, halved
- 1 cup black olives, pitted and halved
- 1 tablespoon avocado oil
- 2 red hot chilies, chopped
- 1 tablespoon balsamic vinegar

Directions:

1. In the multi level air fryer's pan, combine the mango with the corn and the other ingredients.
2. Put the pan in the instant pot and seal with the air fryer lid.
3. Cook on Bake mode at 350 degrees F for 10 minutes.
4. Divide into bowls and serve as an appetizer.

Nutrition:

calories 100, fat 1, fiber 0, carbs 6, protein 2

Shallots Dip

Prep time: 2 minutes | **Cooking:** 12 minutes | **Servings:** 4

Ingredients:

- 1 cup heavy cream
- ½ cup shallots, chopped
- 2 tablespoons balsamic vinegar
- Salt and black pepper to the taste
- 1 tablespoon chives, chopped

Directions:

1. In the multi level air fryer's pan, combine the shallots with the cream and the other ingredients and whisk.
2. Put the pan in the instant pot and seal with the air fryer lid.
3. Cook on Bake mode at 360 degrees F for 12 minutes.
4. Blend using an immersion blender, divide into bowls and serve.

Nutrition:

calories 20, fat 0, fiber 2, carbs 3, protein 1

Apple Bites

Prep time: 3 minutes | **Cooking:** 15 minutes | **Servings:** 4

Ingredients:

- 2 pounds apples, cored and cubed
- 1 tablespoon honey
- 1 tablespoon cinnamon powder
- 1 tablespoon ginger, grated

Directions:

1. In the multi level air fryer's pan, combine the apples with the other ingredients and toss.
2. Put the pan in the instant pot and seal with the air fryer lid.
3. Cook on Air fry mode at 360 degrees F for 15 minutes and serve as a snack.

Nutrition:

calories 151, fat 8, fiber 4, carbs 11, protein 5

Corn and Olives Salsa

Prep time: 5 minutes | **Cooking:** 15 minutes | **Servings:** 4

Ingredients:

- 2 cups corn
- 1 red onion, chopped
- ½ cup black olives, pitted and halved
- ½ cup kalamata olives, pitted and halved
- Juice of 1 lime
- Salt and black pepper to the taste
- 1 tablespoon balsamic vinegar
- 1 tablespoon dill, chopped

Directions:

1. In the multi level air fryer's pan, combine the corn with the onion and the other ingredients and toss.
2. Put the pan in the instant pot and seal with the air fryer lid.
3. Cook on Bake mode at 370 degrees F for 15 minutes and serve.

Nutrition:

calories 131, fat 7, fiber 4, carbs 9, protein 3

Hot Ginger and Chili Dip

Prep time: 5 minutes | **Cooking:** 14 minutes | **Servings:** 4

Ingredients:

- 1 cup heavy cream
- ½ cup Greek yogurt
- 4 red chili peppers, chopped
- 2 tablespoons ginger, grated
- 1 tablespoon balsamic vinegar

Directions:

1. In the multi level air fryer's pan, combine the peppers with the yogurt and the other ingredients and whisk.
2. Put the pan in the instant pot and seal with the air fryer lid.
3. Cook on Bake mode at 370 degrees F for 14 minutes and serve as a snack.

Nutrition:

calories 100, fat 1, fiber 3, carbs 7, protein 4

Turmeric Cream Dip

Prep time: 10 minutes | **Cooking:** 20 minutes | **Servings:** 4

Ingredients:

- 6 tablespoons butter, soft
- 2 cups heavy cream
- Juice of 1 lime
- Salt and black pepper to the taste
- ½ teaspoon turmeric powder

Directions:
1. In the multi level air fryer's pan, combine the cream with lime juice and the other ingredients and toss.
2. Put the pan in the instant pot and seal with the air fryer lid.
3. Cook on Bake mode at 370 degrees F for 20 minutes and serve as a snack.

Nutrition:
calories 151, fat 2, fiber 4, carbs 9, protein 4

Cranberry and Tomato Salsa

Prep time: 10 minutes | **Cooking:** 20 minutes | **Servings:** 4

Ingredients:
- 2 cups cranberries, cooked
- 1 cup corn
- 1 cup cherry tomatoes, halved
- 2 teaspoons olive oil
- A pinch of salt and black pepper
- 2 tablespoons balsamic vinegar

Directions:
1. In the multi level air fryer's pan, combine the cranberries with the corn and the other ingredients and toss.
2. Put the pan in the instant pot and seal with the air fryer lid.
3. Cook on Bake mode at 370 degrees F for 20 minutes and serve.

Nutrition:
calories 121, fat 1, fiber 3, carbs 7, protein 3

Greek Cucumber and Onions Dip

Prep time: 10 minutes | **Cooking:** 20 minutes | **Servings:** 4

Ingredients:
- 1 cup spring onions, chopped
- 1 cup Greek yogurt
- 1 cucumber, cubed
- 2 garlic cloves, minced
- A pinch of salt and black pepper

Directions:
1. In the multi level air fryer's pan, combine the onions with the cucumber and the other ingredients and toss.
2. Put the pan in the instant pot and seal with the air fryer lid.
3. Cook on Bake mode at 370 degrees F for 20 minutes.
4. Blend using an immersion blender, divide into bowls and serve.

Nutrition:
calories 100, fat 1, fiber 2, carbs 7, protein 4

Eggplant, Corn and Tomato Salsa

Prep time: 10 minutes | **Cooking:** 15 minutes | **Servings:** 4

Ingredients:
- 1 pound eggplants, cubed
- ½ cup tomato sauce
- 2 teaspoons olive oil
- 1 cup cherry tomatoes, halved
- 1 cup corn
- ½ teaspoon turmeric powder
- 1 tablespoon lemon juice
- Salt and black pepper to the taste
- ¼ cup parsley, chopped

Directions:
1. In the multi level air fryer's pan, combine the eggplants with the tomatoes and the other ingredients and toss.
2. Put the pan in the instant pot and seal with the air fryer lid.
3. Cook on Bake mode at 380 degrees F for 15 minutes and serve.

Nutrition:
calories 151, fat 8, fiber 6, carbs 11, protein 5

Chili Sprouts Bites

Prep time: 10 minutes | **Cooking:** 15 minutes | **Servings:** 4

Ingredients:
- 1 pound Brussels sprouts, trimmed and quartered
- 1 tablespoon olive oil
- Juice of 1 lime
- ½ teaspoon chili powder
- Salt and black pepper to the taste

Directions:
1. In the multi level air fryer's basket, combine the sprouts with the oil and the other ingredients and toss.
2. Put the basket in the instant pot and seal with the air fryer lid.
3. Cook on Air fry mode at 390 degrees F for 15 minutes.
4. Divide and serve as a snack.

Nutrition:
calories 151, fat 4, fiber 7, carbs 12, protein 5

Cayenne Leeks Spread

Prep time: 10 minutes | **Cooking:** 15 minutes | **Servings:** 6

Ingredients:
- 1 pound leeks, sliced
- 1 cup Greek yogurt
- 1 teaspoon turmeric powder
- Salt and black pepper to the taste
- A pinch of cayenne pepper
- 1 tablespoon dill, chopped

Directions:
1. In the multi level air fryer's pan, combine the leeks with the yogurt and the other ingredients and toss.
2. Put the pan in the instant pot and seal with the air fryer lid.
3. Cook on Bake mode at 380 degrees F for 15 minutes.
4. Blend a bit using an immersion blender, divide into bowls and serve.

Nutrition:
calories 151, fat 4, fiber 5, carbs 13, protein 5

Apple Salsa

Prep time: 10 minutes | **Cooking:** 10 minutes | **Servings:** 6

Ingredients:
- 2 cups apples, cored, peeled and cubed
- 1 cup mango, peeled and cubed
- 2 teaspoons avocado oil
- 1 tablespoon lemon juice
- A pinch of cayenne pepper

Directions:
1. In the multi level air fryer's pan, combine the apples with the mango and the other ingredients.
2. Put the pan in the instant pot and seal with the air fryer lid.
3. Cook on Bake mode at 370 degrees F for 10 minutes.
4. Divide into bowls and serve.

Nutrition:
calories 100, fat 1, fiber 3, carbs 9, protein 3

Fennel Salsa

Prep time: 10 minutes | **Cooking:** 15 minutes | **Servings:** 4

Ingredients:
- 2 fennel bulbs, sliced
- 1 cup cherry tomatoes, halved
- 1 cup corn
- 2 tablespoons balsamic vinegar
- 2 tablespoons olive oil
- Salt and black pepper to the taste

Directions:

1. In the multi level air fryer's pan, combine the fennel with the tomatoes and the other ingredients and toss.
2. Put the pan in the instant pot and seal with the air fryer lid.
3. Cook on Bake mode at 360 degrees F for 15 minutes.

Nutrition:
calories 100, fat 2, fiber 2, carbs 11, protein 4

Corn Dip

Prep time: 5 minutes | **Cooking:** 15 minutes | **Servings:** 6

Ingredients:
- 2 leeks, sliced
- 1 cup corn
- 1 cup heavy cream
- 1 teaspoon turmeric powder
- 2 tablespoons butter, melted
- Juice of 1 lime
- Salt and black pepper to the taste

Directions:
1. In the multi level air fryer's pan, combine the leeks with the corn and the other ingredients.
2. Put the pan in the instant pot and seal with the air fryer lid.
3. Cook on Bake mode at 380 degrees F for 15 minutes.
4. Transfer this to a blender, pulse, divide into bowls and serve cold.

Nutrition:
calories 161, fat 8, fiber 2, carbs 14, protein 6

Corn and Radish Salsa

Prep time: 5 minutes | **Cooking:** 15 minutes | **Servings:** 6

Ingredients:
- 3 spring onions, chopped
- 2 cups radishes, halved
- 1 cup corn
- 1 tablespoon parsley, chopped
- 2 tablespoons balsamic vinegar
- Salt and white pepper to the taste

Directions:
1. In the multi level air fryer's pan, combine the radishes with the corn and the other ingredients and toss.
2. Put the pan in the instant pot and seal with the air fryer lid.
3. Cook on Bake mode at 370 degrees F for 15 minutes and serve as a snack.

Nutrition:
calories 100, fat 2, fiber 5, carbs 11, protein 3

Shallots and Olives Dip

Prep time: 5 minutes | **Cooking:** 15 minutes | **Servings:** 6

Ingredients:
- 1 cup shallots, chopped
- 1 cup Greek yogurt
- 1 tablespoon olive oil
- 2 red chilies, minced
- 1 cup kalamata olives, pitted and halved
- Salt and black pepper to the taste
- 2 tablespoons cilantro, chopped

Directions:
1. In the multi level air fryer's pan, combine the shallots with the olives and the other ingredients and toss.
2. Put the pan in the instant pot and seal with the air fryer lid.
3. Cook on Bake mode at 390 degrees F for 15 minutes.
4. Blend a bit using an immersion blender, divide into bowls and serve.

Nutrition:
calories 131, fat 5, fiber 4, carbs 14, protein 3

Creamy Lime Dip

Prep time: 5 minutes | **Cooking:** 20 minutes | **Servings:** 4

Ingredients:
- 3 spring onions, chopped
- 1 tablespoon olive oil
- 1 cup heavy cream
- Juice of 1 lime
- Zest of 1 lime, grated
- 2 cups corn kernels
- Salt and black pepper to the taste

Directions:
1. In the multi level air fryer's pan, combine the cream with lime juice and the other ingredients and toss.
2. Put the pan in the instant pot and seal with the air fryer lid.
3. Cook on Bake mode at 390 degrees F for 20 minutes.
4. Blend a bit using an immersion blender, divide into bowls and serve.

Nutrition:
calories 151, fat 2, fiber 5, carbs 14, protein 4

Chicken and Peppers Dip

Prep time: 5 minutes | **Cooking:** 20 minutes | **Servings:** 4

Ingredients:
- 1 pound chicken breast, skinless, boneless, ground and browned
- 1 cup cheddar cheese, shredded
- 1 red bell pepper, chopped
- 1 green bell pepper, chopped
- 1 red onion, chopped
- Salt and black pepper to the taste
- A drizzle of olive oil
- 1 tablespoon chives, chopped

Directions:
1. In the multi level air fryer's pan, mix the meat with the peppers and the other ingredients except the cheese and toss.
2. Sprinkle the cheese on top, put the pan in the instant pot, seal with the air fryer lid and cook on Bake mode at 370 degrees F for 20 minutes.
3. Divide into bowls and serve as an appetizer.

Nutrition:
calories 202, fat 12, fiber 2, carbs 4, protein 7

Beet and Tomatoes Salsa

Prep time: 5 minutes | **Cooking:** 20 minutes | **Servings:** 4

Ingredients:
- 2 cups beets, peeled and cubed
- 1 cup kalamata olives, pitted and halved
- 1 cup cherry tomatoes, halved
- 1 tablespoon olive oil
- A pinch of salt and black pepper
- 1 tablespoon balsamic vinegar
- ¼ teaspoon sweet paprika

Directions:
1. In the multi level air fryer's pan, combine the beets with the olives and the other ingredients and toss.
2. Put the pan in the instant pot and seal with the air fryer lid.
3. Cook on Bake mode at 370 degrees F for 20 minutes and serve.

Nutrition:
calories 170, fat 2, fiber 3, carbs 4, protein 6

Carrot Chips

Prep time: 5 minutes | **Cooking:** 15 minutes | **Servings:** 4

Ingredients:
- 1 pound carrots, peeled and sliced
- 1 tablespoon olive oil
- A pinch of salt and black pepper
- 1 teaspoon sweet paprika

Directions:

1. In the multi level air fryer's basket, combine the carrots with the rest of the ingredients and toss.
2. Put the basket in the instant pot and seal with the air fryer lid.
3. Cook on Air fry mode at 400 degrees F for 15 minutes and serve as a snack.

Nutrition:
calories 150, fat 4, fiber 3, carbs 4, protein 6

Zucchini and Spring Onions Cakes

Prep time: 5 minutes | **Cooking:** 16 minutes | **Servings:** 6

Ingredients:
- Cooking spray
- 1 pound zucchinis, grated
- ½ cup coconut flour
- 1 teaspoon turmeric powder
- 2 eggs, whisked
- 2 garlic cloves, minced
- Salt and black pepper to the taste
- 3 spring onions, chopped

Directions:
1. In a bowl, mix all the zucchinis with the flour and the other ingredients except the cooking spray, stir well and shape medium cakes out of this mixture.
2. Place the cakes in your multi level air fryer's basket and grease them with cooking spray.
3. Put the basket in the instant pot, seal with the air fryer lid and cook on Air fry mode at 380 degrees F for 8 minutes on each side.
4. Serve them as an appetizer.

Nutrition:
calories 165, fat 5, fiber 2, carbs 3, protein 7

Mushroom, Olives and Beets Bowls

Prep time: 5 minutes | **Cooking:** 15 minutes | **Servings:** 4

Ingredients:
- 1 pound wild mushrooms, halved
- 1 cup red beets, peeled and cubed
- 1 cup kalamata olives, pitted and halved
- 1 tablespoon rosemary, chopped
- 2 tablespoons olive oil
- Juice of 1 lime
- 2 garlic clove, minced

Directions:
1. In the multi level air fryer's pan, combine the mushrooms with the beets and the other ingredients.
2. Put the pan in the instant pot and seal with the air fryer lid.
3. Cook on Bake mode at 380 degrees F for 15 minutes and serve.

Nutrition:
calories 151, fat 2, fiber 1, carbs 3, protein 6

Chili Mushroom Meatballs

Prep time: 5 minutes | **Cooking:** 15 minutes | **Servings:** 6

Ingredients:
- 1 pound white mushrooms, chopped
- 1 cup almond flour
- 2 eggs, whisked
- 1 tablespoon chives, chopped
- 1 teaspoon chili powder
- Cooking spray
- Salt and black pepper to the taste

Directions:
1. In a bowl, mix the mushrooms with the flour and the other ingredients except the cooking spray, stir and shape medium meatballs out of this mix.
2. Arrange the meatballs in your multi level air fryer's basket and grease them with the cooking spray.
3. Put the basket in the instant pot, seal with the air fryer lid, cook on Air fry mode at 350 degrees F for 15 minutes and serve.

Nutrition:
calories 120, fat 4, fiber 2, carbs 3, protein 5

Avocado and Cucumber Bowls

Prep time: 5 minutes | **Cooking:** 8 minutes | **Servings:** 4

Ingredients:
- 2 avocados, peeled, pitted and cubed
- 1 cup cherry tomatoes, halved
- 1 cup cucumbers, cubed
- Juice of 1 lime
- 1 tablespoon basil, chopped
- 1 tablespoon chives, chopped
- A pinch of salt and black pepper
- 1 tablespoon balsamic vinegar

Directions:
1. In the multi level air fryer's pan, combine the avocados with the cucumber and the other ingredients.
2. Put the pan in the instant pot and seal with the air fryer lid.
3. Cook on Bake mode at 360 degrees F for 8 minutes and serve.

Nutrition:
calories 161, fat 4, fiber 2, carbs 4, protein 6

Wrapped Carrot Bites

Prep time: 5 minutes | **Cooking:** 20 minutes | **Servings:** 12

Ingredients:
- 12 bacon strips
- 12 carrot sliced
- A pinch of salt and black pepper
- 1 teaspoon sweet paprika
- A drizzle of olive oil

Directions:
1. Wrap each carrot slice in a bacon strip, season with salt, pepper and paprika, brush them with the oil and put them in your multi level air fryer's basket.
2. Put the basket in the instant pot, seal with the air fryer lid and cook on Air fry mode at 370 degrees F for 20 minutes.
3. Arrange on a platter and serve as an appetizer.

Nutrition:
calories 140, fat 5, fiber 2, carbs 4, protein 4

Bacon Corn Dip

Prep time: 5 minutes | **Cooking:** 12 minutes | **Servings:** 4

Ingredients:
- ½ cup bacon, cooked and chopped
- 2 cups corn
- 1 cup heavy cream
- A pinch of salt and black pepper

Directions:
1. In the multi level air fryer's pan, combine the bacon with the other ingredients.
2. Put the pan in the instant pot and seal with the air fryer lid.
3. Cook on Bake mode at 350 degrees F for 12 minutes and serve as a party dip.

Nutrition:
calories 151, fat 4, fiber 2, carbs 4, protein 8

Corn and Avocado Spread

Prep time: 5 minutes | **Cooking:** 20 minutes | **Servings:** 4

Ingredients:
- ½ cup mayonnaise
- 1 cup corn
- 1 cup avocado, peeled, pitted and cubed
- 1 cup heavy cream
- A pinch of salt and black

pepper
- 1 teaspoon turmeric powder

Directions:
1. In the multi level air fryer's pan, combine the corn with the other ingredients and toss.
2. Put the pan in the instant pot and seal with the air fryer lid.
3. Cook on Bake mode at 380 degrees F for 20 minutes and serve as a snack.
4. Blend using an immersion blender, divide into bowls and serve as an appetizer.

Nutrition:
calories 100, fat 4, fiber 2, carbs 3, protein 4

Avocado Balls

Prep time: 5 minutes | **Cooking:** 8 minutes | **Servings:** 4

Ingredients:
- 1 cup avocado, peeled, pitted and mashed
- 1 tablespoon basil, chopped
- 1 tablespoon oregano, chopped
- 3 tablespoons almond flour
- 2 garlic cloves, minced
- 1 tablespoon lime juice
- A pinch of salt and black pepper
- 2 eggs, whisked
- Cooking spray

Directions:
1. In a bowl, mix all the avocado with the basil, oregano and the other ingredients except the cooking spray, stir well and shape medium balls out of this mix.
2. Place them in your multi level air fryer's basket and grease with cooking spray.
3. Put the basket in the instant pot, seal with the air fryer lid and cook at 370 degrees F for 8 minutes.
4. Serve as an appetizer.

Nutrition:
calories 160, fat 6, fiber 3, carbs 4, protein 6

Shrimp and Avocado Salsa

Prep time: 5 minutes | **Cooking:** 15 minutes | **Servings:** 4

Ingredients:
- 1 pound shrimp, peeled and deveined
- 1 cup avocado, peeled, pitted and cubed
- 1 cup cherry tomatoes, halved
- Juice of 1 lime
- 1 tablespoon olive oil
- A pinch of salt and black pepper
- 1 tablespoon cilantro, chopped

Directions:
1. In the multi level air fryer's pan, combine the shrimp with the avocado and the other ingredients and toss.
2. Put the pan in the instant pot and seal with the air fryer lid.
3. Cook on Bake mode at 350 degrees F for 15 minutes and serve.

Nutrition:
calories 184, fat 5, fiber 2, carbs 4, protein 7

Cashew and Lemon Dip

Prep time: 5 minutes | **Cooking:** 12 minutes | **Servings:** 6

Ingredients:
- 1 cup cashews, soaked in water for 4 hours and drained
- 1 cup heavy cream
- 1 tablespoon lemon zest, grated
- 1 tablespoon lemon juice
- A pinch of salt and black pepper
- 1 tablespoon chives, chopped

Directions:
1. In a blender, combine all the ingredients, pulse well and transfer to a ramekin.
2. Put the ramekin in your multi level air fryer's basket, put the basket in the instant pot, seal with the air fryer lid and cook on Bake mode at 350 degrees F for 12 minutes.
3. Serve as a party dip.

Nutrition:
calories 144, fat 2, fiber 1, carbs 3, protein 4

Salmon Salad

Prep time: 5 minutes | **Cooking:** 10 minutes | **Servings:** 4

Ingredients:
- 4 ounces smoked salmon, skinless, boneless and cubed
- 1 cup kalamata olives, pitted and halved
- 1 cup corn
- 1 cup baby spinach
- 2 tablespoons lemon juice
- 1 teaspoon avocado oil
- 1 tablespoon chives, chopped
- A pinch of salt and black pepper

Directions:
1. In the multi level air fryer's pan, combine the salmon with the olives and the other ingredients.
2. Put the pan in the instant pot and seal with the air fryer lid.
3. Cook on Bake mode at 350 degrees F for 10 minutes and serve.

Nutrition:
calories 100, fat 2, fiber 1, carbs 2, protein 2

Salmon Balls

Prep time: 5 minutes | **Cooking:** 20 minutes | **Servings:** 6

Ingredients:
- 1 pound salmon fillets, boneless, skinless and ground
- 2 eggs, whisked
- ¼ cup almond flour
- ½ teaspoon sweet paprika
- 1 teaspoon garlic powder
- A pinch of salt and black pepper
- 1 tablespoon parsley, chopped
- Cooking spray

Directions:
1. In a bowl, mix the salmon with the eggs and the other ingredients except the cooking spray, stir well and shape medium balls out of this mix.
2. Pace them in your multi level air fryer's basket and grease with cooking spray.
3. Put the basket in the instant pot, seal with the air fryer lid and cook on Air fry mode at 360 degrees F for 20 minutes.
4. Serve as an appetizer.

Nutrition:
calories 180, fat 5, fiber 2, carbs 5, protein 7

Chicken Meatballs

Prep time: 5 minutes | **Cooking:** 20 minutes | **Servings:** 8

Ingredients:
- 1 and ½ pounds chicken breast, skinless, boneless and ground
- 2 eggs, whisked
- 1 tablespoon oregano, chopped
- 1 tablespoon chives, chopped
- ¼ cup almond flour
- A pinch of salt and black pepper
- 2 garlic cloves, minced
- 2 spring onions, chopped
- Cooking spray

Directions:
1. In a bowl, mix the meat with the eggs and the other ingredients except the cooking spray, stir well and shape medium meatballs

out of this mix.
2. Arrange the meatballs in your multi level air fryer's basket and grease them with cooking spray.
3. Put the basket in the instant pot, seal with the air fryer lid and cook on Air fry mode at 360 degrees F for 20 minutes.
4. Serve as an appetizer.

Nutrition:

calories 257, fat 14, fiber 1, carbs 3, protein 17

Ginger and Shallots Dip

Prep time: 5 minutes | **Cooking:** 20 minutes | **Servings:** 6

Ingredients:

- 1 cup Greek yogurt
- ½ cup heavy cream
- 2 tablespoons ginger, grated
- 2 shallots, chopped
- 1 tablespoon chives, chopped
- A pinch of salt and black pepper
- Cooking spray

Directions:

1. In the multi level air fryer's pan, combine the yogurt with the cream and the other ingredients.
2. Put the pan in the instant pot and seal with the air fryer lid.
3. Cook on Bake mode at 380 degrees F for 20 minutes and serve.

Nutrition:

calories 200, fat 12, fiber 2, carbs 3, protein 14

Asparagus Salsa

Prep time: 5 minutes | **Cooking:** 15 minutes | **Servings:** 8

Ingredients:

- ½ pound asparagus, roughly chopped
- 1 cup black olives, pitted and halved
- 1 cup kalamata olives, pitted and halved
- 1 cup baby spinach
- Juice of 1 lime
- 2 tablespoons olive oil
- A pinch of salt and black pepper

Directions:

1. In the multi level air fryer's pan, combine the asparagus with the olives and the other ingredients.
2. Put the pan in the instant pot and seal with the air fryer lid.
3. Cook on Bake mode at 390 degrees F for 15 minutes and serve.

Nutrition:

calories 173, fat 4, fiber 2, carbs 3, protein 6

Radish Bites

Prep time: 5 minutes | **Cooking:** 15 minutes | **Servings:** 4

Ingredients:

- 1 pound radishes, halved
- 1 cup walnuts
- 1 teaspoon chili powder
- 1 teaspoon sweet paprika
- A pinch of salt and black pepper
- 2 tablespoons avocado oil

Directions:

1. In the multi level air fryer's basket, mix the radishes with the walnuts and the other ingredients and toss.
2. Put the basket in the instant pot, seal with the air fryer lid and cook on Air fry mode at 400 degrees F for 15 minutes.
3. Serve as a snack.

Nutrition:

calories 174, fat 5, fiber 1, carbs 3, protein 6

Olives and Yogurt Dip

Prep time: 5 minutes | **Cooking:** 5 minutes | **Servings:** 6

Ingredients:

- 1 cup black olives, pitted and chopped
- 1 cup kalamata olives, pitted and chopped
- 1 cup green olives, pitted and chopped
- 1 cup Greek yogurt
- 1 tablespoon olive oil
- 3 tablespoons lemon juice
- 1 cup basil, chopped
- A pinch of salt and black pepper

Directions:

1. In a blender, combine the olives with the yogurt and the other ingredients, pulse well and transfer to a ramekin.
2. Place the ramekin in your multi level air fryer's basket.
3. Put the basket in the instant pot, seal with the air fryer lid and cook on Air fry mode at 350 degrees F for 5 minutes.
4. Serve as a party dip.

Nutrition:

calories 120, fat 5, fiber 2, carbs 3, protein 7

Fish and Seafood Recipes

Herbed Cod

Prep time: 5 minutes | **Cooking:** 15 minutes | **Servings:** 4

Ingredients:

- 4 cod fillets, boneless
- 2 tablespoons balsamic vinegar
- Salt and black pepper to the taste
- ½ teaspoon rosemary, dried
- ½ teaspoon coriander, dried
- A drizzle of olive oil
- 1 tablespoon chives, chopped

Directions:

1. In the multi level air fryer's basket, mix the cod with the vinegar and the other ingredients and toss.
2. Put the basket in the instant pot, seal with the air fryer lid and cook on Air fry mode at 370 degrees F for 15 minutes.
3. Divide between plates and serve.

Nutrition:

calories 220, fat 12, fiber 2, carbs 5, protein 13

Orange Salmon

Prep time: 5 minutes | **Cooking:** 15 minutes | **Servings:** 4

Ingredients:

- 4 salmon fillets, boneless
- 3 tablespoons ghee, melted
- Juice of 1 orange
- Salt and black pepper to the taste
- 1 tablespoon dill, chopped

Directions:

1. In the multi level air fryer's pan, combine the salmon with orange juice and the other ingredients.
2. Put the pan in the instant pot and seal with the air fryer lid.
3. Cook on Bake mode at 370 degrees F for 15 minutes.
4. Divide the mix between plates and serve.

Nutrition:

calories 240, fat 12, fiber 2, carbs 5, protein 11

Coriander Salmon

Prep time: 5 minutes | **Cooking:** 20 minutes | **Servings:** 4

Ingredients:

- 4 salmon fillets, boneless
- Juice of 1 lemon
- Zest of 1 lemon, grated
- ½ teaspoon coriander, ground
- A pinch of salt and black pepper
- 2 garlic cloves, minced
- ¼ cup spring onions, chopped

Directions:

1. In the multi level air fryer's pan, combine the salmon with lemon juice and the other ingredients.
2. Put the pan in the instant pot and seal with the air fryer lid.
3. Cook on Bake mode at 370 degrees F for 20 minutes.
4. Divide everything between plates and serve.

Nutrition:

calories 220, fat 14, fiber 2, carbs 5, protein 12

Chives Citrus Shrimp

Prep time: 5 minutes | **Cooking:** 15 minutes | **Servings:** 4

Ingredients:

- 1 pound shrimp, peeled and deveined
- 1 tablespoon olive oil
- 1 orange, peeled and cut into segments
- Juice of 1 orange
- 1 tablespoon chives, chopped
- A pinch of salt and black pepper
- 2 tablespoons green onions, chopped

Directions:

1. In the multi level air fryer's pan, combine the shrimp with the orange and the other ingredients.
2. Put the pan in the instant pot and seal with the air fryer lid.
3. Cook on Bake mode at 350 degrees F for 15 minutes.
4. Divide the mix into bowls and serve.

Nutrition:

calories 221, fat 12, fiber 2, carbs 5, protein 14

Lime Cod Mix

Prep time: 5 minutes | **Cooking:** 15 minutes | **Servings:** 4

Ingredients:

- 2 pounds cod fillets, boneless
- 1 cup avocado, peeled, pitted and cut into wedges
- Juice of 1 lime
- Zest of 1 lime, grated
- 1 teaspoon turmeric powder
- A pinch of salt and black pepper
- 2 tablespoons cilantro, chopped

Directions:

1. In the multi level air fryer's pan, combine the cod with the avocado and the other ingredients and toss gently.
2. Put the pan in the instant pot and seal with the air fryer lid.
3. Cook on Bake mode at 360 degrees F for 15 minutes.
4. Divide between plates and serve.

Nutrition:

calories 280, fat 14, fiber 3, carbs 5, protein 14

Dill Tilapia

Prep time: 5 minutes | **Cooking:** 20 minutes | **Servings:** 4

Ingredients:

- 4 tilapia fillets, boneless
- 2 tablespoons oregano, chopped
- 1 tablespoon avocado oil
- Juice of 1 lime
- A pinch of salt and black pepper
- 1 teaspoon garlic powder
- 1 tablespoon dill, chopped

Directions:

1. In the multi level air fryer's pan, combine the fish with oregano and the other ingredients and toss.
2. Put the pan in the instant pot and seal with the air fryer lid.
3. Cook on Bake mode at 360 degrees F for 20 minutes.
4. Divide between plates and serve hot.

Nutrition:

calories 224, fat 10, fiber 0, carbs 2, protein 18

Balsamic Salmon

Prep time: 5 minutes | **Cooking:** 15 minutes | **Servings:** 4

Ingredients:

- 2 pounds salmon fillets, boneless and cubed
- 1 cup coconut cream
- 1 tablespoon olive oil
- 2 tablespoons balsamic vinegar
- 1 teaspoon rosemary, dried
- A pinch of salt and black pepper

Directions:

1. In the multi level air fryer's pan, combine the salmon with the other ingredients and toss.
2. Put the pan in the instant pot and seal with the air fryer lid.
3. Cook on Bake mode at 350 degrees F for 15 minutes.
4. Divide everything between plates and serve.

Nutrition:

calories 267, fat 18, fiber 2, carbs 5, protein 20

Lime Shrimp

Prep time: 5 minutes | **Cooking:** 14 minutes | **Servings:** 4

Ingredients:

- 2 pounds shrimp, peeled and deveined
- 5 garlic cloves, minced
- Juice of 1 lime
- Salt and black pepper to the taste
- ½ teaspoon sweet paprika
- 1 tablespoon chives, chopped

Directions:

1. In the multi level air fryer's pan, combine the shrimp with the other ingredients and toss.
2. Put the pan in the instant pot and seal with the air fryer lid.
3. Cook on Bake mode at 360 degrees F for 14 minutes.
4. Divide into bowls and serve.

Nutrition:

calories 240, fat 12, fiber 2, carbs 4, protein 12

Fennel Salmon

Prep time: 5 minutes | **Cooking:** 20 minutes | **Servings:** 4

Ingredients:

- 4 salmon fillets, boneless
- 1 tablespoon sweet paprika
- ½ teaspoon turmeric powder
- ½ teaspoon fennel seeds, crushed
- 1 tablespoon olive oil
- Salt and black pepper to the taste
- Juice of 1 lime

Directions:

1. In the multi level air fryer's pan, combine the salmon with the other ingredients and toss.
2. Put the pan in the instant pot and seal with the air fryer lid.
3. Cook on Bake mode at 350 degrees F for 10 minutes.
4. Divide the mix between plates and serve with a side salad.

Nutrition:

calories 240, fat 14, fiber 2, carbs 4, protein 16

Chili Salmon

Prep time: 5 minutes | **Cooking:** 15 minutes | **Servings:** 4

Ingredients:

- 1 pound salmon fillets, boneless, skinless and cubed
- 1 tablespoon sesame seeds, toasted
- Juice of 1 orange
- 1 tablespoon olive oil
- A pinch of salt and black pepper
- 1 teaspoon chili powder

Directions:

1. In the multi level air fryer's pan, combine the salmon with the other ingredients and toss.
2. Put the pan in the instant pot and seal with the air fryer lid.
3. Cook on Bake mode at 360 degrees F for 15 minutes.
4. Divide between plates and serve.

Nutrition:

calories 206, fat 8, fiber 1, carbs 4, protein 13

Shrimp and Beets

Prep time: 5 minutes | **Cooking:** 14 minutes | **Servings:** 4

Ingredients:

- 1 tablespoon olive oil
- 1 cup corn
- 1 cup red beets, peeled and cubed
- 1 tablespoon balsamic vinegar
- 1 pound shrimp, peeled and deveined
- A pinch of salt and black pepper
- 1 tablespoon chives, chopped

Directions:

1. In the multi level air fryer's pan, combine the shrimp with the other ingredients and toss.
2. Put the pan in the instant pot and seal with the air fryer lid.
3. Cook on Bake mode at 370 degrees F for 14 minutes.
4. Divide the mix into bowls and serve.

Nutrition:

calories 195, fat 11, fiber 2, carbs 4, protein 11

Mustard Tuna

Prep time: 5 minutes | **Cooking:** 15 minutes | **Servings:** 4

Ingredients:

- 2 pounds tuna fillets, boneless
- 2 tablespoons mustard
- 2 tablespoons capers, drained
- 1 tablespoon olive oil
- Juice of 1 lime
- 1 teaspoon mustard seeds, crushed
- A pinch of salt and black pepper
- 1 tablespoon cilantro, chopped

Directions:

1. In the multi level air fryer's pan, combine the with tuna with the other ingredients and toss.
2. Put the pan in the instant pot and seal with the air fryer lid.
3. Cook on Bake mode at 380 degrees F for 15 minutes.
4. Divide between plates and serve.

Nutrition:

calories 240, fat 13, fiber 3, carbs 6, protein 15

Salmon and Spring Onions Sauce

Prep time: 5 minutes | **Cooking:** 20 minutes | **Servings:** 4

Ingredients:

- 4 salmon fillets, boneless
- ½ cup lime juice
- ½ cup heavy cream
- 1 teaspoon lime zest, grated
- 4 spring onions, chopped
- ½ teaspoon turmeric powder
- A pinch of salt and black pepper

Directions:

1. In the multi level air fryer's pan, combine the salmon with the other ingredients and toss.
2. Put the pan in the instant pot and seal with the air fryer lid.
3. Cook on Bake mode at 360 degrees F for 20 minutes.
4. Divide between plates and serve.

Nutrition:

calories 227, fat 12, fiber 2, carbs 4, protein 9

Chives Shrimp

Prep time: 10 minutes | **Cooking:** 14 minutes | **Servings:** 4

Ingredients:

- 1 pound shrimp, peeled and deveined
- 2 tablespoons mustard
- 2 tablespoons lemon juice
- ½ teaspoon cumin, ground
- Salt and black pepper to the taste
- 1 tablespoon chives, chopped

Directions:

1. In the multi level air fryer's pan, combine the shrimp with the other ingredients and toss.
2. Put the pan in the instant pot and seal with the air fryer lid.
3. Cook on Bake mode at 370 degrees F for 14 minutes.
4. Divide between plates and serve.

Nutrition:

calories 270, fat 14, fiber 3, carbs 5, protein 12

Rosemary Salmon and Potatoes

Prep time: 5 minutes | **Cooking:** 20 minutes | **Servings:** 4

Ingredients:

- 1 pound salmon fillets, boneless
- 2 sweet potatoes, peeled and cut into wedges
- Juice of ½ lemon
- 1 teaspoon rosemary, dried
- 2 garlic cloves, minced
- 4 shallots, chopped
- Salt and black pepper to the taste

Directions:

1. In the multi level air fryer's pan, combine the salmon with potatoes and the other ingredients and toss.
2. Put the pan in the instant pot and seal with the air fryer lid.
3. Cook on Bake mode at 380 degrees F for 20 minutes.
4. Divide between plates and serve.

Nutrition:
calories 270, fat 12, fiber 2, carbs 4, protein 17

Lime Cod and Fennel

Prep time: 5 minutes | **Cooking:** 20 minutes | **Servings:** 4

Ingredients:

- 2 pounds cod fillets, boneless
- 2 fennel bulbs, sliced
- 1 teaspoon coriander, ground
- ½ teaspoon cumin, ground
- Juice of 1 lime
- 2 tablespoons olive oil
- Salt and back pepper to the taste

Directions:

1. In the multi level air fryer's pan, combine the cod with the other ingredients and toss.
2. Put the pan in the instant pot and seal with the air fryer lid.
3. Cook on Bake mode at 350 degrees F for 20 minutes.
4. Divide between plates and serve right away.

Nutrition:
calories 243, fat 13, fiber 3, carbs 6, protein 14

Tuna Steaks and Lime Sauce

Prep time: 5 minutes | **Cooking:** 14 minutes | **Servings:** 4

Ingredients:

- 1 pound tuna steaks, boneless and cubed
- ½ cup green onions, chopped
- 1 cup coconut cream
- 2 tablespoons lime juice
- 1 teaspoon olive oil
- Salt and black pepper to the taste

Directions:

1. In the multi level air fryer's pan, combine the tuna steaks with the other ingredients and toss.
2. Put the pan in the instant pot and seal with the air fryer lid.
3. Cook on Bake mode at 370 degrees F for 14 minutes.
4. Divide between plates and serve.

Nutrition:
calories 226, fat 12, fiber 2, carbs 4, protein 15

Cilantro Shrimp Mix

Prep time: 5 minutes | **Cooking:** 15 minutes | **Servings:** 4

Ingredients:

- 1 pound shrimp, peeled and deveined
- 1 cup cherry tomatoes, halved
- 1 tablespoon olive oil
- Juice of 1 lime
- Salt and black pepper to the taste
- 1 teaspoon rosemary, dried
- 2 tablespoons cilantro, chopped

Directions:

1. In the multi level air fryer's pan, combine the shrimp with the other ingredients and toss.
2. Put the pan in the instant pot and seal with the air fryer lid.
3. Cook on Bake mode at 370 degrees F for 15 minutes.
4. Divide everything between plates and serve.

Nutrition:
calories 248, fat 11, fiber 2, carbs 5, protein 11

Balsamic Sea Bass Mix

Prep time: 5 minutes | **Cooking:** 20 minutes | **Servings:** 4

Ingredients:

- 4 sea bass fillets, boneless
- 1 cup cherry tomatoes, halved
- 1 tablespoon avocado oil
- 2 tablespoons balsamic vinegar
- Salt and black pepper to the taste
- ¼ cup tomato sauce
- 1 tablespoon chives, chopped
- 1 teaspoon oregano, dried

Directions:

1. In the multi level air fryer's pan, combine the sea bass with the tomatoes and the other ingredients and toss.
2. Put the pan in the instant pot and seal with the air fryer lid.
3. Cook on Bake mode at 380 degrees F for 15 minutes.
4. Divide everything between plates and serve.

Nutrition:
calories 250, fat 9, fiber 2, carbs 5, protein 14

Rosemary Shrimp and Beets

Prep time: 5 minutes | **Cooking:** 12 minutes | **Servings:** 4

Ingredients:

- 2 pounds shrimp, peeled and deveined
- 2 beets, peeled and cubed
- 1 tablespoon olive oil
- 1 teaspoon rosemary, dried
- Juice of ½ lemon
- A pinch of salt and black pepper
- 2 tablespoons parsley, chopped

Directions:

1. In the multi level air fryer's pan, combine the shrimp with the other ingredients and toss.
2. Put the pan in the instant pot and seal with the air fryer lid.
3. Cook on Bake mode at 350 degrees F for 12 minutes.
4. Divide everything into bowls and serve.

Nutrition:
calories 202, fat 8, fiber 2, carbs 5, protein 14

Paprika Lemon Sea Bass

Prep time: 5 minutes | **Cooking:** 20 minutes | **Servings:** 4

Ingredients:

- 1 pound sea bass fillets, boneless
- 3 garlic cloves, minced
- ½ cup fish stock
- ½ teaspoon sweet paprika
- 1 teaspoon cumin, ground
- 2 tablespoons lemon juice
- 2 tablespoons olive oil
- A pinch of salt and black pepper
- 1 tablespoon chives, chopped

Directions:

1. In the multi level air fryer's pan, combine the sea bass with the garlic and the other ingredients and toss.
2. Put the pan in the instant pot and seal with the air fryer lid.
3. Cook on Bake mode at 370 degrees F for 20 minutes.
4. Divide everything between plates and serve.

Nutrition:
calories 220, fat 11, fiber 2, carbs 5, protein 12

Oregano Cod and Green Beans

Prep time: 5 minutes | **Cooking:** 15 minutes | **Servings:** 4

Ingredients:

- 1 pound cod fillets, boneless
- ½ cup veggie stock
- ½ teaspoon sweet paprika
- A pinch of salt and black pepper
- ½ pound green beans, trimmed and halved
- 2 tablespoons oregano, chopped

Directions:
1. In the multi level air fryer's pan, combine the cod with the green beans and the other ingredients and toss.
2. Put the pan in the instant pot and seal with the air fryer lid.
3. Cook on Bake mode at 380 degrees F for 15 minutes.
4. Divide everything between plates and serve.

Nutrition:
calories 222, fat 8, fiber 3, carbs 5, protein 10

Herbed Shrimp

Prep time: 5 minutes | **Cooking:** 12 minutes | **Servings:** 4

Ingredients:
- 1 pound shrimp, peeled and deveined
- ½ teaspoon oregano, dried
- ½ teaspoon coriander, ground
- ½ teaspoon rosemary, dried
- Juice of 1 lime
- A pinch of salt and black pepper
- 1 tablespoon sesame seeds, toasted
- ½ teaspoon Italian seasoning
- 1 tablespoon avocado oil

Directions:
1. In the multi level air fryer's pan, combine the shrimp with the other ingredients and toss.
2. Put the pan in the instant pot and seal with the air fryer lid.
3. Cook on Bake mode at 370 degrees F for 12 minutes.
4. Divide into bowls and serve.

Nutrition:
calories 199, fat 11, fiber 2, carbs 4, protein 11

Cod and Herbed Roasted Peppers

Prep time: 5 minutes | **Cooking:** 15 minutes | **Servings:** 4

Ingredients:
- 4 cod fillets, boneless
- 2 cups roasted red peppers, chopped
- ½ cup tomato sauce
- 1 teaspoon cayenne pepper
- 2 teaspoons olive oil
- 1 tablespoon parsley, chopped
- 1 teaspoon basil, dried
- Salt and black pepper to the taste

Directions:
1. In the multi level air fryer's pan, combine the cod with the other ingredients and toss.
2. Put the pan in the instant pot and seal with the air fryer lid.
3. Cook on Bake mode at 380 degrees F for 15 minutes.
4. Divide everything between plates and serve.

Nutrition:
calories 194, fat 7, fiber 2, carbs 4, protein 12

Paprika Shrimp and Radishes

Prep time: 5 minutes | **Cooking:** 12 minutes | **Servings:** 4

Ingredients:
- 1 pound shrimp, peeled and deveined
- 2 cups radishes, halved
- 2 teaspoons olive oil
- ½ teaspoon sweet paprika
- ½ teaspoon fennel seeds, crushed
- Salt and black pepper to the taste
- 1 tablespoon rosemary, chopped

Directions:
1. In the multi level air fryer's pan, combine the shrimp with the other ingredients and toss.
2. Put the pan in the instant pot and seal with the air fryer lid.
3. Cook on Bake mode at 380 degrees F for 12 minutes.
4. Divide everything into bowls and serve.

Nutrition:
calories 220, fat 14, fiber 2, carbs 6, protein 15

Parmesan Lemon Shrimp

Prep time: 5 minutes | **Cooking:** 12 minutes | **Servings:** 4

Ingredients:
- 2 pounds shrimp, peeled and deveined
- 1 cup parmesan, grated
- 2 teaspoons olive oil
- 2 tablespoons lemon juice
- 1 tablespoon cilantro, chopped
- ¼ cup parmesan, grated
- A pinch of salt and black pepper

Directions:
1. In the multi level air fryer's pan, combine the shrimp with the other ingredients and toss.
2. Put the pan in the instant pot and seal with the air fryer lid.
3. Cook on Bake mode at 360 degrees F for 12 minutes.
4. Divide everything into bowls and serve.

Nutrition:
calories 240, fat 10, fiber 1, carbs 4, protein 12

Black Cod and Veggies

Prep time: 5 minutes | **Cooking:** 15 minutes | **Servings:** 4

Ingredients:
- 1 tablespoon olive oil
- 1 cup corn
- 1 cup black olives, pitted and halved
- Juice of 1 lime
- 4 black cod fillets, boneless
- 1 teaspoon chili powder
- Salt and black pepper to the taste

Directions:
1. In the multi level air fryer's pan, combine the cod with the other ingredients and toss.
2. Put the pan in the instant pot and seal with the air fryer lid.
3. Cook on Bake mode at 370 degrees F for 15 minutes.
4. Divide everything between plates and serve.

Nutrition:
calories 204, fat 12, fiber 3, carbs 5, protein 15

Lime Cod and Zucchinis

Prep time: 5 minutes | **Cooking:** 15 minutes | **Servings:** 4

Ingredients:
- 1 pound cod fillets, boneless
- 2 zucchinis, roughly cubed
- 2 teaspoons olive oil
- 1 teaspoon sweet paprika
- A pinch of salt and black pepper
- Juice of 1 lime
- 1 tablespoon dill, chopped

Directions:
1. In the multi level air fryer's pan, combine the cod with the other ingredients and toss.
2. Put the pan in the instant pot and seal with the air fryer lid.
3. Cook on Bake mode at 370 degrees F for 15 minutes.
4. Divide everything between plates and serve.

Nutrition:
calories 221, fat 9, fiber 2, carbs 15, protein 11

Shrimp with Peppers and Spinach

Prep time: 5 minutes | **Cooking:** 12 minutes | **Servings:** 4

Ingredients:

- 1 pound shrimp, peeled and deveined
- 2 cups baby spinach
- 2 teaspoons olive oil
- 1 red bell pepper, chopped
- Juice of 1 lime
- 2 tablespoons parsley, chopped
- A pinch of salt and black pepper

Directions:

1. In the multi level air fryer's pan, combine the shrimp with the other ingredients and toss.
2. Put the pan in the instant pot and seal with the air fryer lid.
3. Cook on Bake mode at 380 degrees F for 12 minutes.
4. Divide everything between plates and serve.

Nutrition:

calories 251, fat 12, fiber 3, carbs 6, protein 15

Lime Salmon and Sprouts

Prep time: 5 minutes | **Cooking:** 20 minutes | **Servings:** 4

Ingredients:

- 4 salmon fillets, boneless
- ½ pound Brussels sprouts, trimmed and halved
- Juice of 1 lime
- 1 tablespoon olive oil
- ½ teaspoon rosemary, dried
- ½ teaspoon sweet paprika
- Salt and black pepper to the taste
- ½ cup chicken stock
- 1 tablespoon chives, chopped

Directions:

1. In the multi level air fryer's pan, combine the salmon with the other ingredients and toss.
2. Put the pan in the instant pot and seal with the air fryer lid.
3. Cook on Bake mode at 360 degrees F for 20 minutes.
4. Divide everything between plates and serve.

Nutrition:

calories 241, fat 12, fiber 2, carbs 6, protein 12

Minty Shrimp and Pine Nuts Mix

Prep time: 5 minutes | **Cooking:** 15 minutes | **Servings:** 4

Ingredients:

- 2 pounds shrimp, peeled and deveined
- 2 tablespoons avocado oil
- 1 tablespoon mint, chopped
- Juice of 1 lemon
- A pinch of salt and black pepper
- 1/3 pine nuts, toasted
- 1 tablespoon chives, chopped

Directions:

1. In the multi level air fryer's pan, combine the shrimp with the other ingredients and toss.
2. Put the pan in the instant pot and seal with the air fryer lid.
3. Cook on Bake mode at 380 degrees F for 15 minutes.
4. Divide everything into bowls and serve.

Nutrition:

calories 240, fat 12, fiber 4, carbs 6, protein 9

Turmeric Cod and Asparagus

Prep time: 5 minutes | **Cooking:** 20 minutes | **Servings:** 4

Ingredients:

- 4 cod fillets, boneless
- 8 asparagus spears, trimmed and halved
- Juice of 1 lime
- ½ teaspoon sweet paprika
- ½ teaspoon turmeric powder
- 1 tablespoon dill, chopped
- A pinch of salt and black pepper

Directions:

1. In the multi level air fryer's pan, combine the cod with the other ingredients and toss.
2. Put the pan in the instant pot and seal with the air fryer lid.
3. Cook on Bake mode at 380 degrees F for 20 minutes.
4. Divide everything between plates and serve.

Nutrition:

calories 240, fat 12, fiber 4, carbs 6, protein 9

Rosemary Trout

Prep time: 5 minutes | **Cooking:** 15 minutes | **Servings:** 4

Ingredients:

- 4 trout fillets, boneless
- ½ cup chives, chopped
- 2 teaspoons olive oil
- Zest of 1 lemon, grated
- ½ teaspoon rosemary, dried
- Juice of ½ lemon
- Salt and black pepper to the taste

Directions:

1. In the multi level air fryer's pan, combine the trout with the other ingredients and toss.
2. Put the pan in the instant pot and seal with the air fryer lid.
3. Cook on Bake mode at 370 degrees F for 15 minutes.
4. Divide everything between plates and serve.

Nutrition:

calories 240, fat 12, fiber 5, carbs 6, protein 14

Garlic Mackerel

Prep time: 5 minutes | **Cooking:** 20 minutes | **Servings:** 4

Ingredients:

- 4 mackerel fillets, boneless
- 1 tablespoon oregano, chopped
- 2 teaspoons olive oil
- 1 red onion, chopped
- 1 red bell pepper, chopped
- 2 garlic cloves, minced
- 1 tablespoon balsamic vinegar
- A pinch of salt and black pepper

Directions:

1. In the multi level air fryer's pan, combine the mackerel with the other ingredients and toss.
2. Put the pan in the instant pot and seal with the air fryer lid.
3. Cook on Bake mode at 370 degrees F for 20 minutes.
4. Divide everything between plates and serve.

Nutrition:

calories 261, fat 14, fiber 5, carbs 6, protein 14

Cilantro Trout Mix

Prep time: 5 minutes | **Cooking:** 15 minutes | **Servings:** 4

Ingredients:

- 4 trout fillets, boneless
- 1 cup walnuts, chopped
- 2 teaspoons olive oil
- Juice of 1 lime
- A pinch of salt and black pepper
- 1 tablespoon cilantro, chopped

Directions:

1. In the multi level air fryer's pan, combine the trout with the other ingredients and toss.
2. Put the pan in the instant pot and seal with the air fryer lid.
3. Cook on Bake mode at 370 degrees F for 15 minutes.
4. Divide everything between plates and serve.

Nutrition:

calories 271, fat 13, fiber 4, carbs 6, protein 12

Indian Sea Bass

Prep time: 5 minutes | **Cooking:** 20 minutes | **Servings:** 4

Ingredients:

- 4 sea bass fillets, boneless
- 1 yellow onion, chopped
- 1 teaspoon turmeric powder
- ½ teaspoon garam masala
- 1 cup heavy cream
- Juice of 1 lemon
- 1 tablespoon olive oil
- A pinch of salt and black pepper
- ¼ cup cilantro, chopped

Directions:
1. In the multi level air fryer's pan, combine the sea bass fillets with the other ingredients and toss gently.
2. Put the pan in the instant pot and seal with the air fryer lid.
3. Cook on Bake mode at 380 degrees F for 20 minutes.
4. Divide everything between plates and serve.

Nutrition:
calories 254, fat 10, fiber 4, carbs 6, protein 11

Butter Shrimp and Rice

Prep time: 5 minutes | **Cooking:** 25 minutes | **Servings:** 4

Ingredients:
- 1 pound shrimp, peeled and deveined
- 1 cup wild rice
- 2 cups chicken stock
- ½ teaspoon sweet paprika
- ½ teaspoon coriander, ground
- A pinch of salt and black pepper
- 1 tablespoon butter, melted
- 1 tablespoon parsley, chopped

Directions:
1. In the multi level air fryer's pan, combine the shrimp with the other ingredients except the shrimp and toss.
2. Put the pan in the instant pot and seal with the air fryer lid.
3. Cook on Bake mode at 380 degrees F for 15 minutes.
4. Add the shrimp and cook the mix for 10 minutes more.
5. Divide everything between plates and serve.

Nutrition:
calories 261, fat 12, fiber 4, carbs 6, protein 11

Creamy Trout and Okra

Prep time: 5 minutes | **Cooking:** 20 minutes | **Servings:** 4

Ingredients:
- 4 trout fillets, boneless
- 1 cup okra, sliced
- 1 tablespoon olive oil
- 1 cup heavy cream
- 1 teaspoon coriander, ground
- A pinch of salt and black pepper
- 2 spring onions, chopped
- Juice of 1 lime

Directions:
1. In the multi level air fryer's pan, combine the trout with the other ingredients and toss.
2. Put the pan in the instant pot and seal with the air fryer lid.
3. Cook on Bake mode at 380 degrees F for 20 minutes.
4. Divide everything between plates and serve.

Nutrition:
calories 261, fat 12, fiber 5, carbs 6, protein 11

Cilantro Mussels

Prep time: 5 minutes | **Cooking:** 20 minutes | **Servings:** 4

Ingredients:
- 1 pound mussels, de-bearded
- Juice of 1 lemon
- 1 tablespoon lemon zest, grated
- A pinch of salt and black pepper
- 2 tablespoons cilantro, chopped
- 1 teaspoon olive oil

Directions:
1. In the multi level air fryer's pan, combine the mussels with the other ingredients and toss.
2. Put the pan in the instant pot and seal with the air fryer lid.
3. Cook on Bake mode at 390 degrees F for 20 minutes.
4. Divide everything into bowls and serve.

Nutrition:
calories 231, fat 6, fiber 2, carbs 6, protein 10

Cod with Eggplants and Tomato Sauce

Prep time: 5 minutes | **Cooking:** 20 minutes | **Servings:** 4

Ingredients:
- 4 cod fillets, boneless
- 2 eggplants, cubed
- 1 teaspoon sweet paprika
- ½ teaspoon cumin, ground
- 2 tablespoons avocado oil
- ½ cup tomato sauce
- A pinch of salt and black pepper
- 1 tablespoon thyme, chopped

Directions:
1. In the multi level air fryer's pan, combine the cod with eggplants and the other ingredients and toss.
2. Put the pan in the instant pot and seal with the air fryer lid.
3. Cook on Bake mode at 380 degrees F for 20 minutes.
4. Divide everything between plates and serve.

Nutrition:
calories 241, fat 12, fiber 4, carbs 7, protein 11

Lemongrass and Orange Shrimp

Prep time: 5 minutes | **Cooking:** 15 minutes | **Servings:** 4

Ingredients:
- 2 pounds shrimp, peeled and deveined
- 1 tablespoon olive oil
- Juice of 1 lime
- 1 cup orange juice
- A pinch of salt and black pepper
- 4 lemongrass, chopped
- 1 tablespoon chives, chopped

Directions:
1. In the multi level air fryer's pan, combine the shrimp with the other ingredients and toss.
2. Put the pan in the instant pot and seal with the air fryer lid.
3. Cook on Bake mode at 380 degrees F for 15 minutes.
4. Divide everything into bowls and serve.

Nutrition:
calories 271, fat 12, fiber 4, carbs 6, protein 12

Coconut Trout

Prep time: 5 minutes | **Cooking:** 20 minutes | **Servings:** 4

Ingredients:
- 1 pound trout fillets, boneless and roughly cubed
- 1 cup coconut cream
- ½ teaspoon garam masala
- ½ teaspoon turmeric powder
- A drizzle of olive oil
- ½ teaspoon coriander, ground
- Salt and black pepper to the taste
- 1 teaspoon red pepper flakes, crushed
- 1 tablespoon chives, chopped

Directions:
1. In the multi level air fryer's pan, combine the trout with the other ingredients and toss.
2. Put the pan in the instant pot and seal with the air fryer lid.
3. Cook on Bake mode at 390 degrees F for 20 minutes.
4. Divide everything into bowls and serve.

Nutrition:
calories 261, fat 12, fiber 6, carbs 7, protein 12

Balsamic Tuna and Onions

Prep time: 5 minutes | **Cooking:** 20 minutes | **Servings:** 4

Ingredients:
- 1 pound tuna fillets, boneless
- 2 red onions, chopped
- 2 tablespoons balsamic vinegar
- ½ teaspoon sweet paprika
- 2 tablespoons olive oil
- A pinch of salt and black pepper

Directions:
1. In the multi level air fryer's pan, combine the tuna and the other ingredients.
2. Put the pan in the instant pot and seal with the air fryer lid.
3. Cook on Bake mode at 380 degrees F for 20 minutes.
4. Divide everything between plates and serve.

Nutrition:
calories 261, fat 6, fiber 8, carbs 16, protein 6

Cod with Spring Onions and Mango

Prep time: 5 minutes | **Cooking:** 15 minutes | **Servings:** 4

Ingredients:
- 4 cod fillets, boneless
- 1 cup mango, peeled and cubed
- 1 tablespoon avocado oil
- 2 tablespoons lime juice
- 2 spring onions, chopped
- A pinch of salt and black pepper
- 3 garlic cloves, minced
- 1 tablespoon cilantro, chopped

Directions:
1. In the multi level air fryer's pan, combine the cod with spring onions and the other ingredients and toss.
2. Put the pan in the instant pot and seal with the air fryer lid.
3. Cook on Bake mode at 380 degrees F for 15 minutes.
4. Divide everything between plates and serve.

Nutrition:
calories 261, fat 11, fiber 4, carbs 7, protein 11

Thyme Sea Bass

Prep time: 5 minutes | **Cooking:** 20 minutes | **Servings:** 4

Ingredients:
- 4 sea bass fillets, boneless
- 4 tablespoons butter, melted
- Juice of 1 lime
- A pinch of salt and black pepper
- 1 tablespoon thyme, chopped
- 1 tablespoon chives, chopped

Directions:
1. In the multi level air fryer's pan, combine the sea bass and the other ingredients and toss.
2. Put the pan in the instant pot and seal with the air fryer lid.
3. Cook on Bake mode at 400 degrees F for 20 minutes.
4. Divide everything between plates and serve.

Nutrition:
calories 251, fat 14, fiber 5, carbs 6, protein 12

Tuna and Rhubarb

Prep time: 5 minutes | **Cooking:** 20 minutes | **Servings:** 4

Ingredients:
- 1 pound tuna fillets, boneless and roughly cubed
- ½ cup rhubarb, sliced
- 1 cup okra, sliced
- 2 tablespoons olive oil
- 2 tablespoons balsamic vinegar
- A pinch of salt and black pepper
- 1 tablespoon parsley, chopped

Directions:
1. In the multi level air fryer's pan, combine the tuna and the other ingredients and toss.
2. Put the pan in the instant pot and seal with the air fryer lid.
3. Cook on Bake mode at 380 degrees F for 20 minutes.
4. Divide everything into bowls and serve.

Nutrition:
calories 251, fat 10, fiber 3, carbs 4, protein 8

Garlic Rosemary Cod Mix

Prep time: 5 minutes | **Cooking:** 20 minutes | **Servings:** 4

Ingredients:
- 4 cod fillets, boneless
- 2 tablespoons soy sauce
- 1 teaspoon rosemary, dried
- 2 garlic cloves, minced
- A pinch of salt and black pepper
- ½ teaspoon stevia
- 2 tablespoons olive oil

Directions:
1. In the multi level air fryer's pan, combine the cod and the other ingredients and toss.
2. Put the pan in the instant pot and seal with the air fryer lid.
3. Cook on Bake mode at 390 degrees F for 20 minutes.
4. Divide everything between plates and serve.

Nutrition:
calories 251, fat 13, fiber 3, carbs 5, protein 10

Trout and Balsamic Mushrooms Mix

Prep time: 5 minutes | **Cooking:** 20 minutes | **Servings:** 4

Ingredients:
- 4 trout fillets, boneless
- ½ pound white mushrooms, halved
- 1 tablespoon balsamic vinegar
- A pinch of salt and black pepper
- 2 teaspoons olive oil
- 1 tablespoon dill, chopped
- 1 tablespoon thyme, chopped

Directions:
1. In the multi level air fryer's pan, combine the trout and the other ingredients and toss.
2. Put the pan in the instant pot and seal with the air fryer lid.
3. Cook on Bake mode at 390 degrees F for 20 minutes.
4. Divide everything between plates and serve.

Nutrition:
calories 271, fat 12, fiber 4, carbs 6, protein 11

Parsley Trout

Prep time: 10 minutes | **Cooking:** 20 minutes | **Servings:** 4

Ingredients:
- 4 trout fillets, boneless
- 2 tablespoons lemon juice
- 3 tablespoons parsley, chopped
- 2 tablespoons olive oil
- Salt and black pepper to the taste
- 1 teaspoon sweet paprika

Directions:
1. In a blender, mix the lemon juice with the parsley and the other ingredients except the fish, pulse well and rub the fish with this mix.
2. Put the fish in your multi level air fryer's basket.
3. Put the basket in the instant pot, seal with the air fryer lid and cook on Air fry mode at 390 degrees F for 10 minutes on each side.
4. Divide between plates and serve with a side salad.

Nutrition:
calories 221, fat 11, fiber 4, carbs 6, protein 9

Smoked Shrimp Mix

Prep time: 5 minutes | **Cooking:** 20 minutes | **Servings:** 4

Ingredients:

- 1 pound shrimp, peeled and deveined
- 2 tablespoons tarragon, chopped
- 1 teaspoon smoked paprika
- ½ cup chicken stock
- Salt and black pepper to the taste

Directions:
1. In the multi level air fryer's pan, combine the shrimp and the other ingredients and toss.
2. Put the pan in the instant pot and seal with the air fryer lid.
3. Cook on Bake mode at 350 degrees F for 20 minutes.
4. Divide everything into bowls and serve.

Nutrition:
calories 271, fat 12, fiber 4, carbs 6, protein 11

Shrimp and Chives Sauce

Prep time: 5 minutes | **Cooking:** 20 minutes | **Servings:** 4

Ingredients:
- 2 tablespoons avocado oil
- 1 pound shrimp, peeled and deveined
- 1 cup tomato sauce
- 4 garlic cloves, chopped
- ½ teaspoon garlic powder
- 1 teaspoon sweet paprika
- A pinch of salt and black pepper
- 1 tablespoon chives, chopped

Directions:
1. In the multi level air fryer's pan, combine the shrimp and the other ingredients and toss.
2. Put the pan in the instant pot and seal with the air fryer lid.
3. Cook on Bake mode at 380 degrees F for 20 minutes.
4. Divide everything into bowls and serve.

Nutrition:
calories 261, fat 11, fiber 4, carbs 6, protein 10

Coriander Sea Bass and Broccoli

Prep time: 5 minutes | **Cooking:** 20 minutes | **Servings:** 4

Ingredients:
- 4 sea bass fillets, boneless
- 1 teaspoon sweet paprika
- ½ teaspoon coriander, ground
- 1 pound broccoli florets
- 2 tablespoons olive oil
- 1 cup chicken stock
- A pinch of salt and black pepper

Directions:
1. In the multi level air fryer's pan, combine the sea bass with the other ingredients and toss.
2. Put the pan in the instant pot and seal with the air fryer lid.
3. Cook on Bake mode at 380 degrees F for 20 minutes.
4. Divide everything between plates and serve.

Nutrition:
calories 251, fat 15, fiber 4, carbs 6, protein 12

Orange Snapper

Prep time: 5 minutes | **Cooking:** 15 minutes | **Servings:** 4

Ingredients:
- 4 snapper fillets, boneless
- 1 tablespoon hot paprika
- Juice of 1 orange
- ½ teaspoon red pepper flakes, crushed
- 2 tablespoons olive oil
- A pinch of salt and black pepper

Directions:
1. In the multi level air fryer's basket, combine the snapper fillets with the paprika and the other ingredients and toss.
2. Put the basket in the instant pot, seal with the air fryer lid and cook on Air fry mode at 390 degrees F for 15 minutes, flipping the fish halfway.
3. Divide between plates and serve with a side salad.

Nutrition:
calories 241, fat 12, fiber 4, carbs 6, protein 13

Cod with Caraway Chard

Prep time: 5 minutes | **Cooking:** 20 minutes | **Servings:** 4

Ingredients:
- 4 cod fillets, boneless
- 1 cup red chard, torn
- 1 cup tomato sauce
- 1 tablespoon olive oil
- Juice of 1 lime
- A pinch of salt and black pepper
- 1 teaspoon caraway seeds
- 1 tablespoon chives, chopped

Directions:
1. In the multi level air fryer's pan, combine the cod with the other ingredients and toss.
2. Put the pan in the instant pot and seal with the air fryer lid.
3. Cook on Bake mode at 390 degrees F for 20 minutes.
4. Divide everything between plates and serve.

Nutrition:
calories 251, fat 16, fiber 4, carbs 6, protein 13

Cod and Bok Choy

Prep time: 5 minutes | **Cooking:** 20 minutes | **Servings:** 4

Ingredients:
- 4 cod fillets, boneless
- 1 cup bok choy, torn
- 1 red chili pepper, minced
- 1 teaspoon chili powder
- ½ cup chicken stock
- A pinch of salt and black pepper
- 1 tablespoon hot chili paste
- 2 tablespoons olive oil

Directions:
1. In the multi level air fryer's pan, combine the cod with the other ingredients and toss.
2. Put the pan in the instant pot and seal with the air fryer lid.
3. Cook on Bake mode at 380 degrees F for 20 minutes.
4. Divide everything between plates and serve.

Nutrition:
calories 220, fat 13, fiber 4, carbs 6, protein 11

Herbed Tuna

Prep time: 5 minutes | **Cooking:** 20 minutes | **Servings:** 4

Ingredients:
- 4 tuna fillets, boneless
- 2 tablespoons olive oil
- 1 tablespoon oregano, chopped
- 1 tablespoon chives, chopped
- A pinch of salt and black pepper
- 1 tablespoon parsley, chopped
- 1 tablespoon basil, chopped
- 1 tablespoon lemon juice

Directions:
1. In the multi level air fryer's basket, mix the tuna with the oregano, chives and the other ingredients.
2. Put the basket in the instant pot, seal with the air fryer lid and cook on Air fry mode at 380 degrees F for 20 minutes.
3. Divide everything between plates and serve.

Nutrition:
calories 220, fat 12, fiber 2, carbs 6, protein 10

Tuna with Tomatoes and Pineapples

Prep time: 5 minutes | **Cooking:** 20 minutes | **Servings:** 2

Ingredients:
- 1 pound tuna fillets, boneless and roughly cubed
- 1 cup pineapple, peeled and cubed

- 1 tablespoon avocado oil
- 1 cup cherry tomatoes, halved
- A pinch of salt and black pepper
- 2 tablespoons capers, drained
- 1 tablespoon balsamic vinegar
- 2 tablespoons chives, chopped

Directions:
1. In the multi level air fryer's pan, combine the tuna with the other ingredients and toss.
2. Put the pan in the instant pot and seal with the air fryer lid.
3. Cook on Bake mode at 390 degrees F for 20 minutes.
4. Divide everything into bowls and serve.

Nutrition:
calories 280, fat 12, fiber 4, carbs 6, protein 11

Basil Tuna

Prep time: 5 minutes | **Cooking:** 20 minutes | **Servings:** 4

Ingredients:
- 4 tuna fillets, boneless
- Juice of 1 lemon
- 1 tablespoon basil, chopped
- 1 tablespoon pine nuts, toasted
- 1 tablespoon olive oil
- A pinch of salt and black pepper

Directions:
1. In a blender, combine the lemon juice with the other ingredients except the tuna an pulse well.
2. Brush the fish with this mix, place it in your multi level air fryer's basket.
3. Put the basket in the instant pot, seal with the air fryer lid and cook on Air fry mode for 10 minutes on each side at 380 degrees F.
4. Divide between plates and serve with a side salad.

Nutrition:
calories 216, fat 11, fiber 3, carbs 6, protein 12

Mackerel and Radish

Prep time: 5 minutes | **Cooking:** 20 minutes | **Servings:** 4

Ingredients:
- 4 mackerel fillets, boneless
- Juice of 1 lime
- 1 cup radishes, halved
- 2 tablespoons olive oil
- 4 shallots, chopped
- A pinch of salt and black pepper

Directions:
1. In the multi level air fryer's pan, combine the mackerel with the other ingredients and toss.
2. Put the pan in the instant pot and seal with the air fryer lid.
3. Cook on Bake mode at 390 degrees F for 20 minutes.
4. Divide everything between plates and serve.

Nutrition:
calories 270, fat 12, fiber 4, carbs 6, protein 12

Sea Bass and Rosemary Tomatoes

Prep time: 5 minutes | **Cooking:** 20 minutes | **Servings:** 4

Ingredients:
- 4 black sea bass fillets, boneless and skin scored
- 2 cups cherry tomatoes, halved
- Juice of 1 lime
- A pinch of salt and black pepper
- 1 tablespoon rosemary, chopped
- Juice of 1 lime

Directions:
1. In the multi level air fryer's pan, combine the sea bass with the other ingredients and toss.
2. Put the pan in the instant pot and seal with the air fryer lid.
3. Cook on Bake mode at 380 degrees F for 20 minutes.
4. Divide everything between plates and serve.

Nutrition:
calories 220, fat 12, fiber 4, carbs 6, protein 10

Poultry Recipes

Cheesy Chicken Bake

Prep time: 5 minutes | Cooking: 35 minutes | Servings: 4

Ingredients:

- A pinch of salt and black pepper
- 1 cup mozzarella, shredded
- 1 pound chicken breast, skinless, boneless and cut into strips
- 1 cup red bell pepper, chopped
- 2 red onions, chopped
- ½ cup heavy cream
- 2 tablespoons butter, melted
- 1 teaspoon chili powder
- 1 garlic clove, minced
- 1 tablespoon parsley, chopped

Directions:

1. Heat up a pan with the butter over medium heat, add the meat and onions, brown for 10 minutes and transfer to the multi level air fryer pan.
2. Add the rest of the ingredients except the cheese and toss.
3. Sprinkle the cheese on top, put the pan in instant pot, seal with air fryer lid and cook on Roast mode at 380 degrees F for 25 minutes.
4. Divide between plates and serve.

Nutrition:

calories 280, fat 14, fiber 4, carbs 6, protein 20

Turkey and Herbed Green Beans

Prep time: 5 minutes | Cooking: 30 minutes | Servings: 4

Ingredients:

- 1 pound turkey breast, skinless, boneless, browned and sliced
- 1 tablespoon olive oil
- 1 teaspoon basil, dried
- 2 cups green beans, trimmed and halved
- ½ teaspoon sweet paprika
- ½ teaspoon rosemary, dried
- ½ cup chicken stock
- A pinch of salt and black pepper
- 1 tablespoon parsley, chopped

Directions:

1. In the multi level air fryer's pan, combine the browned turkey with the other ingredients and toss.
2. Put the pan in the instant pot and seal with the air fryer lid.
3. Cook on Roast mode at 380 degrees F for 30 minutes.
4. Divide everything between plates and serve.

Nutrition:

calories 241, fat 11, fiber 5, carbs 6, protein 14

Chicken with Peppers and Sauce

Prep time: 5 minutes | Cooking: 25 minutes | Servings: 4

Ingredients:

- 1 pound chicken breasts, skinless, boneless and halved
- 1 red bell pepper, cut into strips
- 1 green bell pepper, cut into strips
- ½ cup tomato sauce
- ½ teaspoon cumin, ground
- ½ teaspoon coriander, ground
- 2 tablespoons olive oil
- 1 tablespoon chives, chopped

Directions:

1. In the multi level air fryer's pan, combine the chicken with the other ingredients and toss.
2. Put the pan in the instant pot and seal with the air fryer lid.
3. Cook on Bake mode at 380 degrees F for 25 minutes.
4. Divide everything between plates and serve.

Nutrition:

calories 280, fat 12, fiber 4, carbs 6, protein 14

Paprika Chicken

Prep time: 5 minutes | Cooking: 20 minutes | Servings: 4

Ingredients:

- 2 pounds chicken breasts, skinless, boneless and sliced
- 2 tablespoons smoked paprika
- 2 tablespoons olive oil
- 1 teaspoon chili powder
- A pinch of salt and black pepper
- 1 tablespoon cilantro, chopped

Directions:

1. In the multi level air fryer's basket, combine the chicken with the other ingredients and toss.
2. Put the basket in the instant pot and seal with the air fryer lid.
3. Cook on Air fry mode at 350 degrees F for 20 minutes.
4. Divide everything between plates and serve.

Nutrition:

calories 222, fat 11, fiber 4, carbs 6, protein 12

Garlic Chicken Thighs

Prep time: 5 minutes | Cooking: 30 minutes | Servings: 4

Ingredients:

- 4 chicken thighs, boneless and skinless
- 3 tablespoons butter, melted
- Juice of 1 lime
- A pinch of salt and black pepper
- 4 garlic cloves, minced
- 1 tablespoon thyme, chopped

Directions:

1. In the multi level air fryer's pan, combine the chicken thighs with the other ingredients and toss.
2. Put the pan in the instant pot and seal with the air fryer lid.
3. Cook on Roast mode at 370 degrees F for 30 minutes.
4. Divide everything between plates and serve.

Nutrition:

calories 270, fat 12, fiber 4, carbs 6, protein 14

Turmeric Chicken Wings

Prep time: 5 minutes | Cooking: 30 minutes | Servings: 4

Ingredients:

- 2 pounds chicken wings, halved
- 3 tablespoons honey
- 1 tablespoon olive oil
- Juice of 1 lime
- ½ teaspoon turmeric powder
- A pinch of salt and black pepper
- 2 garlic cloves, minced

Directions:

1. In your multi level air fryer's basket, mix the chicken with the honey and the other ingredients and toss.
2. Put the basket in the instant pot, seal with the air fryer lid and cook on Roast mode at 400 degrees F for 30 minutes, shaking halfway.
3. Divide between plates and serve with a side salad.

Nutrition:

calories 263, fat 14, fiber 4, carbs 6, protein 15

Creamy Oregano Turkey

Prep time: 5 minutes | Cooking: 30 minutes | Servings: 4

Ingredients:

- 2 pounds turkey breast, skinless, boneless and cubed
- 1 tablespoon olive oil
- 1 red onion, chopped
- 1 cup heavy cream
- Salt and black pepper to the taste
- 3 garlic cloves, minced
- ½ teaspoon oregano, dried
- ¼ cup chives, chopped

Directions:
1. In the multi level air fryer's pan, combine the turkey with the other ingredients and toss.
2. Put the pan in the instant pot and seal with the air fryer lid.
3. Cook on Bake mode at 380 degrees F for 30 minutes.
4. Divide everything between plates and serve.

Nutrition:
calories 270, fat 12, fiber 3, carbs 6, protein 17

Orange Turkey Mix

Prep time: 5 minutes | **Cooking:** 20 minutes | **Servings:** 4

Ingredients:
- 1 pound turkey breast, skinless, boneless and cubed
- 1 cup oranges, peeled and cut into segments
- 1 tablespoon balsamic vinegar
- 1 tablespoon olive oil
- Salt and black pepper to the taste
- 1 tablespoon orange zest, grated

Directions:
1. In the multi level air fryer's pan, combine the turkey with the other ingredients and toss.
2. Put the pan in the instant pot and seal with the air fryer lid.
3. Cook on Bake mode at 380 degrees F for 20 minutes.
4. Divide everything between plates and serve.

Nutrition:
calories 256, fat 12, fiber 4, carbs 6, protein 14

Lemon Chicken and Asparagus

Prep time: 15 minutes | **Cooking:** 25 minutes | **Servings:** 4

Ingredients:
- 1 pound chicken breast, skinless, boneless and sliced
- ¼ pound asparagus spears, trimmed
- 1 tablespoon avocado oil
- Juice of 1 lemon
- ½ teaspoon sweet paprika
- 1 teaspoon oregano, dried
- A pinch of salt and black pepper

Directions:
1. In the multi level air fryer's pan, combine the chicken with the other ingredients and toss.
2. Put the pan in the instant pot and seal with the air fryer lid.
3. Cook on Bake mode at 380 degrees F for 25 minutes.
4. Divide everything between plates and serve.

Nutrition:
calories 280, fat 11, fiber 4, carbs 6, protein 17

Herbed Turkey and Olives

Prep time: 10 minutes | **Cooking:** 30 minutes | **Servings:** 4

Ingredients:
- 2 pounds turkey breast, skinless, boneless and cubed
- 1 cup black olives, pitted and halved
- 1 cup tomato sauce
- 1 tablespoon avocado oil
- A pinch of salt and black pepper
- 1 teaspoon oregano, dried
- ½ teaspoon garlic powder
- ½ teaspoon sweet paprika

Directions:
1. In the multi level air fryer's pan, combine the turkey with the other ingredients and toss.
2. Put the pan in the instant pot and seal with the air fryer lid.
3. Cook on Bake mode at 370 degrees F for 30 minutes.
4. Divide everything between plates and serve.

Nutrition:
calories 270, fat 14, fiber 4, carbs 6, protein 18

Chicken and Walnuts

Prep time: 10 minutes | **Cooking:** 25 minutes | **Servings:** 4

Ingredients:
- ½ cup pine nuts, toasted
- 2 pounds chicken breast, skinless, boneless and cubed
- 1 tablespoon avocado oil
- 1 red onion, sliced
- ½ cup walnuts, chopped
- A pinch of salt and black pepper
- 1 teaspoon chili powder

Directions:
1. In the multi level air fryer's pan, combine the chicken with the other ingredients and toss.
2. Put the pan in the instant pot and seal with the air fryer lid.
3. Cook on Bake mode at 380 degrees F for 25 minutes.
4. Divide everything between plates and serve.

Nutrition:
calories 244, fat 11, fiber 4, carbs 6, protein 17

Creamy Chicken

Prep time: 5 minutes | **Cooking:** 25 minutes | **Servings:** 4

Ingredients:
- 2 pounds chicken breast, skinless, boneless and cubed
- 1 cup coconut cream
- 1 red onion, sliced
- ½ teaspoon sweet paprika
- 1 tablespoon olive oil
- A pinch of salt and black pepper
- 1 tablespoon thyme, chopped
- 3 garlic cloves, minced

Directions:
1. In the multi level air fryer's pan, combine the chicken with the other ingredients and toss.
2. Put the pan in the instant pot and seal with the air fryer lid.
3. Cook on Bake mode at 370 degrees F for 25 minutes.
4. Divide everything between plates and serve.

Nutrition:
calories 275, fat 12, fiber 4, carbs 6, protein 17

Lemon Chicken

Prep time: 5 minutes | **Cooking:** 25 minutes | **Servings:** 4

Ingredients:
- 2 pounds chicken breast, skinless, boneless and cubed
- 4 garlic cloves, minced
- 2 tablespoons lemon juice
- 2 tablespoons lemon zest, grated
- ½ cup heavy cream
- Salt and black pepper to the taste
- 1 teaspoon olive oil
- ¼ cup cilantro, chopped

Directions:
1. In the multi level air fryer's pan, combine the chicken with the other ingredients and toss.
2. Put the pan in the instant pot and seal with the air fryer lid.
3. Cook on Bake mode at 370 degrees F for 25 minutes.
4. Divide everything between plates and serve.

Nutrition:
calories 267, fat 11, fiber 4, carbs 6, protein 16

Basil Turkey and Spinach

Prep time: 5 minutes | **Cooking:** 25 minutes | **Servings:** 4

Ingredients:
- 2 pounds turkey breast, skinless, boneless and cubed

- 1 cup baby spinach
- 1 tablespoon avocado oil
- Juice of 1 lime
- A pinch of salt and black pepper
- 1 teaspoon Italian seasoning
- 1 tablespoon basil, chopped

Directions:
1. In the multi level air fryer's pan, combine the turkey with the other ingredients and toss.
2. Put the pan in the instant pot and seal with the air fryer lid.
3. Cook on Bake mode at 370 degrees F for 25 minutes.
4. Divide everything between plates and serve.

Nutrition:
calories 285, fat 12, fiber 4, carbs 7, protein 15

Cayenne Chicken Wings

Prep time: 5 minutes | **Cooking:** 30 minutes | **Servings:** 4

Ingredients:
- 1 tablespoon olive oil
- 2 pounds chicken wings
- Juice of 1 lime
- 1 teaspoon coriander, ground
- 1 teaspoon cayenne pepper
- Salt and black pepper to the taste

Directions:
1. In the multi level air fryer's basket, mix the chicken wings with the oil, lime juice and the other ingredients and toss.
2. Put the basket in the instant pot, seal with the air fryer lid and cook on Air fry mode at 380 degrees F for 15 minutes on each side.
3. Divide between plates and serve with a side salad.

Nutrition:
calories 280, fat 13, fiber 3, carbs 6, protein 14

Chicken with Soy Sauce

Prep time: 5 minutes | **Cooking:** 20 minutes | **Servings:** 4

Ingredients:
- 4 chicken breasts, skinless, boneless and cubed
- 2 tablespoons soy sauce
- 1 tablespoon olive oil
- 1 teaspoon rosemary, dried
- A pinch of salt and black pepper
- 1 tablespoon chives, chopped

Directions:
1. In the multi level air fryer's pan, combine the chicken with the other ingredients and toss.
2. Put the pan in the instant pot and seal with the air fryer lid.
3. Cook on Bake mode at 400 degrees F for 20 minutes.
4. Divide everything between plates and serve.

Nutrition:
calories 250, fat 12, fiber 4, carbs 6, protein 15

Balsamic Chili Chicken

Prep time: 10 minutes | **Cooking:** 25 minutes | **Servings:** 4

Ingredients:
- 2 pounds chicken wings, halved
- 3 tablespoons balsamic vinegar
- A pinch of salt and black pepper
- 1 tablespoon lemon juice
- ½ teaspoon chili powder

Directions:
1. In your multi level air fryer's basket, mix the chicken with the vinegar and the other ingredients and toss.
2. Put the basket in the instant pot, seal with air fryer lid and cook on Air fry mode at 380 degrees F for 25 minutes.
3. Divide everything between plates and serve.

Nutrition:
calories 254, fat 14, fiber 4, carbs 6, protein 15

Cinnamon Chicken

Prep time: 5 minutes | **Cooking:** 30 minutes | **Servings:** 4

Ingredients:
- 2 pounds chicken breast, skinless, boneless and cubed
- 2 tablespoons cinnamon powder
- A pinch of salt and black pepper
- 2 tablespoons olive oil

Directions:
1. In the multi level air fryer's basket, mix the chicken with the cinnamon and the other ingredients and toss.
2. Put the basket in the instant pot, seal with the air fryer lid and cook on Air fry mode at 360 degrees F for 15 minutes on each side.
3. Divide between plates and serve.

Nutrition:
calories 271, fat 12, fiber 4, carbs 6, protein 13

Masala Turkey and Okra

Prep time: 5 minutes | **Cooking:** 20 minutes | **Servings:** 4

Ingredients:
- 1 pound turkey breast, skinless, boneless and cubed
- 1 cup okra
- 1 tablespoon olive oil
- A pinch of salt and black pepper
- Juice of 1 lemon
- 1 tablespoon chives, chopped
- 1 teaspoon garam masala
- 1 teaspoon chili powder

Directions:
1. In the multi level air fryer's pan, combine the turkey with the other ingredients and toss.
2. Put the pan in the instant pot and seal with the air fryer lid.
3. Cook on Bake mode at 370 degrees F for 20 minutes.
4. Divide everything between plates and serve.

Nutrition:
calories 230, fat 13, fiber 4, carbs 6, protein 16

Cilantro Turkey Mix

Prep time: 5 minutes | **Cooking:** 30 minutes | **Servings:** 4

Ingredients:
- 2 pounds turkey breast, skinless, boneless and cubed
- 2 teaspoons turmeric powder
- ¼ cup chicken stock
- 4 garlic cloves, minced
- Salt and black pepper to the taste
- 1 tablespoon olive oil
- 1 tablespoon cilantro, chopped

Directions:
1. In the multi level air fryer's pan, combine the turkey with the other ingredients and toss.
2. Put the pan in the instant pot and seal with the air fryer lid.
3. Cook on Bake mode at 370 degrees F for 20 minutes.
4. Divide everything between plates and serve.

Nutrition:
calories 250, fat 12, fiber 4, carbs 6, protein 15

Buttery Turkey

Prep time: 10 minutes | **Cooking:** 25 minutes | **Servings:** 4

Ingredients:

- 2 pounds turkey breasts, skinless, boneless and halved
- 4 tablespoons butter, melted
- 2 tablespoons sage, chopped
- ½ teaspoon turmeric powder
- A pinch of salt and black pepper
- ½ cup chicken stock

Directions:
1. In the multi level air fryer's pan, combine the turkey with the other ingredients and toss.
2. Put the pan in the instant pot and seal with the air fryer lid.
3. Cook on Bake mode at 390 degrees F for 25 minutes.
4. Divide everything between plates and serve.

Nutrition:
calories 284, fat 14, fiber 2, carbs 6, protein 20

Coriander Turkey

Prep time: 5 minutes | **Cooking:** 25 minutes | **Servings:** 4

Ingredients:
- 1 pound turkey breast, skinless, boneless and cubed
- 1 tablespoon rosemary, chopped
- A pinch of salt and black pepper
- ½ teaspoon coriander, ground
- 2 tablespoons butter, melted

Directions:
1. In the multi level air fryer's basket, mix the turkey with the rosemary and the other ingredients and toss.
2. Put the basket in the instant pot, seal with the air fryer lid and cook on Air fry mode at 380 degrees F for 25 minutes.
3. Divide between plates and serve with a side salad.

Nutrition:
calories 236, fat 12, fiber 4, carbs 6, protein 13

Cumin Chicken

Prep time: 5 minutes | **Cooking:** 30 minutes | **Servings:** 4

Ingredients:
- 1 pound chicken breast, skinless, boneless and cubed
- 1 cup shallots, chopped
- Juice of 1 lime
- ½ cup chicken stock
- 1 tablespoon olive oil
- ¼ teaspoon cumin, ground
- Salt and black pepper to the taste
- 1 tablespoon parsley, chopped

Directions:
1. In the multi level air fryer's pan, combine the chicken with the other ingredients and toss.
2. Put the pan in the instant pot and seal with the air fryer lid.
3. Cook on Bake mode at 370 degrees F for 30 minutes.
4. Divide everything between plates and serve.

Nutrition:
calories 236, fat 12, fiber 4, carbs 6, protein 15

Turkey with Onion and Fennel

Prep time: 5 minutes | **Cooking:** 20 minutes | **Servings:** 4

Ingredients:
1 pound turkey breast, skinless, boneless and cubed
1 red onion, chopped
2 fennel bulbs, sliced
½ cup chicken stock
Salt and black pepper to the taste
1 tablespoon olive oil
1 tablespoon chives, chopped

Directions:
1. In the multi level air fryer's pan, combine the turkey with the other ingredients and toss.
2. Put the pan in the instant pot and seal with the air fryer lid.
3. Cook on Bake mode at 360 degrees F for 20 minutes.
4. Divide everything between plates and serve.

Nutrition:
calories 240, fat 12, fiber 4, carbs 6, protein 15

Chicken with Artichokes

Prep time: 5 minutes | **Cooking:** 30 minutes | **Servings:** 4

Ingredients:
- 1 pound chicken breast, skinless, boneless and cubed
- 1 cup canned artichoke hearts, drained and quartered
- 1 red onion, chopped
- 1 tablespoon olive oil
- 1 teaspoon turmeric powder
- ½ cup chicken stock
- A pinch of salt and black pepper
- 1 tablespoon chives, chopped

Directions:
1. In the multi level air fryer's pan, combine the chicken with the other ingredients and toss.
2. Put the pan in the instant pot and seal with the air fryer lid.
3. Cook on Bake mode at 380 degrees F for 30 minutes.
4. Divide everything between plates and serve.

Nutrition:
calories 283, fat 12, fiber 3, carbs 5, protein 15

Parsley Turkey Mix

Prep time: 5 minutes | **Cooking:** 25 minutes | **Servings:** 4

Ingredients:
- 1 pound turkey breast, skinless, boneless, cubed
- 1 tablespoon tarragon, chopped
- 1 tablespoon olive oil
- Juice of 1 lime
- ¼ cup chicken stock
- 1 tablespoon parsley, chopped
- A pinch of salt and black pepper

Directions:
1. In the multi level air fryer's pan, combine the turkey with the other ingredients and toss.
2. Put the pan in the instant pot and seal with the air fryer lid.
3. Cook on Bake mode at 380 degrees F for 25 minutes.
4. Divide everything between plates and serve.

Nutrition:
calories 284, fat 13, fiber 3, carbs 5, protein 15

Coconut Chicken and Almonds

Prep time: 5 minutes | **Cooking:** 25 minutes | **Servings:** 2

Ingredients:
- 1 pound chicken breast, skinless, boneless and cubed
- ½ cup almonds, chopped
- ½ cup coconut cream
- ½ teaspoon turmeric powder
- Salt and black pepper to the taste
- 2 tablespoons butter, melted
- 1 tablespoon chives, chopped

Directions:
1. In the multi level air fryer's pan, combine the chicken with the other ingredients and toss.
2. Put the pan in the instant pot and seal with the air fryer lid.
3. Cook on Bake mode at 370 degrees F for 25 minutes.
4. Divide everything between plates and serve.

Nutrition:
calories 274, fat 12, fiber 3, carbs 5, protein 14

Lime Chicken and Radishes

Prep time: 5 minutes | **Cooking:** 30 minutes | **Servings:** 4

Ingredients:

- 2 pounds chicken breast, skinless, boneless and cut into strips
- A pinch of salt and black pepper
- 1 cup radishes, halved
- Juice of 1 lime
- 1 tablespoon olive oil
- ½ cup chicken stock
- ½ teaspoon sweet paprika
- 2 tablespoon chives, chopped

Directions:

1. In the multi level air fryer's pan, combine the chicken with the other ingredients and toss.
2. Put the pan in the instant pot and seal with the air fryer lid.
3. Cook on Bake mode at 380 degrees F for 25 minutes.
4. Divide everything between plates and serve.

Nutrition:

calories 257, fat 12, fiber 4, carbs 5, protein 14

Chicken and Cilantro Tomatoes

Prep time: 5 minutes | **Cooking:** 25 minutes | **Servings:** 4

Ingredients:

- 1 pound chicken breast, skinless, boneless and cubed
- 1 cup cherry tomatoes, halved
- 1 tablespoon olive oil
- 1 teaspoon chili powder
- A pinch of salt and black pepper
- ½ cup chicken stock
- 1 tablespoon cilantro, chopped

Directions:

1. In the multi level air fryer's pan, combine the chicken with the other ingredients and toss.
2. Put the pan in the instant pot and seal with the air fryer lid.
3. Cook on Bake mode at 380 degrees F for 25 minutes.
4. Divide everything between plates and serve.

Nutrition:

calories 267, fat 13, fiber 4, carbs 6, protein 16

Turmeric Lemon Turkey

Prep time: 5 minutes | **Cooking:** 30 minutes | **Servings:** 4

Ingredients:

- 1 pound turkey breast, skinless, boneless and sliced
- 1 tablespoon cumin, ground
- 1 tablespoon olive oil
- Juice of ½ lemon
- 4 garlic cloves, minced
- 1 teaspoon turmeric powder
- 1 tablespoon garlic powder

Directions:

1. In the multi level air fryer's pan, combine the turkey with the other ingredients and toss.
2. Put the pan in the instant pot and seal with the air fryer lid.
3. Cook on Bake mode at 380 degrees F for 30 minutes.
4. Divide everything between plates and serve.

Nutrition:

calories 285, fat 12, fiber 3, carbs 6, protein 16

Chicken and Butter Mushrooms

Prep time: 5 minutes | **Cooking:** 25 minutes | **Servings:** 4

Ingredients:

- 2 pounds chicken breast, skinless, boneless and cubed
- 1 cup white mushrooms, halved
- 1 tablespoon butter, melted
- 1 tablespoon lime juice
- A pinch of salt and black pepper
- ½ teaspoon turmeric powder
- ½ teaspoon coriander, ground
- 1 cup chicken stock

Directions:

1. In the multi level air fryer's pan, combine the chicken with the other ingredients and toss.
2. Put the pan in the instant pot and seal with the air fryer lid.
3. Cook on Bake mode at 370 degrees F for 25 minutes.
4. Divide everything between plates and serve.

Nutrition:

calories 285, fat 11, fiber 3, carbs 5, protein 14

Rosemary Turkey and Corn

Prep time: 5 minutes | **Cooking:** 25 minutes | **Servings:** 4

Ingredients:

- 1 pound turkey breast, skinless, boneless and sliced
- 2 cups corn
- 1 tablespoon olive oil
- 2 garlic cloves, minced
- ½ teaspoon rosemary, dried
- ½ cup heavy cream
- A pinch of salt and black pepper

Directions:

1. In the multi level air fryer's pan, combine the turkey with the other ingredients and toss.
2. 'Put the pan in the instant pot and seal with the air fryer lid.
3. Cook on Bake mode at 380 degrees F for 25 minutes.
4. Divide everything between plates and serve.

Nutrition:

calories 240, fat 12, fiber 3, carbs 5, protein 13

Turkey with Garlic Quinoa

Prep time: 5 minutes | **Cooking:** 25 minutes | **Servings:** 4

Ingredients:

- 1 pound turkey breast, skinless, boneless and cubed
- 1 cup quinoa
- 1 cup chicken stock
- A pinch of salt and black pepper
- ½ teaspoon turmeric powder
- 2 teaspoons olive oil
- 2 garlic cloves, minced
- ¼ cup parsley, chopped

Directions:

1. In the multi level air fryer's pan, combine the turkey with the other ingredients and toss.
2. Put the pan in the instant pot and seal with the air fryer lid.
3. Cook on Bake mode at 380 degrees F for 30 minutes.
4. Divide everything between plates and serve.

Nutrition:

calories 264, fat 14, fiber 4, carbs 6, protein 16

Chicken and Veggies Mix

Prep time: 5 minutes | **Cooking:** 20 minutes | **Servings:** 4

Ingredients:

- 1 pound chicken meat, ground and browned
- 1 zucchini, cubed
- 1 sweet potato, cubed
- ½ cup tomato sauce
- 1 eggplant, cubed
- 1 cup cherry tomatoes, halved
- 1 teaspoon chili powder
- A pinch of salt and black pepper
- 2 tablespoons olive oil
- 1 teaspoon garlic powder
- 1 tablespoon parsley, chopped

Directions:

1. In the multi level air fryer's pan, combine the chicken with the other ingredients and toss.
2. Put the pan in the instant pot and seal with the air fryer lid.

3. Cook on Bake mode at 370 degrees F for 20 minutes.
4. Divide everything between plates and serve.

Nutrition:
calories 274, fat 12, fiber 3, carbs 6, protein 15

Chicken and Tomato Sprouts

Prep time: 5 minutes | **Cooking:** 25 minutes | **Servings:** 4

Ingredients:
- 2 pound chicken breast, skinless, boneless sand cubed
- 1 cup Brussels sprouts, trimmed and halved
- 1 cup tomato sauce
- ½ tablespoon olive oil
- 1 red onion, chopped
- A pinch of salt and black pepper
- 1 tablespoon sweet paprika, chopped
- 1 tablespoon parsley, chopped

Directions:
1. In the multi level air fryer's pan, combine the chicken with the other ingredients and toss.
2. Put the pan in the instant pot and seal with the air fryer lid.
3. Cook on Bake mode at 380 degrees F for 25 minutes.
4. Divide everything between plates and serve.

Nutrition:
calories 284, fat 13, fiber 4, carbs 5, protein 14

Chicken and Wine Sauce

Prep time: 5 minutes | **Cooking:** 20 minutes | **Servings:** 4

Ingredients:
- 1 pound chicken breast, skinless, boneless and cubed
- 1 cup plums, pitted and halved
- Juice of 1 lime
- ¼ cup red wine
- Salt and black pepper to the taste
- ½ teaspoon sweet paprika
- ¼ teaspoon garlic powder
- 1 tablespoon olive oil

Directions:
1. In the multi level air fryer's pan, combine the chicken with the other ingredients and toss.
2. Put the pan in the instant pot and seal with the air fryer lid.
3. Cook on Bake mode at 380 degrees F for 20 minutes.
4. Divide everything between plates and serve.

Nutrition:
calories 240, fat 11, fiber 2, carbs 5, protein 12

Turkey and Balsamic Broccoli

Prep time: 5 minutes | **Cooking:** 25 minutes | **Servings:** 4

Ingredients:
- 2 pounds turkey breast, skinless, boneless and cubed
- 2 cups broccoli florets
- 1 tablespoon olive oil
- 2 garlic cloves, minced
- 1 tablespoon balsamic vinegar
- A pinch of salt and black pepper
- 1 tablespoon dill, chopped

Directions:
1. In the multi level air fryer's pan, combine the turkey with the other ingredients and toss.
2. Put the pan in the instant pot and seal with the air fryer lid.
3. Cook on Bake mode at 380 degrees F for 25 minutes.
4. Divide everything between plates and serve.

Nutrition:
calories 274, fat 11, fiber 3, carbs 6, protein 12

Chicken with Chili Kale and Sauce

Prep time: 5 minutes | **Cooking:** 25 minutes | **Servings:** 4

Ingredients:
- 1 pound chicken breast, skinless, boneless and cubed
- 2 cups baby kale
- 1 cup tomato sauce
- A pinch of salt and black pepper
- 2 tablespoons olive oil
- 1 tablespoon garlic, chopped
- 1 red chili pepper, chopped
- ½ tablespoon cilantro, chopped

Directions:
1. In the multi level air fryer's pan, combine the chicken with the other ingredients and toss.
2. Put the pan in the instant pot and seal with the air fryer lid.
3. Cook on Bake mode at 380 degrees F for 25 minutes.
4. Divide everything between plates and serve.

Nutrition:
calories 261, fat 12, fiber 2, carbs 5, protein 13

Turkey with Peppers and Bok Choy

Prep time: 5 minutes | **Cooking:** 25 minutes | **Servings:** 4

Ingredients:
- 1 pound turkey breast, skinless, boneless and cubed
- 1 cup bok choy, torn
- 1 red onion, sliced
- 1 tablespoon olive oil
- A pinch of salt and black pepper
- 1 green bell pepper, chopped
- 1 teaspoon sweet paprika
- ½ cup chicken stock

Directions:
1. In the multi level air fryer's pan, combine the turkey with the other ingredients and toss.
2. Put the pan in the instant pot and seal with the air fryer lid.
3. Cook on Bake mode at 380 degrees F for 25 minutes.
4. Divide everything between plates and serve.

Nutrition:
calories 274, fat 12, fiber 4, carbs 6, protein 15

Italian Turkey Mix

Prep time: 5 minutes | **Cooking:** 25 minutes | **Servings:** 4

Ingredients:
- 1 pound turkey breast, skinless, boneless and sliced
- 2 eggplants, roughly cubed
- 1 tablespoon olive oil
- 1 cup chicken stock
- 2 tablespoons tomato paste
- 1 teaspoon Italian seasoning
- Salt and black pepper to the taste
- 1 tablespoon oregano, chopped

Directions:
1. In the multi level air fryer's pan, combine the turkey with the other ingredients and toss.
2. Put the pan in the instant pot and seal with the air fryer lid.
3. Cook on Bake mode at 370 degrees F for 25 minutes.
4. Divide everything between plates and serve.

Nutrition:
calories 263, fat 12, fiber 3, carbs 6, protein 16

Chicken and Rice

Prep time: 5 minutes | **Cooking:** 25 minutes | **Servings:** 4

Ingredients:
- 1 pound chicken breast, skinless, boneless and cubed
- 1 cup white rice
- 2 cups chicken stock
- ½ cup peas
- ½ teaspoon turmeric powder

- ½ teaspoon chili powder
- A pinch of salt and black pepper
- 2 tablespoons parsley, chopped

Directions:
1. In the multi level air fryer's pan, combine the chicken with the other ingredients and toss.
2. Put the pan in the instant pot and seal with the air fryer lid.
3. Cook on Bake mode at 380 degrees F for 25 minutes.
4. Divide everything between plates and serve.

Nutrition:
calories 268, fat 12, fiber 4, carbs 6, protein 17

Salsa Chicken

Prep time: 5 minutes | **Cooking:** 25 minutes | **Servings:** 4

Ingredients:
- 2 pounds chicken breast, skinless, boneless and cubed
- 1 cup salsa Verde
- 1 tablespoon avocado oil
- 3 spring onions, chopped
- A pinch of salt and black pepper
- ¼ cup chicken stock
- 4 garlic cloves, minced
- 1 tablespoon chives, chopped

Directions:
1. In the multi level air fryer's pan, combine the chicken with the other ingredients and toss.
2. Put the pan in the instant pot and seal with the air fryer lid.
3. Cook on Bake mode at 370 degrees F for 25 minutes.
4. Divide everything between plates and serve.

Nutrition:
calories 265, fat 14, fiber 3, carbs 5, protein 14

Spiced Duck Mix

Prep time: 5 minutes | **Cooking:** 25 minutes | **Servings:** 4

Ingredients:
- 2 pounds duck breast, skinless, boneless and cubed
- 1 tablespoon avocado oil
- 1 teaspoon allspice, ground
- 1 teaspoon turmeric powder
- 2 garlic cloves, minced
- ¼ cup chicken stock
- A pinch of salt and black pepper
- 1 tablespoon coriander, chopped

Directions:
1. In the multi level air fryer's pan, combine the duck with the other ingredients and toss.
2. Put the pan in the instant pot and seal with the air fryer lid.
3. Cook on Bake mode at 380 degrees F for 25 minutes.
4. Divide everything between plates and serve.

Nutrition:
calories 287, fat 12, fiber 4, carbs 6, protein 17

Creamy Turkey Mix

Prep time: 5 minutes | **Cooking:** 30 minutes | **Servings:** 4

Ingredients:
- 2 pounds turkey breast, skinless, boneless and cubed
- 2 tablespoons mustard
- 1 cup heavy cream
- A pinch of salt and black pepper
- ½ teaspoon thyme, dried
- 1 teaspoon cumin, ground
- 2 tablespoons olive oil

Directions:
1. In the multi level air fryer's pan, combine the turkey with the other ingredients and toss.
2. Put the pan in the instant pot and seal with the air fryer lid.
3. Cook on Bake mode at 380 degrees F for 30 minutes.
4. Divide everything between plates and serve.

Nutrition:
calories 274, fat 11, fiber 4, carbs 6, protein 14

Rosemary Duck Mix

Prep time: 5 minutes | **Cooking:** 20 minutes | **Servings:** 2

Ingredients:
- 1 pound duck breast, boneless and skin scored
- 2 tablespoons balsamic vinegar
- 2 tablespoons olive oil
- ½ teaspoon rosemary, dried
- 1 teaspoon chili powder
- A pinch of salt and black pepper

Directions:
1. In your multi level air fryer's basket, mix the duck with the vinegar, oil and the other ingredients and rub.
2. Put the basket in the instant pot, seal with the air fryer lid and cook on Air fry at 380 degrees F for 10 minutes on each side.
3. Divide everything between plates and serve.

Nutrition:
calories 294, fat 12, fiber 4, carbs 6, protein 15

Cardamom Chives Chicken

Prep time: 5 minutes | **Cooking:** 30 minutes | **Servings:** 4

Ingredients:
- 2 pounds chicken breast, skinless, boneless and cubed
- 2 tablespoons olive oil
- ½ teaspoon sweet paprika
- 1 tablespoon cardamom, crushed
- 2 tablespoons chives, chopped
- A pinch of salt and black pepper

Directions:
1. In the multi level air fryer's pan, combine the chicken with the other ingredients and toss.
2. Put the pan in the instant pot and seal with the air fryer lid.
3. Cook on Bake mode at 380 degrees F for 30 minutes.
4. Divide everything between plates and serve.

Nutrition:
calories 284, fat 12, fiber 4, carbs 6, protein 18

Lime Duck with Rhubarb

Prep time: 5 minutes | **Cooking:** 25 minutes | **Servings:** 2

Ingredients:
- 2 duck legs, skin scored
- 1 cup rhubarb, sliced
- ½ cup chicken stock
- 1 teaspoon sweet paprika
- 1 tablespoon olive oil
- A pinch of salt and black pepper
- Juice of ½ lime
- 1 tablespoon rosemary, chopped

Directions:
1. In the multi level air fryer's pan, combine the duck with the other ingredients and toss.
2. Put the pan in the instant pot and seal with the air fryer lid.
3. Cook on Bake mode at 400 degrees F for 25 minutes.
4. Divide everything between plates and serve.

Nutrition:
calories 276, fat 12, fiber 4, carbs 6, protein 14

Peppercorn and Coriander Chicken

Prep time: 5 minutes | **Cooking:** 30 minutes | **Servings:** 4

Ingredients:
- 2 pounds chicken breast, skinless, boneless and cubed
- 1 tablespoon olive oil
- 10 peppercorns, crushed
- 1 tablespoon lemon juice
- ½ teaspoon coriander, ground
- 1 tablespoon olive oil
- A pinch of salt and black pepper

Directions:
1. In the multi level air fryer's pan, combine the chicken with the other ingredients and toss.
2. Put the pan in the instant pot and seal with the air fryer lid.
3. Cook on Bake mode at 380 degrees F for 30 minutes.
4. Divide everything between plates and serve.

Nutrition:
calories 271, fat 13, fiber 4, carbs 6, protein 15

Duck and Mushrooms Mix

Prep time: 5 minutes | **Cooking:** 25 minutes | **Servings:** 4

Ingredients:
- 1 pound duck breast, skinless, boneless and cubed
- 1 tablespoon olive oil
- 1 tablespoon soy sauce
- A pinch of salt and black pepper
- ¼ pound oyster mushrooms, sliced
- 1 tablespoon rosemary, chopped
- 3 garlic cloves, minced

Directions:
1. In the multi level air fryer's pan, combine the duck with the other ingredients and toss
2. Put the pan in the instant pot and seal with the air fryer lid.
3. Cook on Bake mode at 380 degrees F for 25 minutes.
4. Divide everything between plates and serve.

Nutrition:
calories 2764, fat 12, fiber 4, carbs 6, protein 14

Balsamic Duck and Peppers

Prep time: 5 minutes | **Cooking:** 25 minutes | **Servings:** 4

Ingredients:
- 2 pounds duck breast, skinless, boneless and cubed
- 1 cup roasted peppers, chopped
- 1 tablespoon balsamic vinegar
- 1 tablespoon avocado oil
- 1 teaspoon sage, dried
- A pinch of salt and black pepper
- 1 tablespoon lemon juice

Directions:
1. In the multi level air fryer's pan, combine the duck with the other ingredients and toss.
2. Put the pan in the instant pot and seal with the air fryer lid.
3. Cook on Bake mode at 370 degrees F for 25 minutes.
4. Divide everything between plates and serve.

Nutrition:
calories 270, fat 14, fiber 3, carbs 6, protein 16

Parsley Duck and Zucchini Mix

Prep time: 5 minutes | **Cooking:** 25 minutes | **Servings:** 4

Ingredients:
- 1 pound duck breasts, skinless, boneless and cubed
- 2 zucchinis, cubed
- 1 tablespoon olive oil
- 1 tablespoon balsamic vinegar
- A pinch of salt and black pepper
- 2 tablespoons parsley, chopped

Directions:
1. In the multi level air fryer's pan, combine the duck with the other ingredients and toss.
2. Put the pan in the instant pot and seal with the air fryer lid.
3. Cook on Bake mode at 370 degrees F for 25 minutes.
4. Divide everything between plates and serve.

Nutrition:
calories 285, fat 14, fiber 4, carbs 6, protein 16

Curry Turkey

Prep time: 5 minutes | **Cooking:** 25 minutes | **Servings:** 4

Ingredients:
- 2 pounds turkey breast, skinless, boneless and cubed
- 1 tablespoon red curry paste
- 1 cup tomato sauce
- 1 tablespoon olive oil
- 2 shallots, chopped
- Salt and black pepper to the taste
- ½ tablespoon parsley, chopped

Directions:
1. In the multi level air fryer's pan, combine the turkey with the other ingredients and toss.
2. Put the pan in the instant pot and seal with the air fryer lid.
3. Cook on Bake mode at 370 degrees F for 25 minutes.
4. Divide everything between plates and serve.

Nutrition:
calories 274, fat 14, fiber 4, carbs 7, protein 16

Turkey and Lemon Beans

Prep time: 5 minutes | **Cooking:** 25 minutes | **Servings:** 4

Ingredients:
- 2 pounds turkey breast, skinless, boneless and cubed
- 1 cup canned red kidney beans, drained
- 1 cup canned black beans, drained
- 1 tablespoon lemon juice
- ½ cup tomato sauce
- A drizzle of olive oil
- Salt and black pepper to the taste

Directions:
1. In the multi level air fryer's pan, combine the turkey with the other ingredients and toss.
2. Put the pan in the instant pot and seal with the air fryer lid.
3. Cook on Bake mode at 370 degrees F for 25 minutes.
4. Divide everything between plates and serve.

Nutrition:
calories 263, fat 12, fiber 4, carbs 6, protein 14

Mint Buttery Duck

Prep time: 5 minutes | **Cooking:** 20 minutes | **Servings:** 4

Ingredients:
- 2 duck breasts, boneless, skinless and cubed
- 2 tablespoons butter, melted
- 2 tablespoons mint, chopped
- Juice of 1 lime
- A pinch of salt and black pepper
- 2 shallots, sliced
- ½ teaspoon mustard seeds, crushed

Directions:
1. In the multi level air fryer's pan, combine the duck with the other ingredients and toss.
2. Put the pan in the instant pot and seal with the air fryer lid.
3. Cook on Bake mode at 370 degrees F for 20 minutes.
4. Divide everything between plates and serve.

Nutrition:

calories 241, fat 10, fiber 2, carbs 5, protein 15

Chicken and Creamy Sauce

Prep time: 5 minutes | **Cooking:** 25 minutes | **Servings:** 4

Ingredients:

- 2 pounds chicken breast, skinless, boneless and cubed
- A pinch of salt and black pepper
- 1 tablespoon olive oil
- ¼ cup balsamic vinegar
- ½ cup cranberries
- 1 cup heavy cream

Directions:

1. In the multi level air fryer's pan, combine the chicken with the other ingredients and toss.
2. Put the pan in the instant pot and seal with the air fryer lid.
3. Cook on Bake mode at 380 degrees F for 25 minutes.
4. Divide everything between plates and serve.

Nutrition:

calories 287, fat 12, fiber 4, carbs 6, protein 16

Chicken, Kale and Tomatoes Salad

Prep time: 10 minutes | **Cooking:** 25 minutes | **Servings:** 4

Ingredients:

- 2 pounds chicken breast, skinless, boneless and cubed
- 1 cup baby kale
- 1 cup cherry tomatoes, halved
- 1 cup kalamata olives, pitted and halved
- Juice of 1 lime
- 2 tablespoons olive oil
- 2 tablespoons parsley, chopped
- Salt and black pepper to the taste
- 1 tablespoon chives, chopped

Directions:

1. In the multi level air fryer's pan, combine the chicken with the other ingredients and toss.
2. Put the pan in the instant pot and seal with the air fryer lid.
3. Cook on Bake mode at 380 degrees F for 25 minutes.
4. Divide everything into bowls and serve.

Nutrition:

calories 274, fat 14, fiber 4, carbs 6, protein 16

Duck and Creamy Berries

Prep time: 5 minutes | **Cooking:** 25 minutes | **Servings:** 4

Ingredients:

- 2 pounds duck breasts, boneless, skinless and roughly cubed
- 2 tablespoons avocado oil
- 1 cup blackberries
- 1 cup blueberries
- ¼ teaspoon coriander, ground
- 1 cup heavy cream
- Salt and black pepper to the taste
- 1 cup basil, chopped

Directions:

1. In the multi level air fryer's pan, combine the duck with the other ingredients and toss.
2. Put the pan in the instant pot and seal with the air fryer lid.
3. Cook on Bake mode at 380 degrees F for 25 minutes.
4. Divide everything between plates and serve.

Nutrition:

calories 274, fat 13, fiber 3, carbs 5, protein 16

Turkey with Lime Avocado

Prep time: 5 minutes | **Cooking:** 25 minutes | **Servings:** 4

Ingredients:

- 1 yellow onion, chopped
- 2 tablespoons olive oil
- 2 pounds turkey breast, skinless, boneless and cubed
- 1 cup avocado, peeled, pitted and cubed
- Juice of 1 lime
- 4 garlic cloves, minced
- 1 teaspoon cumin, ground
- Salt and black pepper to the taste
- 1 tablespoon cilantro, chopped

Directions:

1. In the multi level air fryer's pan, combine the turkey with the other ingredients and toss.
2. Put the pan in the instant pot and seal with the air fryer lid.
3. Cook on Bake mode at 370 degrees F for 25 minutes.
4. Divide everything between plates and serve.

Nutrition:

calorie 284, fat 12, fiber 4, carbs 6, protein 17

Garlic Lime Turkey Mix

Prep time: 10 minutes | **Cooking:** 20 minutes | **Servings:** 4

Ingredients:

- 2 pounds turkey breast, skinless, boneless and cubed
- 2 tablespoons sesame seeds
- 4 spring onions, chopped
- Juice of 1 lime
- Salt and black pepper to the taste
- 1 tablespoon olive oil
- 2 garlic cloves, minced
- 1 tablespoon coriander, chopped

Directions:

1. In the multi level air fryer's pan, combine the turkey with the other ingredients and toss.
2. Put the pan in the instant pot and seal with the air fryer lid.
3. Cook on Bake mode at 380 degrees F for 20 minutes.
4. Divide everything between plates and serve.

Nutrition:

calories 264, fat 12, fiber 4, carbs 6, protein 17

Cumin Duck Mix

Prep time: 5 minutes | **Cooking:** 25 minutes | **Servings:** 4

Ingredients:

- 1 pound duck breasts, skinless, boneless and cubed
- 1 tablespoon sweet paprika
- 2 tablespoons butter, melted
- Salt and black pepper to the taste
- ½ cup chicken stock
- ½ teaspoon cumin, ground

Directions:

1. In the multi level air fryer's pan, combine the duck with the other ingredients and toss.
2. Put the pan in the instant pot and seal with the air fryer lid.
3. Cook on Bake mode at 380 degrees F for 25 minutes.
4. Divide everything between plates and serve.

Nutrition:

calories 264, fat 14, fiber 4, carbs 6, protein 18

Chicken and Ginger Beets

Prep time: 10 minutes | **Cooking:** 20 minutes | **Servings:** 4

Ingredients:

- 2 pounds chicken legs, boneless
- 2 beets, peeled and cubed
- 1 tablespoon olive oil
- ½ teaspoon coriander, ground
- 2 tablespoons ginger, grated
- Salt and black pepper to the taste
- ½ cup chicken stock

Directions:

1. In the multi level air fryer's pan, combine the chicken with the other ingredients and toss.
2. Put the pan in the instant pot and seal with the air fryer lid.
3. Cook on Bake mode at 380 degrees F for 20 minutes.
4. Divide everything between plates and serve.

Nutrition:

calories 300, fat 4, fiber 12, carbs 22, protein 20

Meat Recipes

Pork and Tomato Peppers

Prep time: 5 minutes | **Cooking:** 25 minutes | **Servings:** 4

Ingredients:

- 1 pound pork stew meat, cubed
- ¼ cup tomato sauce
- 2 teaspoons olive oil
- 1 red bell pepper, chopped
- 1 green bell pepper, chopped
- ½ teaspoon garlic powder
- ½ teaspoon chili powder
- ½ teaspoon cumin, ground

Directions:

1. In the multi level air fryer's pan, combine the pork with the other ingredients and toss.
2. Put the pan in the instant pot and seal with the air fryer lid.
3. Cook on Roast mode at 400 degrees F for 25 minutes.
4. Divide everything between plates and serve.

Nutrition:

calories 284, fat 13, fiber 4, carbs 6, protein 17

Dill Lamb Mix

Prep time: 5 minutes | **Cooking:** 25 minutes | **Servings:** 4

Ingredients:

- 1 pound lamb stew meat, cubed
- 1 teaspoon sweet paprika
- 1 tablespoon olive oil
- 1 teaspoon cumin, ground
- 1 teaspoon coriander, ground
- A pinch of salt and black pepper
- 1 tablespoon dill, chopped

Directions:

1. In the multi level air fryer's pan, combine the lamb with the other ingredients and toss.
2. Put the pan in the instant pot and seal with the air fryer lid.
3. Cook on Roast mode at 390 degrees F for 25 minutes.
4. Divide everything between plates and serve.

Nutrition:

calories 273, fat 12, fiber 4, carbs 6, protein 20

Rosemary Pork Chops

Prep time: 5 minutes | **Cooking:** 25 minutes | **Servings:** 4

Ingredients:

- 2 pounds pork chops
- 1 teaspoon rosemary, dried
- 1 teaspoon chili powder
- 1 tablespoon olive oil
- 2 tablespoons balsamic vinegar
- A pinch of salt and black pepper

Directions:

1. In the multi level air fryer's pan, combine the pork chops with the other ingredients and toss.
2. Put the pan in the instant pot and seal with the air fryer lid.
3. Cook on Roast mode at 390 degrees F for 25 minutes.
4. Divide everything between plates and serve.

Nutrition:

calories 276, fat 12, fiber 4, carbs 6, protein 22

Spiced Pork Chops

Prep time: 5 minutes | **Cooking:** 25 minutes | **Servings:** 4

Ingredients:

- 2 pounds pork chops
- 1 tablespoon oregano, chopped
- 1 teaspoon sweet paprika
- 1 teaspoon cumin, ground
- A pinch of salt and black pepper
- ½ teaspoon onion powder
- ¼ teaspoon garlic powder
- 10 ounces beef stock

Directions:

1. In the multi level air fryer's pan, combine the pork chops with the other ingredients and toss.
2. Put the pan in the instant pot and seal with the air fryer lid.
3. Cook on Bake mode at 400 degrees F for 25 minutes.
4. Divide everything between plates and serve.

Nutrition:

calories 284, fat 14, fiber 4, carbs 6, protein 22

Paprika Pork Chops

Prep time: 5 minutes | **Cooking:** 25 minutes | **Servings:** 4

Ingredients:

- 2 tablespoons avocado oil
- 2 pounds pork chops
- 5 garlic cloves, minced
- 1 teaspoon rosemary, dried
- 1 teaspoon smoked paprika
- A pinch of salt and black pepper

Directions:

1. In the multi level air fryer's pan, combine the pork chops with the other ingredients and toss.
2. Put the pan in the instant pot and seal with the air fryer lid.
3. Cook on Bake mode at 400 degrees F for 25 minutes.
4. Divide everything between plates and serve.

Nutrition:

calories 273, fat 13, fiber 4, carbs 6, protein 22

Turmeric Pork

Prep time: 5 minutes | **Cooking:** 25 minutes | **Servings:** 4

Ingredients:

- 1 pound pork stew meat, cubed
- 3 tablespoons butter, melted
- Juice of 1 lime
- A pinch of salt and black pepper
- ½ teaspoon turmeric powder
- 1 teaspoon sweet paprika

Directions:

1. In the multi level air fryer's pan, combine the pork with the other ingredients and toss.
2. Put the pan in the instant pot and seal with the air fryer lid.
3. Cook on Bake mode at 380 degrees F for 25 minutes.
4. Divide everything between plates and serve.

Nutrition:

calories 284, fat 12, fiber 4, carbs 6, protein 19

Hot Lamb

Prep time: 5 minutes | **Cooking:** 25 minutes | **Servings:** 4

Ingredients:

- 2 pounds lamb stew meat, cubed
- 2 red chilies, minced
- 1 teaspoon chili powder
- 1 red onion, chopped
- ½ cup beef stock
- 2 tablespoons olive oil
- Salt and black pepper to the taste

Directions:

1. In the multi level air fryer's pan, combine the lamb with the other ingredients and toss.
2. Put the pan in the instant pot and seal with the air fryer lid.
3. Cook on Bake mode at 400 degrees F for 25 minutes.
4. Divide everything between plates and serve.

Nutrition:

calories 267, fat 12, fiber 4, carbs 6, protein 18

Creamy Lamb

Prep time: 5 minutes | **Cooking:** 25 minutes | **Servings:** 4

Ingredients:
- 2 pounds lamb stew meat, cubed
- 2 tablespoons basil, chopped
- 1 cup heavy cream
- A pinch of salt and black pepper
- 2 teaspoons olive oil
- 1 teaspoon coriander, ground
- ½ teaspoon chili powder

Directions:
1. In the multi level air fryer's pan, combine the lamb with the other ingredients and toss.
2. Put the pan in the instant pot and seal with the air fryer lid.
3. Cook on Bake mode at 400 degrees F for 25 minutes.
4. Divide everything between plates and serve.

Nutrition:
calories 274, fat 13, fiber 4, carbs 6, protein 18

Masala Pork Chops

Prep time: 5 minutes | **Cooking:** 25 minutes | **Servings:** 4

Ingredients:
- 2 pounds pork chops
- A pinch of salt and black pepper
- 1 teaspoon garlic powder
- ½ teaspoon garam masala
- 2 tablespoons olive oil
- 1 teaspoon cayenne pepper

Directions:
1. In the multi level air fryer's basket, mix the pork chops with the cayenne and the other ingredients and rub.
2. Put the basket in the instant pot, seal with the air fryer lid and cook on Air fry mode at 400 degrees F for 25 minutes.
3. Divide everything between plates and serve.

Nutrition:
calories 280, fat 13, fiber 4, carbs 6, protein 18

Mustard Garlic Lamb

Prep time: 10 minutes | **Cooking:** 25 minutes | **Servings:** 4

Ingredients:
- 2 pounds lamb stew meat, cubed
- 2 tablespoons mustard
- 1 cup heavy cream
- 1 teaspoon turmeric powder
- 2 tablespoons olive oil
- A pinch of salt and black pepper
- 2 garlic cloves, minced

Directions:
1. In the multi level air fryer's pan, combine the lamb with the other ingredients and toss.
2. Put the pan in the instant pot and seal with the air fryer lid.
3. Cook on Bake mode at 390 degrees F for 25 minutes.
4. Divide everything between plates and serve.

Nutrition:
calories 287, fat 13, fiber 4, carbs 6, protein 20

Balsamic Beef and Eggplant Mix

Prep time: 5 minutes | **Cooking:** 30 minutes | **Servings:** 4

Ingredients:
- 1 pound beef stew meat, cubed
- 2 eggplants, cubed
- 1 tablespoon olive oil
- 1 teaspoon sweet paprika
- A pinch of salt and black pepper
- 2 tablespoons balsamic vinegar

Directions:
1. In the multi level air fryer's pan, combine the beef with the other ingredients and toss.
2. Put the pan in the instant pot and seal with the air fryer lid.
3. Cook on Bake mode at 380 degrees F for 30 minutes.
4. Divide everything between plates and serve.

Nutrition:
calories 274, fat 13, fiber 4, carbs 7, protein 22

Herbed Lamb and Green Beans

Prep time: 5 minutes | **Cooking:** 25 minutes | **Servings:** 4

Ingredients:
- 2 pounds lamb stew meat, cubed
- 2 cups green beans, trimmed and halved
- 2 tablespoons avocado oil
- 1 teaspoon cumin, ground
- 1 teaspoon rosemary, dried
- 1 tablespoon lemon juice
- 2 garlic cloves, minced
- A pinch of salt and black pepper

Directions:
1. In the multi level air fryer's pan, combine the lamb with the other ingredients and toss.
2. Put the pan in the instant pot and seal with the air fryer lid.
3. Cook on Bake mode at 390 degrees F for 25 minutes.
4. Divide everything between plates and serve.

Nutrition:
calories 284, fat 13, fiber 4, carbs 6, protein 22

Pork and Tomato Spinach Mix

Prep time: 5 minutes | **Cooking:** 25 minutes | **Servings:** 4

Ingredients:
- 2 pounds pork stew meat, cubed
- 1 tablespoon olive oil
- 2 cups baby spinach
- 2 tablespoons tomato paste
- 1 cup beef stock
- A pinch of salt and black pepper
- 1 tablespoon chives, chopped

Directions:
1. In the multi level air fryer's pan, combine the pork with the other ingredients and toss.
2. Put the pan in the instant pot and seal with the air fryer lid.
3. Cook on Bake mode at 390 degrees F for 25 minutes.
4. Divide everything between plates and serve.

Nutrition:
calories 284, fat 12, fiber 4, carbs 7, protein 22

Pork and Sauce

Prep time: 5 minutes | **Cooking:** 30 minutes | **Servings:** 4

Ingredients:
- 2 pounds pork stew meat, cubed
- ¾ cup beef stock
- 1 cup cherry tomatoes, halved
- 2 tablespoons olive oil
- 3 tablespoons tomato sauce
- 1 teaspoon cumin, ground
- 1 teaspoon coriander, ground
- Salt and black pepper to the taste

Directions:
1. In the multi level air fryer's pan, combine the pork with the other ingredients and toss.
2. Put the pan in the instant pot and seal with the air fryer lid.
3. Cook on Bake mode at 380 degrees F for 30 minutes.
4. Divide everything between plates and serve.

Nutrition:
calories 287, fat 13, fiber 4, carbs 6, protein 18

Pork with Tomato Radishes

Prep time: 5 minutes | **Cooking:** 30 minutes | **Servings:** 4

Ingredients:
- 2 pounds pork chops
- 2 cups radishes, halved
- 1 cup tomato sauce
- A pinch of salt and black pepper
- 2 teaspoons olive oil
- ½ teaspoon chipotle chili powder
- ½ teaspoon allspice, ground

Directions:
1. In the multi level air fryer's pan, combine the pork with the other ingredients and toss.
2. Put the pan in the instant pot and seal with the air fryer lid.
3. Cook on Bake mode at 380 degrees F for 30 minutes.
4. Divide everything between plates and serve.

Nutrition:
calories 287, fat 14, fiber 4, carbs 7, protein 18

Balsamic Pork and Cabbage

Prep time: 5 minutes | **Cooking:** 30 minutes | **Servings:** 4

Ingredients:
- 2 pounds pork stew meat, cubed
- 2 cups red cabbage, shredded
- 1 cup tomato sauce
- 1 red onion, chopped
- ½ cup beef stock
- 2 tablespoons balsamic vinegar
- A pinch of salt and black pepper
- 2 tablespoons cilantro, chopped

Directions:
1. In the multi level air fryer's pan, combine the pork with the other ingredients and toss.
2. Put the pan in the instant pot and seal with the air fryer lid.
3. Cook on Bake mode at 380 degrees F for 30 minutes.
4. Divide everything between plates and serve.

Nutrition:
calories 284, fat 14, fiber 4, carbs 6, protein 17

Italian Pork with Tomatoes and Peppers

Prep time: 5 minutes | **Cooking:** 30 minutes | **Servings:** 2

Ingredients:
- 1 pound pork stew meat, cubed
- 1 tablespoon Italian seasoning
- 2 red bell peppers, cut into strips
- 1 cup canned tomatoes, chopped
- 1 teaspoon sweet paprika
- A pinch of salt and black pepper

Directions:
1. In the multi level air fryer's pan, combine the pork with the other ingredients and toss.
2. Put the pan in the instant pot and seal with the air fryer lid.
3. Cook on Roast mode at 390 degrees F for 30 minutes.
4. Divide everything between plates and serve.

Nutrition:
calories 284, fat 13, fiber 4, carbs 6, protein 19

Cocoa and Rosemary Lamb Chops

Prep time: 5 minutes | **Cooking:** 30 minutes | **Servings:** 4

Ingredients:
- 2 tablespoons cocoa powder
- 2 pounds lamb chops
- 1 tablespoon balsamic vinegar
- ½ teaspoon rosemary, dried
- 2 tablespoons olive oil
- A pinch of salt and black pepper

Directions:
1. In the multi level air fryer's basket, mix the lamb chops with the cocoa powder and the other ingredients.
2. Put the basket in the instant pot, seal with the air fryer lid and cook on Air fry mode at 390 degrees F for 30 minutes.
3. Divide between plates and serve.

Nutrition:
calories 284, fat 14, fiber 5, carbs 7, protein 20

Pork and Red Wine Sauce

Prep time: 5 minutes | **Cooking:** 30 minutes | **Servings:** 4

Ingredients:
- 1 pound pork stew meat, cubed
- ½ cup walnuts, chopped
- ½ cup red wine
- 2 spring onions, chopped
- 1 red bell pepper, sliced
- 1 tablespoon olive oil
- 2 tablespoons chives, chopped
- A pinch of salt and black pepper

Directions:
1. In the multi level air fryer's pan, combine the pork with the other ingredients and toss.
2. Put the pan in the instant pot and seal with the air fryer lid.
3. Cook on Roast mode at 380 degrees F for 30 minutes.
4. Divide everything into bowls and serve.

Nutrition:
calories 274, fat 12, fiber 4, carbs 6, protein 19

Ginger Pork Mix

Prep time: 5 minutes | **Cooking:** 30 minutes | **Servings:** 4

Ingredients:
- 1 pound pork stew meat, cubed
- 1 cup coconut cream
- 1 teaspoon sweet paprika
- 1 teaspoon turmeric powder
- A pinch of salt and black pepper
- 1 tablespoon ginger, grated
- 1 tablespoon chives, chopped

Directions:
1. In the multi level air fryer's pan, combine the pork with the other ingredients and toss.
2. Put the pan in the instant pot and seal with the air fryer lid.
3. Cook on Roast mode at 380 degrees F for 30 minutes.
4. Divide everything between plates and serve.

Nutrition:
calories 284, fat 13, fiber 4, carbs 6, protein 18

Beef Stew

Prep time: 5 minutes | **Cooking:** 20 minutes | **Servings:** 4

Ingredients:
- 2 pounds beef stew meat, cubed
- 1 cup carrots, peeled and sliced
- 1 red onion, chopped
- 2 tablespoons olive oil
- ½ cup tomato sauce
- Salt and black pepper to the taste
- 1 teaspoon sweet paprika

Directions:
1. In the multi level air fryer's pan, combine the beef with the other ingredients and toss.
2. Put the pan in the instant pot and seal with the air fryer lid.
3. Cook on Bake mode at 390 degrees F for 20 minutes.
4. Divide everything between plates and serve.

Nutrition:
calories 294, fat 13, fiber 3, carbs 6, protein 19

Lemon Beef Mix

Prep time: 5 minutes | **Cooking:** 25 minutes | **Servings:** 4

Ingredients:
- 1 pound beef stew meat, cubed and browned
- 2 zucchinis, cubed
- 1 tablespoon olive oil
- 1 tablespoon lemon juice
- 1 tablespoon lemon zest, grated
- 2 tablespoons chives, chopped
- A pinch of salt and black pepper
- 1 teaspoon coriander, ground

Directions:
1. In the multi level air fryer's pan, combine the beef with the other ingredients and toss.
2. Put the pan in the instant pot and seal with the air fryer lid.
3. Cook on Bake mode at 380 degrees F for 25 minutes.
4. Divide everything between plates and serve.

Nutrition:
calories 284, fat 13, fiber 4, carbs 6, protein 16

Almond Beef Mix

Prep time: 5 minutes | **Cooking:** 25 minutes | **Servings:** 4

Ingredients:
- 1 pound beef stew meat, cubed
- 2 tablespoons chives, chopped
- 2 tablespoons soy sauce
- 1 tablespoon avocado oil
- 2 tablespoons almonds, sliced
- A pinch of salt and black pepper

Directions:
1. In the multi level air fryer's pan, combine the beef with the other ingredients and toss.
2. Put the pan in the instant pot and seal with the air fryer lid.
3. Cook on Bake mode at 370 degrees F for 25 minutes.
4. Divide everything into bowls and serve.

Nutrition:
calories 270, fat 12, fiber 4, carbs 6, protein 16

Pork and Garlic Broccoli

Prep time: 5 minutes | **Cooking:** 25 minutes | **Servings:** 4

Ingredients:
- 1 pound pork stew meat, cubed
- 1 tablespoon avocado oil
- 1 cup broccoli florets
- 2 tablespoons balsamic vinegar
- 1 teaspoon rosemary, dried
- A pinch of salt and black pepper
- 2 garlic cloves, minced

Directions:
1. In the multi level air fryer's pan, combine the pork with the other ingredients and toss.
2. Put the pan in the instant pot and seal with the air fryer lid.
3. Cook on Bake mode at 390 degrees F for 25 minutes.
4. Divide everything into bowls and serve.

Nutrition:
calories 274, fat 12, fiber 4, carbs 6, protein 16

Beef and Coconut Mushrooms

Prep time: 5 minutes | **Cooking:** 25 minutes | **Servings:** 4

Ingredients:
- 1 pound beef stew meat, cubed
- 2 cups mushrooms, halved
- 2 tablespoons olive oil
- A pinch of salt and black pepper
- 2 garlic cloves, minced
- ¼ cup coconut cream
- ¼ cup parsley, chopped

Directions:
1. In the multi level air fryer's pan, combine the beef with the other ingredients and toss.
2. Put the pan in the instant pot and seal with the air fryer lid.
3. Cook on Bake mode at 390 degrees F for 25 minutes.
4. Divide everything into bowls and serve.

Nutrition:
calories 280, fat 134, fiber 5, carbs 7, protein 17

Beef and Onions Stew

Prep time: 5 minutes | **Cooking:** 25 minutes | **Servings:** 4

Ingredients:
- 2 pounds beef stew meat, cubed
- 1 cup spring onions, chopped
- 2 garlic cloves, minced
- 1 teaspoon chili powder
- 2 spring onions, chopped
- 1 cup beef stock
- A pinch of salt and black pepper

Directions:
1. In the multi level air fryer's pan, combine the beef with the other ingredients and toss.
2. Put the pan in the instant pot and seal with the air fryer lid.
3. Cook on Bake mode at 390 degrees F for 25 minutes.
4. Divide everything into bowls and serve.

Nutrition:
calories 267, fat 13, fiber 2, carbs 5, protein 15

Pork with Tomato and Fennel Mix

Prep time: 5 minutes | **Cooking:** 20 minutes | **Servings:** 4

Ingredients:
- 2 tablespoons avocado oil
- 2 pounds pork stew meat, cubed
- 2 fennel bulbs, sliced
- 1 teaspoon chili powder
- 1 teaspoon cumin, ground
- Salt and black pepper to the taste
- 1 teaspoon sweet paprika
- ¼ cup tomato sauce

Directions:
1. In the multi level air fryer's pan, combine the pork with the other ingredients and toss.
2. Put the pan in the instant pot and seal with the air fryer lid.
3. Cook on Bake mode at 380 degrees F for 20 minutes.
4. Divide everything between plates and serve.

Nutrition:
calories 284, fat 13, fiber 4, carbs 6, protein 15

Beef with Scallions and Kale

Prep time: 5 minutes | **Cooking:** 25 minutes | **Servings:** 4

Ingredients:
- 2 pounds beef stew meat, cubed
- 2 cups baby kale, torn
- 1 cup tomato sauce
- 2 scallions, chopped
- ½ teaspoon sweet paprika
- 2 garlic cloves, minced
- A pinch of salt and black pepper
- 2 tablespoons olive oil

Directions:
1. In the multi level air fryer's pan, combine the beef with the other ingredients and toss.
2. Put the pan in the instant pot and seal with the air fryer lid.
3. Cook on Bake mode at 390 degrees F for 25 minutes.
4. Divide everything between plates and serve.

Nutrition:
calories 284, fat 14, fiber 2, carbs 6, protein 19

Pork and Passata Mix

Prep time: 5 minutes | **Cooking:** 25 minutes | **Servings:** 4

Ingredients:

- 1 pound beef stew meat, cubed
- 2 red onions, sliced
- 1 tablespoon olive oil
- ½ cup tomato passata
- Salt and black pepper to the taste
- 1 tablespoon parsley, chopped
- 1 teaspoon sweet paprika

Directions:

1. In the multi level air fryer's pan, combine the pork with the other ingredients and toss.
2. Put the pan in the instant pot and seal with the air fryer lid.
3. Cook on Bake mode at 390 degrees F for 25 minutes.
4. Divide everything between plates and serve.

Nutrition:

calories 284, fat 14, fiber 3, carbs 6, protein 18

Butter Beef and Chili Potatoes

Prep time: 5 minutes | **Cooking:** 20 minutes | **Servings:** 4

Ingredients:

- 1 pound beef stew meat, cubed
- 2 sweet potatoes, peeled and cubed
- 1 cup tomato sauce
- 1 teaspoon coriander, ground
- 1 teaspoon chili powder
- Salt and black pepper to the taste
- 1 tablespoon butter, melted

Directions:

1. In the multi level air fryer's pan, combine the beef with the other ingredients and toss.
2. Put the pan in the instant pot and seal with the air fryer lid.
3. Cook on Bake mode at 390 degrees F for 20 minutes.
4. Divide everything between plates and serve.

Nutrition:

calories 280, fat 12, fiber 4, carbs 6, protein 17

Lamb and Onion Stew

Prep time: 5 minutes | **Cooking:** 20 minutes | **Servings:** 4

Ingredients:

- 1 pound lamb stew meat, cubed
- 1 yellow onion, chopped
- ½ cup beef stock
- 1 cup canned tomatoes, crushed
- A pinch of salt and black pepper
- A drizzle of olive oil
- 2 spring onions, chopped
- 2 garlic cloves, minced
- 1 teaspoon chili powder
- 1 teaspoon cumin, ground
- 1 tablespoon cilantro, chopped

Directions:

1. In the multi level air fryer's pan, combine the lamb with the other ingredients and toss.
2. Put the pan in the instant pot and seal with the air fryer lid.
3. Cook on Bake mode at 380 degrees F for 20 minutes.
4. Divide everything into bowls and serve.

Nutrition:

calories 276, fat 12, fiber 3, carbs 6, protein 17

Herbed Beef with Tomatoes and Okra

Prep time: 5 minutes | **Cooking:** 25 minutes | **Servings:** 4

Ingredients:

- 2 pounds beef stew meat, cubed
- 1 cup okra, sliced
- 1 cup tomatoes, cubed
- 1 tablespoon olive oil
- A pinch of salt and black pepper
- 2 tablespoons olive oil
- 2 garlic cloves, minced
- 1 teaspoon coriander, ground
- 1 teaspoon rosemary, dried
- 1 tablespoon parsley, chopped

Directions:

1. In the multi level air fryer's pan, combine the beef with the other ingredients and toss.
2. Put the pan in the instant pot and seal with the air fryer lid.
3. Cook on Bake mode at 380 degrees F for 25 minutes.
4. Divide everything between plates and serve.

Nutrition:

calories 283, fat 14, fiber 4, carbs 6, protein 17

Lamb with Tomatoes

Prep time: 5 minutes | **Cooking:** 25 minutes | **Servings:** 4

Ingredients:

- 2 pounds lamb stew meat, cubed
- 1 cup cherry tomatoes, halved
- 2 gold potatoes, peeled and cubed
- 1 tablespoon olive oil
- A pinch of salt and black pepper
- 1 cup tomato sauce
- 1 teaspoon rosemary, chopped

Directions:

1. In the multi level air fryer's pan, combine the lamb with the other ingredients and toss.
2. Put the pan in the instant pot and seal with the air fryer lid.
3. Cook on Bake mode at 380 degrees F for 25 minutes.
4. Divide everything between plates and serve.

Nutrition:

calories 283, fat 12, fiber 3, carbs 6, protein 17

Basil Lamb

Prep time: 5 minutes | **Cooking:** 25 minutes | **Servings:** 4

Ingredients:

- 1 pound lamb stew meat, cubed
- 1 teaspoon turmeric powder
- 1 teaspoon basil, dried
- ¼ teaspoon garlic powder
- A pinch of salt and black pepper
- ½ cup beef stock
- 1 tablespoon olive oil

Directions:

1. In the air fryer's pan, mix the lamb with the turmeric and the other ingredients, toss and cook at 390 degrees F for 25 minutes.
2. Divide between plates and serve.

Nutrition:

calories 294, fat 12, fiber 3, carbs 6, protein 19

Cilantro Beef Mix

Prep time: 5 minutes | **Cooking:** 30 minutes | **Servings:** 4

Ingredients:

- 2 tablespoons avocado oil
- 2 pounds beef stew meat, cubed
- 1 red onion, chopped
- 1 cup beef stock
- 3 tablespoons tomato sauce
- 2 spring onions, chopped
- 1 tablespoon rosemary, chopped
- 1 garlic clove, minced
- A pinch of salt and black pepper
- 1 tablespoon cilantro, chopped

Directions:

1. In the multi level air fryer's pan, combine the beef with the other ingredients and toss.
2. Put the pan in the instant pot and seal with the air fryer lid.
3. Cook on Bake mode at 370 degrees F for 30 minutes.
4. Divide everything into bowls and serve.

Nutrition:

calories 273, fat 10, fiber 3, carbs 6, protein 15

Basil Lamb Stew

Prep time: 5 minutes | **Cooking:** 25 minutes | **Servings:** 4

Ingredients:

- 2 pounds lamb stew meat, cubed
- 1 cup avocado, peeled, pitted and cubed
- ½ cup beef stock
- 2 scallions, chopped
- ½ cup basil, chopped
- 2 teaspoons olive oil
- A pinch of salt and black pepper

Directions:

1. In the multi level air fryer's pan, combine the lamb with the other ingredients and toss.
2. Put the pan in the instant pot and seal with the air fryer lid.
3. Cook on Bake mode at 380 degrees F for 25 minutes.
4. Divide everything between plates and serve.

Nutrition:

calories 273, fat 12, fiber 3, carbs 6, protein 18

Parsley Beef and Carrots Stew

Prep time: 5 minutes | **Cooking:** 30 minutes | **Servings:** 4

Ingredients:

- 1 tablespoon olive oil
- 2 pounds beef stew meat, cubed
- 1 cup carrots, peeled and sliced
- 2 tablespoons balsamic vinegar
- 1 bunch spring onions, chopped
- 1 teaspoon chili powder
- A pinch of salt and black pepper
- 1 tablespoon parsley, chopped

Directions:

1. In the multi level air fryer's pan, combine the beef with the other ingredients and toss.
2. Put the pan in the instant pot and seal with the air fryer lid.
3. Cook on Bake mode at 380 degrees F for 30 minutes.
4. Divide everything between plates and serve.

Nutrition:

calories 273, fat 13, fiber 4, carbs 6, protein 18

Lamb and Tomato Artichokes Stew

Prep time: 5 minutes | **Cooking:** 30 minutes | **Servings:** 4

Ingredients:

- 2 pounds lamb stew meat
- 1 cup canned artichoke hearts, drained
- 1 cup tomato sauce
- ¼ cup beef stock
- A pinch of salt and black pepper
- 2 teaspoons avocado oil
- 2 shallots, chopped
- 1 tablespoon chives, chopped

Directions:

1. In the multi level air fryer's pan, combine the lamb with the other ingredients and toss.
2. Put the pan in the instant pot and seal with the air fryer lid.
3. Cook on Bake mode at 380 degrees F for 30 minutes.
4. Divide everything into bowls and serve.

Nutrition:

calories 273, fat 13, fiber 4, carbs 6, protein 18

Curry Beef and Spinach

Prep time: 5 minutes | **Cooking:** 20 minutes | **Servings:** 4

Ingredients:

- 2 pounds beef, cut into strips
- 2 tablespoons red curry paste
- 1 cup heavy cream
- 2 tablespoons olive oil
- 2 cups baby spinach
- Salt and black pepper to the taste

Directions:

1. In the multi level air fryer's pan, combine the beef with the other ingredients and toss.
2. Put the pan in the instant pot and seal with the air fryer lid.
3. Cook on Bake mode at 390 degrees F for 20 minutes.
4. Divide everything into bowls and serve.

Nutrition:

calories 283, fat 14, fiber 2, carbs 6, protein 19

Cumin Beef and Garlic

Prep time: 5 minutes | **Cooking:** 30 minutes | **Servings:** 4

Ingredients:

- 2 tablespoons avocado oil
- 2 pounds beef stew meat, cubed
- 2 tablespoons balsamic vinegar
- 3 garlic cloves, minced
- Salt and black pepper to the taste
- 1 teaspoon rosemary, dried
- 1 teaspoon cumin, ground

Directions:

1. In the multi level air fryer's pan, combine the beef with the other ingredients and toss.
2. Put the pan in the instant pot and seal with the air fryer lid.
3. Cook on Bake mode at 390 degrees F for 30 minutes.
4. Divide everything between plates and serve.

Nutrition:

calories 273, fat 14, fiber 4, carbs 6, protein 19

Lemon Chili Lamb

Prep time: 5 minutes | **Cooking:** 30 minutes | **Servings:** 4

Ingredients:

- 4 scallions, chopped
- 2 pounds lamb stew meat, cubed
- 2 tablespoons lemon juice
- 2 tablespoons lemon zest, grated
- 1 teaspoon chili powder
- A pinch of salt and black pepper
- 1 teaspoon turmeric powder

Directions:

1. In the multi level air fryer's pan, combine the lamb with the other ingredients and toss.
2. Put the pan in the instant pot and seal with the air fryer lid.
3. Cook on Bake mode at 390 degrees F for 30 minutes.
4. Divide everything between plates and serve.

Nutrition:

calories 283, fat 13, fiber 4, carbs 6, protein 15

Mint and Cilantro Lamb Chops

Prep time: 5 minutes | **Cooking:** 25 minutes | **Servings:** 4

Ingredients:

- 2 pounds lamb chops
- 2 tablespoons mint, chopped
- Juice of 1 lime
- A pinch of salt and black pepper
- ½ cup cilantro, chopped
- 1 teaspoon chili powder
- 3 tablespoons olive oil

Directions:

1. In the multi level air fryer's pan, combine the lamb with the other ingredients and toss.
2. Put the pan in the instant pot and seal with the air fryer lid.
3. Cook on Roast mode at 400 degrees F for 25 minutes.
4. Divide everything between plates and serve.

Nutrition:

calories 284, fat 10, fiber 3, carbs 6, protein 16

Lamb with Shallots Sauce

Prep time: 5 minutes | **Cooking:** 25 minutes | **Servings:** 4

Ingredients:

- 2 pounds lamb chops
- 1 cup red wine
- 1 teaspoon rosemary, dried
- A pinch of salt and black pepper
- 1 cup shallots, chopped
- 1 garlic clove, minced
- Juice of 1 lime
- 2 tablespoons avocado oil

Directions:

1. In the multi level air fryer's pan, combine the lamb with the other ingredients and toss.
2. Put the pan in the instant pot and seal with the air fryer lid.
3. Cook on Bake mode at 400 degrees F for 25 minutes.
4. Divide everything between plates and serve.

Nutrition:
calories 284, fat 14, fiber 3, carbs 6, protein 16

Lamb with Rosemary Apples

Prep time: 10 minutes | **Cooking:** 30 minutes | **Servings:** 4

Ingredients:

- 2 pounds lamb stew meat, cubed
- 2 green apples, cored and cut into wedges
- 2 tablespoons olive oil
- ½ teaspoon rosemary, dried
- 2 tablespoons lemon juice
- ½ cup red wine
- A pinch of salt and black pepper

Directions:

1. In the multi level air fryer's pan, combine the lamb with the other ingredients and toss.
2. Put the pan in the instant pot and seal with the air fryer lid.
3. Cook on Bake mode at 380 degrees F for 30 minutes.
4. Divide everything between plates and serve.

Nutrition:
calories 274, fat 12, fiber 3, carbs 6, protein 16

Beef and Tomato Olives Sauce

Prep time: 5 minutes | **Cooking:** 30 minutes | **Servings:** 4

Ingredients:

- 2 pounds beef stew meat, cubed
- 1 cup kalamata olives, pitted and halved
- 1 cup black olives, pitted and halved
- 2 tablespoons olive oil
- A pinch of salt and black pepper
- ½ cup tomato sauce
- 1 tablespoon rosemary, chopped

Directions:

1. In the multi level air fryer's pan, combine the beef with the other ingredients and toss.
2. Put the pan in the instant pot and seal with the air fryer lid.
3. Cook on Bake mode at 380 degrees F for 30 minutes.
4. Divide everything into bowls and serve.

Nutrition:
calories 274, fat 10, fiber 4, carbs 6, protein 15

Lamb with Lime Endives

Prep time: 5 minutes | **Cooking:** 30 minutes | **Servings:** 4

Ingredients:

- 1 pound lamb stew meat, cubed
- 2 endives, shredded
- Juice of 1 lime
- 2 tablespoons olive oil
- A pinch of salt and black pepper
- 2 garlic cloves, minced
- 1 tablespoon chives, chopped
- ½ teaspoon Italian seasoning

Directions:

1. In the multi level air fryer's pan, combine the lamb with the other ingredients and toss.
2. Put the pan in the instant pot and seal with the air fryer lid.
3. Cook on Bake mode at 370 degrees F for 30 minutes.
4. Divide everything between plates and serve.

Nutrition:
calories 283, fat 13, fiber 4, carbs 6, protein 15

Mexican Lamb Mix

Prep time: 5 minutes | **Cooking:** 30 minutes | **Servings:** 4

Ingredients:

- 1 tablespoon olive oil
- 2 pounds lamb stew meat, cubed
- 1 cup mild salsa
- 1 cup cherry tomatoes, halved
- A pinch of salt and black pepper
- 2 spring onions, chopped
- Juice of ½ lemon
- 1 tablespoon dill, chopped

Directions:

1. In the multi level air fryer's pan, combine the lamb with the other ingredients and toss.
2. Put the pan in the instant pot and seal with the air fryer lid.
3. Cook on Bake mode at 380 degrees F for 30 minutes.
4. Divide everything between plates and serve.

Nutrition:
calories 284, fat 13, fiber 3, carbs 6, protein 14

Green Curry Beef

Prep time: 5 minutes | **Cooking:** 30 minutes | **Servings:** 4

Ingredients:

- 1 tablespoon avocado oil
- 2 pounds beef stew meat, cubed
- 1 teaspoon chili powder
- 2 tablespoons green curry paste
- 2 cups canned tomatoes, crushed
- Juice of 2 limes
- 1 teaspoon sweet paprika

Directions:

1. In the multi level air fryer's pan, combine the beef with the other ingredients and toss.
2. Put the pan in the instant pot and seal with the air fryer lid.
3. Cook on Bake mode at 380 degrees F for 30 minutes.
4. Divide everything into bowls and serve.

Nutrition:
calories 284, fat 12, fiber 3, carbs 5, protein 16

Beef with Balsamic Sun-dried Tomatoes

Prep time: 10 minutes | **Cooking:** 30 minutes | **Servings:** 4

Ingredients:

- 2 pounds beef stew meat, cut into strips
- 1 cup sun-dried tomatoes, chopped
- 1 cup spring onions, chopped
- ½ cup beef stock
- 1 tablespoon avocado oil
- A pinch of salt and black pepper
- 3 garlic cloves, minced
- 2 tablespoons balsamic vinegar
- 1 tablespoon chives, chopped

Directions:

1. In the multi level air fryer's pan, combine the beef with the other ingredients and toss.
2. Put the pan in the instant pot and seal with the air fryer lid.
3. Cook on Bake mode at 380 degrees F for 30 minutes.
4. Divide everything between plates and serve.

Nutrition:
calories 273, fat 13, fiber 4, carbs 6, protein 17

Coriander Lamb Cutlets

Prep time: 5 minutes | **Cooking:** 30 minutes | **Servings:** 4

Ingredients:

- 2 pounds lamb cutlets
- A pinch of salt and black pepper
- 4 tablespoons mustard
- 2 tablespoons butter, melted
- ½ teaspoon coriander, ground
- A pinch of cayenne pepper
- 1 tablespoon rosemary, chopped

Directions:

1. In the multi level air fryer's basket, combine the lamb with the mustard and the other ingredients and rub.
2. Put the basket in the instant pot, seal with the air fryer lid and cook on Air Fry mode at 390 degrees F for 15 minutes on each side.
3. Divide between plates and serve.

Nutrition:

calories 284, fat 13, fiber 3, carbs 6, protein 17

Herbed Lamb Balls

Prep time: 5 minutes | **Cooking:** 30 minutes | **Servings:** 4

Ingredients:

- 2 pounds lamb, ground
- 2 eggs, whisked
- 1 tablespoon parsley, chopped
- 1 tablespoon mint, chopped
- 1 red onion, chopped
- ¼ cup almond flour
- A pinch of salt and black pepper
- 2 garlic cloves, minced
- Cooking spray

Directions:

1. In a bowl, mix the meat with the eggs and the other ingredients except the cooking spray, stir well and shape medium meatballs out of this mix.
2. Grease the meatballs with cooking spray, put them in your multi level air fryer's basket.
3. Put the basket in the instant pot, seal with the air fryer lid and cook on Air fry mode at 380 degrees F for 15 minutes on each side.
4. Divide between plates and serve with a side salad.

Nutrition:

calories 287, fat 12, fiber 3, carbs 6, protein 17

Lime and Cumin Lamb Mix

Prep time: 5 minutes | **Cooking:** 30 minutes | **Servings:** 4

Ingredients:

- 2 pounds lamb chops
- Juice of 1 lime
- Zest of 1 lime, grated
- A pinch of salt and black pepper
- 1 tablespoon olive oil
- 1 teaspoon sweet paprika
- 1 teaspoon cumin, ground
- 1 tablespoon cumin, ground

Directions:

1. In the multi level air fryer's basket, mix the lamb chops with the lime juice and the other ingredients and rub..
2. Put the basket in the instant pot, seal with the air fryer lid and cook on Air fry mode at 380 degrees F for 15 minutes on each side.
3. Serve with a side salad.

Nutrition:

calories 284, fat 13, fiber 3, carbs 5, protein 15

Lamb with Spring Onions and Corn

Prep time: 5 minutes | **Cooking:** 30 minutes | **Servings:** 4

Ingredients:

- 2 pounds lamb stew meat, cubed
- 1 cup corn
- 1 cup spring onions, chopped
- ¼ cup beef stock
- 1 tablespoon olive oil
- A pinch of salt and black pepper
- 2 tablespoons rosemary, chopped

Directions:

1. In the multi level air fryer's pan, combine the lamb with the other ingredients and toss.
2. Put the pan in the instant pot and seal with the air fryer lid.
3. Cook on Bake mode at 380 degrees F for 30 minutes.
4. Divide everything between plates and serve.

Nutrition:

calories 274, fat 12, fiber 3, carbs 5, protein 15

Beef and Squash

Prep time: 10 minutes | **Cooking:** 30 minutes | **Servings:** 4

Ingredients:

- 2 pounds beef stew meat, cubed
- 1 cup butternut squash, peeled and cubed
- 1 tablespoon basil, chopped
- 1 tablespoon oregano, chopped
- A pinch of salt and black pepper
- A drizzle of olive oil
- 2 garlic cloves, minced

Directions:

1. In the multi level air fryer's pan, combine the beef with the other ingredients and toss.
2. Put the pan in the instant pot and seal with the air fryer lid.
3. Cook on Bake mode at 380 degrees F for 30 minutes.
4. Divide everything between plates and serve.

Nutrition:

calories 284, fat 13, fiber 3, carbs 6, protein 14

Masala Beef Mix

Prep time: 5 minutes | **Cooking:** 20 minutes | **Servings:** 4

Ingredients:

- 1 pound beef stew meat, roughly cubed
- 1 tablespoon smoked paprika
- ½ cup beef stock
- ½ teaspoon garam masala
- 2 tablespoons olive oil
- A pinch of salt and black pepper

Directions:

1. In the multi level air fryer's basket, mix the beef with the smoked paprika and the other ingredients and toss.
2. Put the basket in the instant pot, seal with the air fryer lid and cook on Air fry mode at 390 degrees F for 20 minutes on each side.
3. Divide between plates and serve.

Nutrition:

calories 274, fat 12, fiber 4, carbs 6, protein 17

Creamy Marjoram Pork

Prep time: 5 minutes | **Cooking:** 20 minutes | **Servings:** 4

Ingredients:

- 2 pounds pork stew meat, roughly cubed and browned
- 1 tablespoon marjoram, chopped
- 1 cup heavy cream
- 2 tablespoons olive oil
- Salt and black pepper to the taste
- 2 garlic cloves, minced

Directions:

1. In the multi level air fryer's pan, combine the pork with the other ingredients and toss.

2. Put the pan in the instant pot and seal with the air fryer lid.
3. Cook on Bake mode at 400 degrees F for 20 minutes.
4. Divide everything between plates and serve.

Nutrition:
calories 274, fat 14, fiber 3, carbs 6, protein 14

Creamy Spiced Lamb

Prep time: 5 minutes | **Cooking:** 30 minutes | **Servings:** 4

Ingredients:
- 1 pound lamb stew meat, cubed
- 2 teaspoons nutmeg, ground
- 1 teaspoon coriander, ground
- 1 cup heavy cream
- 2 tablespoons olive oil
- 2 tablespoons chives, chopped
- Salt and black pepper to the taste

Directions:
1. In the multi level air fryer's pan, combine the lamb with the other ingredients and toss.
2. Put the pan in the instant pot and seal with the air fryer lid.
3. Cook on Bake mode at 380 degrees F for 30 minutes.
4. Divide everything into bowls and serve.

Nutrition:
calories 287, fat 13, fiber 2, carbs 6, protein 12

Yogurt Beef Mix

Prep time: 5 minutes | **Cooking:** 30 minutes | **Servings:** 4

Ingredients:
- 2 pounds beef stew meat, roughly cubed
- 1 teaspoon coriander, ground
- 1 teaspoon garam masala
- 1 teaspoon cumin, ground
- A pinch of salt and black pepper
- 1 cup Greek yogurt
- ½ teaspoon turmeric powder

Directions:
1. In the multi level air fryer's pan, combine the beef with the other ingredients and toss.
2. Put the pan in the instant pot and seal with the air fryer lid.
3. Cook on Bake mode at 380 degrees F for 30 minutes.
4. Divide everything between plates and serve.

Nutrition:
calories 283, fat 13, fiber 3, carbs 6, protein 15

Beef and Mustard Fennel

Prep time: 5 minutes | **Cooking:** 30 minutes | **Servings:** 4

Ingredients:
- 2 pounds beef stew meat, cut into strips
- 2 fennel bulbs, sliced
- 2 tablespoons mustard
- A pinch of salt and black pepper
- 1 tablespoon black peppercorns, ground
- 2 tablespoons balsamic vinegar
- 2 tablespoons olive oil

Directions:
1. In the multi level air fryer's pan, combine the beef with the other ingredients and toss.
2. Put the pan in the instant pot and seal with the air fryer lid.
3. Cook on Bake mode at 380 degrees F for 30 minutes.
4. Divide everything into bowls and serve.

Nutrition:
calories 283, fat 13, fiber 2, carbs 6, protein 17

Lamb Meatloaf

Prep time: 5 minutes | **Cooking:** 35 minutes | **Servings:** 4

Ingredients:
- 2 pounds lamb stew meat, ground
- 2 eggplants, chopped
- 1 yellow onion, chopped
- A pinch of salt and black pepper
- ½ teaspoon coriander, ground
- Cooking spray
- 2 tablespoons cilantro, chopped
- 1 egg
- 2 tablespoons tomato paste

Directions:
1. In a bowl, mix the lamb with the eggplants of the ingredients except the cooking spray and stir.
2. Grease a loaf pan that fits the multi level air fryer with the cooking spray, add the mix and shape the meatloaf.
3. Put the pan in the instant pot, seal with air fryer lid and cook on Roast mode at 380 degrees F for 35 minutes.
4. Slice and serve with a side salad.

Nutrition:
calories 263, fat 12, fiber 3, carbs 6, protein 15

Pork Chops with Corn

Prep time: 10 minutes | **Cooking:** 25 minutes | **Servings:** 4

Ingredients:
- 2 pounds pork chops
- 1 cup kalamata olives, pitted and halved
- 1 cup black olives, pitted and halved
- 1 cup corn
- Salt and black pepper to the taste
- 1 tablespoons avocado oil
- 2 tablespoons garlic powder
- 2 tablespoons oregano, dried

Directions:
1. In the multi level air fryer's pan, combine the pork chops with the other ingredients and toss.
2. Put the pan in the instant pot and seal with the air fryer lid.
3. Cook on Roast mode at 400 degrees F for 25 minutes.
4. Divide everything between plates and serve.

Nutrition:
calories 281, fat 8, fiber 7, carbs 17, protein 19

Beef and Paprika Broccoli

Prep time: 10 minutes | **Cooking:** 30 minutes | **Servings:** 4

Ingredients:
- 1 pound beef stew meat, cubed
- 2 cups broccoli florets
- ½ cup tomato sauce
- 1 teaspoon sweet paprika
- 2 teaspoons olive oil
- 1 tablespoon cilantro, chopped

Directions:
1. In the multi level air fryer's pan, combine the beef with the other ingredients and toss.
2. Put the pan in the instant pot and seal with the air fryer lid.
3. Cook on Roast mode at 390 degrees F for 30 minutes.
4. Divide everything between plates and serve.

Nutrition:
calories 281, fat 12, fiber 7, carbs 19, protein 20

Cajun Chili Beef

Prep time: 10 minutes | **Cooking:** 30 minutes | **Servings:** 4

Ingredients:
- 2 pounds beef stew meat, cubed
- 1 tablespoon Cajun seasoning
- 1 teaspoon sweet paprika
- 1 teaspoon chili powder
- Salt and black pepper to the taste
- 1 tablespoon olive oil

Directions:

1. In the multi level air fryer's pan, combine the beef with the other ingredients and toss.
2. Put the pan in the instant pot and seal with the air fryer lid.
3. Cook on Roast mode at 400 degrees F for 30 minutes.
4. Divide everything between plates and serve.

Nutrition:
calories 291, fat 8, fiber 7, carbs 19, protein 20

Pork with Sprouts

Prep time: 10 minutes | **Cooking:** 30 minutes | **Servings:** 4

Ingredients:
- 2 pounds pork stew meat, cubed
- 1 cup Brussels sprouts, trimmed and halved
- 1 cup mushrooms, sliced
- Salt and black pepper to the taste
- 1 tablespoon balsamic vinegar
- 1 yellow onion, chopped
- 2 teaspoons olive oil

Directions:
1. In the multi level air fryer's pan, combine the pork with the other ingredients and toss.
2. Put the pan in the instant pot and seal with the air fryer lid.
3. Cook on Roast mode at 390 degrees F for 30 minutes.
4. Divide everything between plates and serve.

Nutrition:
calories 285, fat 8, fiber 2, carbs 18, protein 20

Pork Chops with Turmeric Sauce

Prep time: 10 minutes | **Cooking:** 30 minutes | **Servings:** 4

Ingredients:
- 2 tablespoons avocado oil
- 2 pounds pork chops
- 1 cup yogurt
- 2 garlic cloves, minced
- 1 teaspoon turmeric powder
- Salt and black pepper to the taste
- 2 tablespoon oregano, chopped

Directions:
1. In the multi level air fryer's pan, combine the pork chops with the other ingredients and toss.
2. Put the pan in the instant pot and seal with the air fryer lid.
3. Cook on Roast mode at 400 degrees F for 30 minutes.
4. Divide everything between plates and serve.

Nutrition:
calories 301, fat 7, fiber 5, carbs 19, protein 22

Lamb and Spinach Mix

Prep time: 10 minutes | **Cooking:** 20 minutes | **Servings:** 4

Ingredients:
- 2 pounds lamb stew meat, cubed
- 2 tablespoons macadamia nuts, peeled
- 1 cup baby spinach
- ½ cup beef stock
- 2 garlic cloves, minced
- Salt and black pepper to the taste
- 1 tablespoon oregano, chopped

Directions:
1. In the multi level air fryer's pan, combine the lamb with the other ingredients and toss.
2. Put the pan in the instant pot and seal with the air fryer lid.
3. Cook on Bake mode at 380 degrees F for 20 minutes.
4. Divide everything between plates and serve.

Nutrition:
calories 280, fat 12, fiber 8, carbs 20, protein 19

Beef and Cucumber Mix

Prep time: 10 minutes | **Cooking:** 20 minutes | **Servings:** 4

Ingredients:
- 1 pound beef stew meat, cut into strips
- 2 eggplants, cubed
- 2 cucumbers, sliced
- 2 garlic cloves, minced
- 1 cup heavy cream
- 2 tablespoons olive oil
- Salt and black pepper to the taste

Directions:
1. In the multi level air fryer's pan, combine the beef with the other ingredients and toss.
2. Put the pan in the instant pot and seal with the air fryer lid.
3. Cook on Roast mode at 400 degrees F for 20 minutes.
4. Divide everything between plates and serve.

Nutrition:
calories 283, fat 11, fiber 9, carbs 22, protein 14

Nutmeg Pork and Sour Cream Mix

Prep time: 10 minutes | **Cooking:** 25 minutes | **Servings:** 4

Ingredients:
- 1 pound pork stew meat, cubed
- 1 cup canned artichoke hearts, drained and halved
- 2 tablespoons olive oil
- 2 tablespoons rosemary, chopped
- ½ teaspoon cumin, ground
- ½ teaspoon nutmeg, ground
- ½ cup sour cream
- Salt and black pepper to the taste

Directions:
1. In the multi level air fryer's pan, combine the pork with the other ingredients and toss.
2. Put the pan in the instant pot and seal with the air fryer lid.
3. Cook on Roast mode at 400 degrees F for 25 minutes.
4. Divide everything between plates and serve.

Nutrition:
calories 280, fat 13, fiber 9, carbs 22, protein 18

Nutmeg and Chili Beef

Prep time: 10 minutes | **Cooking:** 30 minutes | **Servings:** 4

Ingredients:
- 2 pounds beef stew meat, cubed
- 1 teaspoon nutmeg, ground
- 2 tablespoons avocado oil
- ½ teaspoon chili powder
- ¼ cup beef stock
- 2 tablespoons chives, chopped
- Salt and black pepper to the taste

Directions:
1. In the multi level air fryer's pan, combine the beef with the other ingredients and toss.
2. Put the pan in the instant pot and seal with the air fryer lid.
3. Cook on Roast mode at 400 degrees F for 30 minutes.
4. Divide everything between plates and serve.

Nutrition:
calories 280, fat 12, fiber 2, carbs 17, protein 14

Lamb with Dill Asparagus

Prep time: 10 minutes | **Cooking:** 30 minutes | **Servings:** 4

Ingredients:
- 2 tablespoons butter, melted
- 2 pounds lamb chops
- 4 asparagus spears, trimmed and halved
- Salt and black pepper to the taste
- 1 tablespoon avocado oil
- ¼ cup beef stock
- 1 tablespoon dill, chopped

Directions:
1. In the multi level air fryer's pan, combine the lamb with the other ingredients and toss.
2. Put the pan in the instant pot and seal with the air fryer lid.
3. Cook on Roast mode at 400 degrees F for 30 minutes.
4. Divide everything into bowls and serve.

Nutrition:
calories 300, fat 11, fiber 4, carbs 18, protein 22

Vegetable Recipes

Masala Artichokes

Prep time: 5 minutes | **Cooking:** 10 minutes | **Servings:** 4

Ingredients:

- 2 cups canned artichoke hearts, halved
- 1 teaspoon garam masala
- 1 teaspoon chili powder
- 2 tablespoons olive oil
- A pinch of salt and black pepper
- 2 tablespoons balsamic vinegar
- 1 tablespoon dill, chopped

Directions:

1. In the multi level air fryer's pan, combine the beef with the other ingredients and toss.
2. Put the pan in the instant pot and seal with the air fryer lid.
3. Cook on Roast mode at 400 degrees F for 30 minutes.
4. Divide everything between plates and serve.

Nutrition:

calories 200, fat 6, fiber 2, carbs 3, protein 6

Chili Beet

Prep time: 5 minutes | **Cooking:** 30 minutes | **Servings:** 4

Ingredients:

- 1 pound red beets, peeled and cut into wedges
- 2 tablespoons avocado oil
- A pinch of salt and black pepper
- 1 teaspoon chili powder
- 1 tablespoon chives, chopped
- Juice of 1 lime

Directions:

1. In your multi level air fryer's basket, combine the beets with the oil and the other ingredients except the chives and toss.
2. Put the basket in the instant pot, seal with the air fryer lid and cook on Air fry mode at 400 degrees F for 30 minutes.
3. Divide between plates and serve with the chives on top,

Nutrition:

calories 200, fat 5, fiber 2, carbs 4, protein 6

Yogurt Potatoes Mix

Prep time: 4 minutes | **Cooking:** 25 minutes | **Servings:** 4

Ingredients:

- 1 pound gold potatoes, peeled and cut into wedges
- 1 teaspoon turmeric powder
- 1 teaspoon coriander, ground
- 2 tablespoons olive oil
- A pinch of salt and black pepper
- 1 cup Greek yogurt
- 1 cup dill, chopped
- 2 garlic cloves, minced

Directions:

1. In the multi level air fryer's pan, combine the potatoes with the other ingredients and toss.
2. Put the pan in the instant pot and seal with the air fryer lid.
3. Cook on Roast mode at 400 degrees F for 25 minutes.
4. Divide everything between plates and serve.

Nutrition:

calories 194, fat 6, fiber 2, carbs 4, protein 8

Chili Tomatoes

Prep time: 5 minutes | **Cooking:** 20 minutes | **Servings:** 4

Ingredients:

- 1 pound cherry tomatoes, halved
- ¼ teaspoon rosemary, dried
- 1 teaspoon chili powder
- ½ cup balsamic vinegar
- 2 tablespoons olive oil
- A pinch of salt and black pepper

Directions:

1. In your multi level air fryer's basket, combine the tomatoes with the other ingredients and toss.
2. Put the basket in the instant pot, seal with air fryer lid and cook on Air fry mode at 400 degrees F for 20 minutes.
3. Divide between plates and serve.

Nutrition:

calories 173, fat 4, fiber 2, carbs 4, protein 8

Garlic Potato Mix

Prep time: 5 minutes | **Cooking:** 30 minutes | **Servings:** 4

Ingredients:

- 2 pounds sweet potatoes, peeled and cut into wedges
- 1 cup bacon, cooked and chopped
- 2 tablespoons olive oil
- 1 teaspoon sweet paprika
- 4 garlic cloves, minced
- Juice of 1 lime

Directions:

1. In the multi level air fryer's pan, combine the potatoes with the other ingredients and toss.
2. Put the pan in the instant pot and seal with the air fryer lid.
3. Cook on Roast mode at 390 degrees F for 30 minutes.
4. Divide everything between plates and serve.

Nutrition:

calories 172, fat 6, fiber 2, carbs 5, protein 8

Creamy Artichokes

Prep time: 5 minutes | **Cooking:** 20 minutes | **Servings:** 4

Ingredients:

- 2 cups canned artichoke hearts, drained and halved
- 2 tablespoons butter, melted
- 2 tablespoons mustard
- 3 garlic cloves, minced
- ½ cup heavy cream

Directions:

1. In the multi level air fryer's pan, combine the artichokes with the other ingredients and toss.
2. Put the pan in the instant pot and seal with the air fryer lid.
3. Cook on Roast mode at 400 degrees F for 20 minutes.
4. Divide everything between plates and serve.

Nutrition:

calories 162, fat 4, fiber 4, carbs 6, protein 9

Cayenne Beets

Prep time: 5 minutes | **Cooking:** 20 minutes | **Servings:** 4

Ingredients:

- 1 pound red beets, peeled and roughly cubed
- A pinch of salt and black pepper
- 1 tablespoon lemon zest, grated
- 1 teaspoon cayenne pepper
- 1 teaspoon chili pepper
- 2 tablespoons avocado oil
- Juice of 1 lemon

Directions:

1. In the multi level air fryer's basket, combine the beets with the other ingredients and toss.
2. Put the basket in the instant pot and seal with the air fryer lid.
3. Cook on Air fry mode at 390 degrees F for 20 minutes.
4. Divide everything between plates and serve.

Nutrition:

calories 175, fat 5, fiber 2, carbs 4, protein 8

Mustard Broccoli

Prep time: 5 minutes | **Cooking:** 30 minutes | **Servings:** 4

Ingredients:

- 1 pound broccoli florets
- 1 cup coconut cream
- 1 teaspoon turmeric powder
- 1 teaspoon cumin, ground
- 1 tablespoon mustard
- ½ cup chicken stock
- A pinch of salt and black pepper
- 1 tablespoon parsley, chopped

Directions:

1. In the multi level air fryer's pan, combine the broccoli with the other ingredients and toss.
2. Put the pan in the instant pot and seal with the air fryer lid.
3. Cook on Roast mode at 380 degrees F for 30 minutes.
4. Divide everything between plates and serve.

Nutrition:

calories 244, fat 12, fiber 3, carbs 5, protein 12

Butter Cauliflower

Prep time: 5 minutes | **Cooking:** 20 minutes | **Servings:** 4

Ingredients:

- 1 pound cauliflower florets
- 1 tablespoon balsamic vinegar
- 2 tablespoons butter, melted
- 2 shallots, chopped
- A pinch of salt and black pepper
- 1 tablespoon dill, chopped
- ¼ cup beef stock

Directions:

1. In the multi level air fryer's pan, combine the cauliflower with the other ingredients and toss.
2. Put the pan in the instant pot and seal with the air fryer lid.
3. Cook on Roast mode at 380 degrees F for 20 minutes.
4. Divide everything between plates and serve.

Nutrition:

calories 173, fat 7, fiber 2, carbs 4, protein 8

Coriander Broccoli and Beets

Prep time: 5 minutes | **Cooking:** 25 minutes | **Servings:** 4

Ingredients:

- 1 pound broccoli florets
- ½ pound beets, peeled and cubed
- 2 tablespoons avocado oil
- 1 teaspoon chili powder
- ½ cup beef stock
- ½ teaspoon coriander, ground
- Salt and black pepper to the taste
- ½ cup tomato sauce

Directions:

1. In the multi level air fryer's pan, combine the broccoli with the other ingredients and toss.
2. Put the pan in the instant pot and seal with the air fryer lid.
3. Cook on Roast mode at 380 degrees F for 25 minutes.
4. Divide everything between plates and serve.

Nutrition:

calories 163, fat 5, fiber 2, carbs 4, protein 8

Paprika Asparagus

Prep time: 5 minutes | **Cooking:** 15 minutes | **Servings:** 4

Ingredients:

- 1 pound asparagus spears, trimmed and halved
- 2 red chilies, minced
- 2 tablespoons avocado oil
- 2 tablespoons chili sauce
- ½ teaspoon sweet paprika
- A pinch of salt and black pepper

Directions:

1. In a bowl, mix the asparagus with the chilies and the other ingredients and rub,
2. Put the asparagus in your multi level air fryer's basket.
3. Put the basket in the instant pot, seal with the air fryer lid and cook on Air fry mode at 400 degrees F for 15 minutes.
4. Divide between plates and serve.

Nutrition:

calories 173, fat 6, fiber 2, carbs 6, protein 8

Parmesan Turmeric Potatoes

Prep time: 5 minutes | **Cooking:** 25 minutes | **Servings:** 4

Ingredients:

- 1 pound red potatoes, peeled and cubed
- 1 cup heavy cream
- 1 teaspoon turmeric powder
- ½ cup parmesan, grated
- Juice of 1 lime
- Salt and black pepper to the taste
- 2 tablespoons olive oil

Directions:

1. In the multi level air fryer's pan, combine the potatoes with the other ingredients and toss.
2. Put the pan in the instant pot and seal with the air fryer lid.
3. Cook on Roast mode at 400 degrees F for 25 minutes.
4. Divide everything between plates and serve.

Nutrition:

calories 172, fat 5, fiber 2, carbs 4, protein 9

Garlic Broccoli Mix

Prep time: 5 minutes | **Cooking:** 20 minutes | **Servings:** 4

Ingredients:

- 1 pound broccoli florets
- ½ pound baby carrots, peeled
- 2 scallions, chopped
- 1 teaspoon sweet paprika
- ½ cup chicken stock
- 2 tablespoons tomato paste
- 3 garlic cloves, minced
- A pinch of salt and black pepper
- 1 tablespoon olive oil

Directions:

1. In the multi level air fryer's pan, combine the broccoli with the other ingredients and toss.
2. Put the pan in the instant pot and seal with the air fryer lid.
3. Cook on Roast mode at 400 degrees F for 20 minutes.
4. Divide everything between plates and serve.

Nutrition:

calories 180, fat 4, fiber 2, carbs 4, protein 6

Lime Carrots

Prep time: 5 minutes | **Cooking:** 25 minutes | **Servings:** 4

Ingredients:

- 1 pound baby carrots, peeled
- 3 tablespoons butter, melted
- Zest of 1 lime, grated
- 1 teaspoon chili powder
- A pinch of salt and black pepper
- 1 teaspoons sweet paprika

Directions:

1. In the multi level air fryer's pan, combine the carrots with the other ingredients and toss.
2. Put the pan in the instant pot and seal with the air fryer lid.
3. Cook on Roast mode at 390 degrees F for 25 minutes.
4. Divide everything between plates and serve.

Nutrition:

calories 130, fat 3, fiber 3, carbs 4, protein 8

Bell Peppers and Tomato Sauce

Prep time: 5 minutes | **Cooking:** 20 minutes | **Servings:** 4

Ingredients:

- 1 pound red bell peppers, cut into strips

- 1 teaspoon sweet paprika
- 1 red onion, sliced
- 1 cup tomato passata
- A pinch of salt and black pepper
- 1 tablespoon olive oil
- 1 tablespoon chives, chopped
- 2 tablespoons lime juice

Directions:
1. In the multi level air fryer's pan, combine the peppers with the other ingredients and toss.
2. Put the pan in the instant pot and seal with the air fryer lid.
3. Cook on Roast mode at 360 degrees F for 20 minutes.
4. Divide everything between plates and serve.

Nutrition:
calories 131, fat 3, fiber 2, carbs 4, protein 5

Masala Carrots

Prep time: 2 minutes | **Cooking:** 25 minutes | **Servings:** 4

Ingredients:
- 2 tablespoons olive oil
- 1 pound carrots, peeled and roughly sliced
- 2 tablespoons balsamic vinegar
- 1 teaspoon garam masala
- 1 teaspoon rosemary, dried
- 3 garlic cloves, minced
- Salt and black pepper to the taste

Directions:
1. In the multi level air fryer's basket, combine the carrot slices with the oil and the other ingredients and rub.
2. Put the basket in the instant pot, seal with the air fryer lid and cook on Air fry mode at 380 degrees F for 25 minutes.
3. Divide between plates and serve.

Nutrition:
calories 122, fat 4, fiber 3, carbs 4, protein 5

Beets and Cream Sauce

Prep time: 5 minutes | **Cooking:** 25 minutes | **Servings:** 4

Ingredients:
- 2 pounds baby beets, peeled and halved
- 1 cup heavy cream
- 1 teaspoon turmeric powder
- A pinch of salt and black pepper
- 2 tablespoons olive oil
- 2 garlic cloves, minced
- Juice of 1 lime
- ½ teaspoon coriander, ground

Directions:
1. In the multi level air fryer's pan, combine the beets with the other ingredients and toss.
2. Put the pan in the instant pot and seal with the air fryer lid.
3. Cook on Roast mode at 400 degrees F for 25 minutes.
4. Divide everything between plates and serve.

Nutrition:
calories 135, fat 3, fiber 2, carbs 4, protein 6

Chard Sauté

Prep time: 5 minutes | **Cooking:** 20 minutes | **Servings:** 4

Ingredients:
- 2 cups red chard, torn
- 1 cup kalamata olives, pitted and halved
- ½ cup tomato sauce
- 1 teaspoon chili powder
- 2 tablespoons olive oil
- Salt and black pepper to the taste

Directions:
1. In the multi level air fryer's pan, combine the chard with the other ingredients and toss.
2. Put the pan in the instant pot and seal with the air fryer lid.
3. Cook on Roast mode at 370 degrees F for 20 minutes.
4. Divide everything between plates and serve.

Nutrition:
calories 154, fat 3, fiber 2, carbs 4, protein 6

Rosemary Mushrooms Mix

Prep time: 5 minutes | **Cooking:** 20 minutes | **Servings:** 4

Ingredients:
- 1 pound white mushrooms, halved
- 1 teaspoon sweet paprika
- 1 red onion, chopped
- 1 teaspoon rosemary, dried
- Salt and black pepper to the taste
- 2 tablespoons olive oil
- 1 cup coconut milk

Directions:
1. In the multi level air fryer's pan, combine the mushrooms with the other ingredients and toss.
2. Put the pan in the instant pot and seal with the air fryer lid.
3. Cook on Roast mode at 380 degrees F for 20 minutes.
4. Divide everything between plates and serve.

Nutrition:
calories 162, fat 4, fiber 1, carbs 3, protein 5

Salsa Kale

Prep time: 5 minutes | **Cooking:** 20 minutes | **Servings:** 4

Ingredients:
- 2 cups baby kale
- 1 pound cherry tomatoes, halved
- 1 cup mild salsa
- 2 scallions, chopped
- 1 tablespoon olive oil
- A pinch of salt and black pepper
- 2 tablespoons chives, chopped

Directions:
1. In the multi level air fryer's pan, combine the kale with the other ingredients and toss.
2. Put the pan in the instant pot and seal with the air fryer lid.
3. Cook on Bake mode at 380 degrees F for 20 minutes.
4. Divide everything between plates and serve.

Nutrition:
calories 140, fat 3, fiber 2, carbs 3, protein 5

Chives Brussels Sprouts

Prep time: 5 minutes | **Cooking:** 20 minutes | **Servings:** 4

Ingredients:
- 1 pound Brussels sprouts, trimmed
- ½ pound cherry tomatoes, halved
- 2 tablespoons tomato paste
- 1 cup chicken stock
- ½ teaspoon sweet paprika
- 1 tablespoon olive oil
- Salt and black pepper to the taste
- 1 tablespoon chives, chopped

Directions:
1. In the multi level air fryer's pan, combine the sprouts with the other ingredients and toss.
2. Put the pan in the instant pot and seal with the air fryer lid.
3. Cook on Bake mode at 380 degrees F for 20 minutes.
4. Divide everything between plates and serve.

Nutrition:
calories 170, fat 5, fiber 3, carbs 4, protein 7

Lime Tomatoes

Prep time: 5 minutes | **Cooking:** 20 minutes | **Servings:** 4

Ingredients:
- 1 pound cherry tomatoes, halved

- 1 teaspoon Italian seasoning
- 1 tablespoon basil, chopped
- Juice of 1 lime
- A pinch of salt and black pepper
- 4 garlic cloves, minced
- 2 tablespoons olive oil

Directions:
1. In the multi level air fryer's pan, combine the tomatoes with the other ingredients and toss.
2. Put the pan in the instant pot and seal with the air fryer lid.
3. Cook on Bake mode at 380 degrees F for 20 minutes.
4. Divide everything between plates and serve.

Nutrition:
calories 173, fat 6, fiber 2, carbs 4, protein 5

Coriander Zucchini

Prep time: 5 minutes | **Cooking:** 20 minutes | **Servings:** 4

Ingredients:
- 1 pound zucchinis, roughly sliced
- 1 cup mild salsa
- 1 red onion, chopped
- Salt and black pepper to the taste
- 2 tablespoons lime juice
- 2 tablespoons olive oil
- 1 teaspoon coriander, ground

Directions:
1. In the multi level air fryer's pan, combine the zucchinis with the other ingredients and toss.
2. Put the pan in the instant pot and seal with the air fryer lid.
3. Cook on Bake mode at 390 degrees F for 20 minutes.
4. Divide everything between plates and serve.

Nutrition:
calories 150, fat 4, fiber 2, carbs 4, protein 5

Balsamic and Garlic Green Beans

Prep time: 5 minutes | **Cooking:** 20 minutes | **Servings:** 4

Ingredients:
- 1 pound green beans, trimmed and halved
- 1 cup black olives, pitted and halved
- 1 cup kalamata olives, pitted and halved
- 1 red onion, sliced
- 2 tablespoons balsamic vinegar
- 1 tablespoon olive oil
- 3 garlic cloves, minced
- ½ cup tomato sauce

Directions:
1. In the multi level air fryer's pan, combine the green beans with the other ingredients and toss.
2. Put the pan in the instant pot and seal with the air fryer lid.
3. Cook on Bake mode at 350 degrees F for 20 minutes.
4. Divide everything between plates and serve.

Nutrition:
calories 180, fat 4, fiber 3, carbs 5, protein 6

Lime Avocado Mix

Prep time: 5 minutes | **Cooking:** 15 minutes | **Servings:** 4

Ingredients:
- 2 small avocados, pitted, peeled and cut into wedges
- 1 tablespoon olive oil
- Zest of 1 lime, grated
- Juice of 1 lime
- 1 tablespoon avocado oil
- A pinch of salt and black pepper
- ½ teaspoon sweet paprika

Directions:
1. In the multi level air fryer's pan, combine the avocado with the other ingredients and toss.
2. Put the pan in the instant pot and seal with the air fryer lid.
3. Cook on Bake mode at 350 degrees F for 15 minutes.
4. Divide everything between plates and serve.

Nutrition:
calories 153, fat 3, fiber 3, carbs 4, protein 6

Chili Black Beans

Prep time: 5 minutes | **Cooking:** 20 minutes | **Servings:** 4

Ingredients:
- 2 cups canned black beans, drained
- 1 tablespoon olive oil
- 1 teaspoon chili powder
- 2 red chilies, minced
- A pinch of salt and black pepper
- ¼ cup tomato sauce

Directions:
1. In the multi level air fryer's pan, combine the black beans with the other ingredients and toss.
2. Put the pan in the instant pot and seal with the air fryer lid.
3. Cook on Bake mode at 380 degrees F for 20 minutes.
4. Divide everything between plates and serve.

Nutrition:
calories 160, fat 4, fiber 3, carbs 5, protein 4

Simple Tomatoes and Peppers

Prep time: 4 minutes | **Cooking:** 20 minutes | **Servings:** 4

Ingredients:
- 1 tablespoon avocado oil
- ½ pound mixed bell peppers, sliced
- 1 pound cherry tomatoes, halved
- 1 red onion, chopped
- A pinch of salt and black pepper
- 1 teaspoon sweet paprika
- ½ tablespoon Cajun seasoning

Directions:
1. In the multi level air fryer's pan, combine the tomatoes with the other ingredients and toss.
2. Put the pan in the instant pot and seal with the air fryer lid.
3. Cook on Bake mode at 390 degrees F for 20 minutes.
4. Divide everything between plates and serve.

Nutrition:
calories 151, fat 3, fiber 2, carbs 4, protein 5

Cilantro Sweet Potatoes

Prep time: 5 minutes | **Cooking:** 25 minutes | **Servings:** 4

Ingredients:
- 1 pound sweet potatoes, peeled and cut into wedges
- 1 cup kalamata olives, pitted and halved
- 1 tablespoon olive oil
- 2 tablespoons balsamic vinegar
- A bunch of cilantro, chopped
- Salt and black pepper to the taste
- 1 tablespoon basil, chopped

Directions:
1. In the multi level air fryer's pan, combine the potatoes with the other ingredients and toss.
2. Put the pan in the instant pot and seal with the air fryer lid.
3. Cook on Bake mode at 370 degrees F for 25 minutes.
4. Divide everything between plates and serve.

Nutrition:
calories 132, fat 4, fiber 2, carbs 4, protein 4

Parsley Sprouts

Prep time: 5 minutes | **Cooking:** 20 minutes | **Servings:** 4

Ingredients:

- 1 pound Brussels sprouts, trimmed and halved
- ½ pound baby spinach
- 1 tablespoon olive oil
- Juice of 1 lime
- Salt and black pepper to the taste
- 1 tablespoon parsley, chopped

Directions:
1. In the multi level air fryer's pan, combine the sprouts with the other ingredients and toss.
2. Put the pan in the instant pot and seal with the air fryer lid.
3. Cook on Bake mode at 380 degrees F for 20 minutes.
4. Divide everything into bowls and serve.

Nutrition:
calories 140, fat 3, fiber 2, carbs 5, protein 6

Coriander Tomatoes

Prep time: 5 minutes | **Cooking:** 20 minutes | **Servings:** 4

Ingredients:
- 2 pounds cherry tomatoes, halved
- 1 teaspoon sweet paprika
- 1 teaspoon coriander, ground
- 2 teaspoons lemon zest, grated
- 2 tablespoons olive oil
- 2 tablespoons lemon juice
- A handful parsley, chopped

Directions:
1. In the multi level air fryer's pan, combine the tomatoes with the other ingredients and toss.
2. Put the pan in the instant pot and seal with the air fryer lid.
3. Cook on Bake mode at 370 degrees F for 20 minutes.
4. Divide everything into bowls and serve.

Nutrition:
calories 151, fat 2, fiber 3, carbs 5, protein 5

Lime and Coriander Green Beans

Prep time: 5 minutes | **Cooking:** 20 minutes | **Servings:** 4

Ingredients:
- 1 pound cherry tomatoes, halved
- ½ pound green beans, trimmed and halved
- Juice of 1 lime
- 1 teaspoon coriander, ground
- 1 teaspoon sweet paprika
- A pinch of salt and black pepper
- 2 tablespoons olive oil

Directions:
1. In the multi level air fryer's pan, combine the green beans with the other ingredients and toss.
2. Put the pan in the instant pot and seal with the air fryer lid.
3. Cook on Bake mode at 380 degrees F for 20 minutes.
4. Divide everything into bowls and serve.

Nutrition:
calories 151, fat 3, fiber 2, carbs 4, protein 4

Chili Tomato and Onions

Prep time: 5 minutes | **Cooking:** 20 minutes | **Servings:** 4

Ingredients:
- 1 pound cherry tomatoes, halved
- 2 red onions, sliced
- 2 tablespoons avocado oil
- 1 teaspoon hot paprika
- 1 tablespoon olive oil
- 2 teaspoons chili powder
- A pinch of salt and black pepper
- 1 tablespoon chives, chopped

Directions:
1. In the multi level air fryer's pan, combine the tomatoes with the other ingredients and toss.
2. Put the pan in the instant pot and seal with the air fryer lid.
3. Cook on Bake mode at 390 degrees F for 20 minutes.
4. Divide everything into bowls and serve.

Nutrition:
calories 173, fat 4, fiber 2, carbs 4, protein 6

Kale and Corn Salad

Prep time: 5 minutes | **Cooking:** 15 minutes | **Servings:** 4

Ingredients:
- 1 pound kale leaves, torn
- 1 cup kalamata olives, pitted and halved
- 1 cup corn
- Salt and black pepper to the taste
- ¼ cup heavy cream
- 1 tablespoon chives, chopped
- 1 cup cherry tomatoes, halved
- Juice of 1 lime

Directions:
1. In the multi level air fryer's pan, combine the kale with the other ingredients and toss.
2. Put the pan in the instant pot and seal with the air fryer lid.
3. Cook on Bake mode at 390 degrees F for 15 minutes.
4. Divide everything into bowls and serve.

Nutrition:
calories 161, fat 2, fiber 2, carbs 4, protein 6

Garlic Paprika Carrots

Prep time: 5 minutes | **Cooking:** 20 minutes | **Servings:** 4

Ingredients:
- 1 tablespoon avocado oil
- 1 pound baby carrots, peeled
- Juice of 1 lime
- ½ teaspoon sweet paprika
- 6 garlic cloves, minced
- 1 tablespoon balsamic vinegar
- Salt and black pepper to the taste

Directions:
1. In the multi level air fryer's pan, combine the carrots with the other ingredients and toss.
2. Put the pan in the instant pot and seal with the air fryer lid.
3. Cook on Bake mode at 380 degrees F for 20 minutes.
4. Divide everything into bowls and serve.

Nutrition:
calories 121, fat 3, fiber 2, carbs 4, protein 6

Creamy Green Beans

Prep time: 5 minutes | **Cooking:** 20 minutes | **Servings:** 4

Ingredients:
- 1 pound green beans, trimmed and halved
- 1 cup walnuts, chopped
- 2 cups cherry tomatoes, halved
- 2 tablespoons olive oil
- A pinch of salt and black pepper
- 1 tablespoon chives, chopped

Directions:
1. In the multi level air fryer's pan, combine the green beans with the other ingredients and toss.
2. Put the pan in the instant pot and seal with the air fryer lid.
3. Cook on Bake mode at 380 degrees F for 20 minutes.
4. Divide everything into bowls and serve.

Nutrition:
calories 141, fat 3, fiber 2, carbs 4, protein 5

Garlic and Lime Corn

Prep time: 5 minutes | **Cooking:** 15 minutes | **Servings:** 4

Ingredients:
- 2 cups corn
- 3 garlic cloves, minced
- 1 tablespoon olive oil
- Juice of 1 lime
- 1 teaspoon sweet paprika
- Salt and black pepper to the

taste
- 2 tablespoons dill, chopped

Directions:
1. In the multi level air fryer's pan, combine the corn with the other ingredients and toss.
2. Put the pan in the instant pot and seal with the air fryer lid.
3. Cook on Bake mode at 390 degrees F for 15 minutes.
4. Divide everything into bowls and serve.

Nutrition:
calories 180, fat 3, fiber 2, carbs 4, protein 6

Green Beans and Spinach Salad
Prep time: 5 minutes | **Cooking:** 20 minutes | **Servings:** 4

Ingredients:
- 1 pound green beans, trimmed and halved
- 1 cup baby spinach
- 1 cup baby kale
- 2 tablespoons olive oil
- 1 cup corn
- 1 tablespoon lime juice
- A pinch of salt and black pepper
- 1 teaspoon rosemary, dried
- 1 teaspoon chili powder

Directions:
1. In the multi level air fryer's pan, combine the green beans with the other ingredients and toss.
2. Put the pan in the instant pot and seal with the air fryer lid.
3. Cook on Bake mode at 400 degrees F for 20 minutes.
4. Divide everything into bowls and serve.

Nutrition:
calories 151, fat 4, fiber 2, carbs 4, protein 6

Red Cabbage Sauté
Prep time: 5 minutes | **Cooking:** 20 minutes | **Servings:** 4

Ingredients:
- 1 pound red cabbage, shredded
- ½ pound cherry tomatoes, halved
- 2 tablespoons olive oil
- Salt and black pepper to the taste
- ½ cup heavy cream
- 1 tablespoon chives, chopped

Directions:
1. In the multi level air fryer's pan, combine the cabbage with the other ingredients and toss.
2. Put the pan in the instant pot and seal with the air fryer lid.
3. Cook on Bake mode at 390 degrees F for 20 minutes.
4. Divide everything into bowls and serve.

Nutrition:
calories 173, fat 5, fiber 3, carbs 5, protein 8

Cabbage and Spring Onions Sauté
Prep time: 5 minutes | **Cooking:** 20 minutes | **Servings:** 4

Ingredients:
- 1 pound Savoy cabbage, shredded
- 2 scallions, chopped
- 2 tablespoons avocado oil
- Juice of 1 lime
- 2 spring onions, chopped
- 2 tablespoons tomato sauce
- Salt and black pepper to the taste
- 1 tablespoon chives, chopped

Directions:
1. In the multi level air fryer's pan, combine the cabbage with the other ingredients and toss.
2. Put the pan in the instant pot and seal with the air fryer lid.
3. Cook on Bake mode at 360 degrees F for 20 minutes.
4. Divide everything into bowls and serve.

Nutrition:
calories 163, fat 4, fiber 3, carbs 6, protein 7

Butter Kale
Prep time: 5 minutes | **Cooking:** 20 minutes | **Servings:** 4

Ingredients:
- 1 pound baby kale
- 1 teaspoon turmeric powder
- 1 red bell pepper, cut into strips
- 1 red onion, chopped
- 2 tablespoons butter, melted
- 1 tablespoon dill, chopped

Directions:
1. In the multi level air fryer's pan, combine the kale with the other ingredients and toss.
2. Put the pan in the instant pot and seal with the air fryer lid.
3. Cook on Bake mode at 380 degrees F for 20 minutes.
4. Divide everything between plates and serve.

Nutrition:
calories 173, fat 5, fiber 3, carbs 6, protein 7

Coriander and Butter Fennel
Prep time: 5 minutes | **Cooking:** 15 minutes | **Servings:** 4

Ingredients:
- 3 tablespoons butter, melted
- 2 fennel bulbs, sliced
- 1 teaspoon turmeric powder
- 1 teaspoon coriander, ground
- 1 tablespoon lemon zest, grated
- A pinch of salt and black pepper
- 1 tablespoon lemon juice

Directions:
1. In the multi level air fryer's pan, combine the fennel with the other ingredients and toss.
2. Put the pan in the instant pot and seal with the air fryer lid.
3. Cook on Bake mode at 350 degrees F for 15 minutes.
4. Divide everything between plates and serve.

Nutrition:
calories 163, fat 4, fiber 3, carbs 5, protein 6

Oregano Kale
Prep time: 5 minutes | **Cooking:** 15 minutes | **Servings:** 4

Ingredients:
- 2 cups baby kale
- 2 scallions, chopped
- Juice of 1 lime
- 1 tablespoon olive oil
- A pinch of salt and black pepper
- 2 tablespoons balsamic vinegar
- 1 tablespoon oregano, chopped

Directions:
1. In the multi level air fryer's pan, combine the kale with the other ingredients and toss.
2. Put the pan in the instant pot and seal with the air fryer lid.
3. Cook on Bake mode at 350 degrees F for 15 minutes.
4. Divide everything between plates and serve.

Nutrition:
calories 143, fat 4, fiber 3, carbs 6, protein 7

Almond Endives
Prep time: 5 minutes | **Cooking:** 15 minutes | **Servings:** 4

Ingredients:
- 2 endives, trimmed and halved
- 1 tablespoon coriander, chopped
- 1 teaspoon sweet paprika
- 2 tablespoons olive oil
- A pinch of salt and black pepper
- 2 tablespoons white vinegar
- ½ cup almonds, chopped

Directions:
1. In the multi level air fryer's pan, combine the endives with the other ingredients and toss.
2. Put the pan in the instant pot and seal with the air fryer lid.
3. Cook on Bake mode at 350 degrees F for 15 minutes.
4. Divide everything between plates and serve.

Nutrition:
calories 154, fat 4, fiber 3, carbs 6, protein 7

Mozzarella Beets

Prep time: 5 minutes | **Cooking:** 30 minutes | **Servings:** 4

Ingredients:
- 2 beets, peeled and roughly cut into wedges
- 1 cup mozzarella, shredded
- 1 red onion, sliced
- A pinch of salt and black pepper
- 1 tablespoon lemon juice
- 2 tablespoons chives, chopped
- 2 tablespoons olive oil

Directions:
1. In the multi level air fryer's basket, mix the beets with the onion and the other ingredients except the cheese and toss.
2. Put the basket in the instant pot, seal with air fryer lid and cook on Air fry mode at 380 degrees F for 30 minutes.
3. Divide the mix between plates and serve with cheese on top.

Nutrition:
calories 140, fat 4, fiber 3, carbs 5, protein 7

Mushrooms with Potatoes and Sauce

Prep time: 5 minutes | **Cooking:** 20 minutes | **Servings:** 4

Ingredients:
- 1 pound white mushrooms, halved
- ½ pound gold potatoes, peeled and halved
- 3 scallions, chopped
- 1 cup heavy cream
- A pinch of salt and black pepper
- 1 tablespoon olive oil
- 1 tablespoon parsley, chopped
- Juice of ½ lemon

Directions:
1. In the multi level air fryer's pan, combine the mushrooms with the other ingredients and toss.
2. Put the pan in the instant pot and seal with the air fryer lid.
3. Cook on Bake mode at 380 degrees F for 20 minutes.
4. Divide everything between plates and serve.

Nutrition:
calories 170, fat 4, fiber 3, carbs 5, protein 8

Herbed Corn and Fennel

Prep time: 5 minutes | **Cooking:** 15 minutes | **Servings:** 4

Ingredients:
- 1 cup corn
- 2 fennel bulbs, sliced
- 2 tablespoons olive oil
- Juice of 1 lime
- A pinch of salt and black pepper
- 2 tablespoons cilantro, chopped
- 2 tablespoons parsley, chopped

Directions:
1. In the multi level air fryer's pan, combine the corn with the other ingredients and toss.
2. Put the pan in the instant pot and seal with the air fryer lid.
3. Cook on Bake mode at 380 degrees F for 15 minutes.
4. Divide everything between plates and serve.

Nutrition:
calories 163, fat 4, fiber 2, carbs 4, protein 7

Greens Sauté

Prep time: 5 minutes | **Cooking:** 20 minutes | **Servings:** 4

Ingredients:
- 1 pound collard greens, torn
- 1 cup black olives, pitted and halved
- 1 cup green olives, pitted and halved
- 4 scallions, chopped
- 2 tablespoons tomato paste
- 2 tablespoons olive oil
- Salt and black pepper to the taste
- ½ tablespoon chives, chopped
- ½ teaspoon coriander, ground

Directions:
1. In the multi level air fryer's pan, combine the collard greens with the other ingredients and toss.
2. Put the pan in the instant pot and seal with the air fryer lid.
3. Cook on Bake mode at 370 degrees F for 20 minutes.
4. Divide everything between plates and serve.

Nutrition:
calories 163, fat 4, fiber 3, carbs 5, protein 6

Chili Mustard Greens

Prep time: 10 minutes | **Cooking:** 20 minutes | **Servings:** 4

Ingredients:
- 1 bunch mustard greens, trimmed and torn
- 1 pound cherry tomatoes, halved
- 2 tablespoons balsamic vinegar
- 2 tablespoons olive oil
- ½ teaspoon chili powder
- 3 garlic cloves, minced
- Salt and black pepper to the taste
- 1 tablespoon chives, chopped

Directions:
1. In the multi level air fryer's pan, combine the mustard greens with the other ingredients and toss.
2. Put the pan in the instant pot and seal with the air fryer lid.
3. Cook on Bake mode at 350 degrees F for 20 minutes.
4. Divide everything between plates and serve.

Nutrition:
calories 163, fat 4, fiber 3, carbs 4, protein 7

Mint Fennel Mix

Prep time: 5 minutes | **Cooking:** 20 minutes | **Servings:** 4

Ingredients:
- 2 fennel bulbs, trimmed and sliced
- 1 cup avocado, peeled, pitted and cubed
- 1 tablespoon avocado oil
- Juice of 1 lime
- 2 tablespoons mint, chopped
- A pinch of salt and black pepper
- 1 teaspoon balsamic vinegar
- 1 teaspoon sweet paprika

Directions:
1. In the multi level air fryer's pan, combine the fennel with the other ingredients and toss.
2. Put the pan in the instant pot and seal with the air fryer lid.
3. Cook on Bake mode at 350 degrees F for 20 minutes.
4. Divide everything between plates and serve.

Nutrition:
calories 162, fat 5, fiber 3, carbs 4, protein 6

Nutmeg and Lemon Potatoes

Prep time: 5 minutes | **Cooking:** 30 minutes | **Servings:** 4

Ingredients:
- 4 gold potatoes, peeled and cut into wedges

- 1 teaspoon nutmeg, ground
- ½ cup veggie stock
- ½ teaspoon sweet paprika
- Salt and black pepper to the taste
- 1 tablespoon olive oil
- 1 tablespoon lemon juice

Directions:
1. In the multi level air fryer's pan, combine the potatoes with the other ingredients and toss.
2. Put the pan in the instant pot and seal with the air fryer lid.
3. Cook on Bake mode at 390 degrees F for 30 minutes.
4. Divide everything between plates and serve.

Nutrition:

calories 162, fat 4, fiber 3, carbs 5, protein 7

Dessert Recipes

Cocoa Cupcakes

Prep time: 5 minutes | **Cooking:** 20 minutes | **Servings:** 4

Ingredients:

- ½ cup almond flour
- ½ cup cocoa powder
- 4 tablespoons sugar
- ½ cup mango, peeled and cubed
- 1 teaspoon baking powder
- 4 eggs, whisked
- 1 teaspoon almond extract
- 4 tablespoons avocado oil
- ¼ cup almond milk
- Cooking spray

Directions:

1. In a bowl, mix the flour with the cocoa powder and the other ingredients except the cooking spray and whisk well.
2. Grease a cupcake tin that fits the multi level air fryer with the cooking spray and pour the mix inside.
3. Put the pan in your instant pot, seal with air fryer lid, cook on Bake mode at 350 degrees F for 20 minutes and serve cold.

Nutrition:

calories 103, fat 4, fiber 2, carbs 6, protein 3

Avocado Vanilla Cookies

Prep time: 5 minutes | **Cooking:** 20 minutes | **Servings:** 6

Ingredients:

- 1 cup almond flour
- 1 cup avocado, peeled, pitted and cubed
- 3 tablespoons sugar
- ½ teaspoon baking powder
- ¼ teaspoon vanilla extract
- 2 eggs, whisked

Directions:

1. In a bowl, mix the avocado with the flour and the other ingredients and toss.
2. Scoop 6 servings of this mix on the multi level air fryer's pan lined with parchment paper.
3. Put the pan in your instant pot, seal with air fryer lid and cook on Bake mode at 350 degrees F for 20 minutes.
4. Serve the cookies cold.

Nutrition:

calories 125, fat 7, fiber 1, carbs 5, protein 4

Creamy Ghee Bars

Prep time: 5 minutes | **Cooking:** 35 minutes | **Servings:** 8

Ingredients:

- 2 cups coconut flour
- 3 tablespoons sugar
- ½ cup walnuts, chopped
- 1 cup ghee, melted
- ½ cup heavy cream
- 2 eggs, whisked
- ½ teaspoon almond extract
- ½ teaspoon vanilla extract

Directions:

1. In a bowl, mix the flour with the sugar, walnuts and the other ingredients and toss.
2. Press this on the bottom of the multi level air fryer's pan lined with parchment paper.
3. Introduce this in the instant pot, seal with air fryer lid and cook on Bake mode at 350 degrees F for 35 minutes.
4. Cool down, cut into bars and serve.

Nutrition:

calories 182, fat 12, fiber 2, carbs 4, protein 4

Lime Pineapple Bars

Prep time: 10 minutes | **Cooking:** 35 minutes | **Servings:** 6

Ingredients:

- ½ cup ghee, melted
- 1 cup pineapple, peeled and chopped
- 3 tablespoons sugar
- 2 cups almond flour
- 2 eggs, whisked
- 1 tablespoon lime juice

Directions:

1. In a bowl, mix the ghee with the pineapple and the other ingredients, stir well and press into the multi level air fryer's pan.
2. Put the pan in your instant pot, seal with air fryer lid and cook on Bake mode at 350 degrees F for 35 minutes.
3. Cool down, cut into bars and serve.

Nutrition:

calories 210, fat 12, fiber 1, carbs 4, protein 8

Squash Coconut Bread

Prep time: 10 minutes | **Cooking:** 40 minutes | **Servings:** 12

Ingredients:

- 2 cups coconut flour
- 1 cup butternut squash, peeled and cubed
- 1 teaspoon baking soda
- 4 tablespoons sugar
- ½ cup butter, melted
- 1 teaspoon almond extract
- 3 eggs, whisked
- Cooking spray

Directions:

1. In a bowl, mix the flour with the squash and the other ingredients except the cooking spray and stir well.
2. Grease the multi level air fryer's pan with the cooking spray, line with parchment paper and pour the squash mix inside.
3. Put the pan in the instant pot, seal with air fryer lid and cook on Bake mode at 370 degrees F for 40 minutes.
4. Cool down, slice and serve.

Nutrition:

calories 143, fat 11, fiber 1, carbs 3, protein 3

Lemon Butter Cream

Prep time: 10 minutes | **Cooking:** 25 minutes | **Servings:** 4

Ingredients:

- 2 eggs, whisked
- 3 tablespoons sugar
- 2 cups heavy cream
- Juice and zest of 1 lemon
- 2 tablespoons butter, melted
- 1 teaspoon vanilla extract
- ½ teaspoon lemon extract
- Cooking spray

Directions:

1. In a bowl, combine the eggs with the sugar and the other ingredients except the cooking spray and stir well.
2. Grease a ramekin that fits the multi level air fryer with the cooking spray and pour the mixture inside.
3. Put the ramekin in the multi level air fryer's basket, put the basket in the instant pot, seal with air fryer lid and cook on Bake mode at 360 degrees F for 25 minutes.
4. Divide into bowls and serve.

Nutrition:

calories 212, fat 15, fiber 2, carbs 6, protein 4

Almond Berry Cake

Prep time: 5 minutes | **Cooking:** 30 minutes | **Servings:** 4

Ingredients:

- 3 eggs, whisked
- 4 tablespoons sugar
- 1 cup strawberries, sliced
- 1 and ½ cups almond flour
- 1 teaspoon almond extract
- 1 teaspoon baking powder
- ½ cup butter, melted
- Cooking spray

Directions:
1. In a bowl, mix the eggs with the sugar and the other ingredients except the cooking spray and whisk everything.
2. Grease the multi level air fryer's pan the cooking spray, and pour the strawberries mix inside
3. Put the pan in the instant pot, seal with air fryer lid and cook on Bake mode at 370 degrees F for 30 minutes.
4. Cool down, slice and serve.

Nutrition:
calories 182, fat 12, fiber 1, carbs 6, protein 5

Almond Donuts

Prep time: 5 minutes | **Cooking:** 20 minutes | **Servings:** 4

Ingredients:
- 2 cups almond flour
- 3 tablespoons sugar
- 1 egg, whisked
- 3 tablespoons butter, melted
- 1 and ½ cups almond milk
- ½ cup carrots, peeled and grated
- 1 teaspoon baking powder

Directions:
1. In a bowl, mix the flour with the sugar and the other ingredients and whisk well.
2. Shape donuts from this mix and place them in your multi level air fryer's basket.
3. Put the basket in the instant pot, seal with air fryer lid and cook on Bake mode at 370 degrees F for 20 minutes.
4. Serve them right away.

Nutrition:
calories 190, fat 12, fiber 1, carbs 4, protein 6

Coconut Cookies

Prep time: 10 minutes | **Cooking:** 20 minutes | **Servings:** 8

Ingredients:
- 2 eggs, whisked
- 1 tablespoon coconut cream
- ½ cup almonds, chopped
- 3 tablespoons sugar
- ½ cup butter, melted
- 1 teaspoon vanilla extract
- 2 cups coconut flour
- Cooking spray

Directions:
1. In a bowl, mix the eggs with the almonds, cream and the other ingredients except the cooking spray and stir well.
2. Shape 8 balls out of this mix, put them on in the multi level air fryer's pan greased with cooking spray and flatten them.
3. Put the pan in the instant pot, seal with air fryer lid, cook on Bake mode at 370 degrees F for 20 minutes and serve the cookies cold.

Nutrition:
calories 234, fat 13, fiber 2, carbs 4, protein 7

Ginger Almond Cream

Prep time: 10 minutes | **Cooking:** 15 minutes | **Servings:** 6

Ingredients:
- 2 cups almond milk
- ½ cup heavy cream
- 1 tablespoon ginger, grated
- 2 tablespoons sugar
- 1 egg, whisked
- 1 teaspoon vanilla extract
- ¼ teaspoon nutmeg, ground

Directions:
1. In a bowl, mix the almond milk with the cream and the other ingredients and whisk well.
2. Transfer this to 6 ramekins and put them in the multi level air fryer's basket.
3. Put the basket in the instant pot, seal with air fryer lid and cook on Bake mode at 360 degrees F for 15 minutes.
4. Cool down and serve.

Nutrition:
calories 220, fat 13, fiber 2, carbs 4, protein 3

Butter Berry Muffins

Prep time: 10 minutes | **Cooking:** 20 minutes | **Servings:** 4

Ingredients:
- 1 cup blueberries
- ¼ cup butter, melted
- 3 tablespoons sugar
- 2 eggs, whisked
- ¼ cup almond flour
- ½ teaspoon baking soda
- ½ teaspoon baking powder
- Cooking spray

Directions:
1. In a bowl, mix the berries with the melted butter and the other ingredients except the cooking spray and whisk well.
2. Grease a muffin pan that fits the multi level air fryer with the cooking spray, pour the muffin mix, put the pan in the instant pot, seal with air fryer lid and cook on Bake mode at 350 degrees F for 20 minutes.
3. Serve the muffins cold.

Nutrition:
calories 223, fat 7, fiber 2, carbs 4, protein 5

Lemon Apple Jam

Prep time: 10 minutes | **Cooking:** 30 minutes | **Servings:** 6

Ingredients:
- ¼ cup sugar
- 1 pound apples, peeled, cored and chopped
- 1 tablespoon lemon juice
- ½ cup water

Directions:
1. In the multi level air fryer's pan, combine the apples with the other ingredients and toss.
2. Put the pan in the instant pot and seal with the air fryer lid.
3. Cook on Bake mode at 380 degrees F for 30 minutes.
4. Divide the mix into cups, cool down and serve.

Nutrition:
calories 100, fat 1, fiber 0, carbs 1, protein 1

Vanilla Cream

Prep time: 4 minutes | **Cooking:** 20 minutes | **Servings:** 4

Ingredients:
- 2 cups strawberries, sliced
- 1 cup heavy cream
- 2 tablespoons sugar
- 1 teaspoon vanilla extract
- 1 teaspoon nutmeg, ground

Directions:
1. In a bowl, mix all the berries with the cream and the other ingredients and whisk well.
2. Divide this into 4 ramekins, put them in the multi level air fryer's basket, put the basket in the instant pot, seal with air fryer lid and cook on Bake mode at 340 degrees F for 20 minutes
3. Cool the cream down and serve.

Nutrition:
calories 123, fat 2, fiber 2, carbs 4, protein 3

Butter Cream

Prep time: 5 minutes | **Cooking:** 20 minutes | **Servings:** 4

Ingredients:
- 2 eggs, whisked
- 3 tablespoons sugar
- 3 tablespoons butter, melted
- 1 cup heavy cream

- 1 teaspoon vanilla extract

Directions:
1. In a bowl, mix the eggs with the sugar and the other ingredients and stir well.
2. Pour this into 4 ramekins, put them in the multi level air fryer's basket, put the basket in the instant pot, seal with air fryer lid and cook on Bake mode at 350 degrees F for 20 minutes.
3. Cool and serve.

Nutrition:
calories 191, fat 12, fiber 2, carbs 4, protein 6

Blackberry Jam

Prep time: 10 minutes | **Cooking:** 30 minutes | **Servings:** 10

Ingredients:
- 2 cups blackberries
- 1 cup water
- ¼ cup sugar
- 3 tablespoons lemon juice

Directions:
1. In the multi level air fryer's pan, combine the berries and the other ingredients.
2. Put the pan in the instant pot and seal with the air fryer lid.
3. Cook on Bake mode at 340 degrees F for 30 minutes.
4. Divide into cups and serve.

Nutrition:
calories 100, fat 2, fiber 1, carbs 3, protein 1

Avocado and Blueberries Cream

Prep time: 5 minutes | **Cooking:** 20 minutes | **Servings:** 6

Ingredients:
- 2 cups avocado, peeled, pitted and mashed
- 1 cup heavy cream
- 1 cup blueberries
- 3 tablespoons sugar
- 1 cup coconut cream

Directions:
1. In a bowl, mix the avocado with the cream and the other ingredients and whisk well.
2. Divide this into 6 ramekins, put them in your multi level air fryer's basket, put the basket in the instant pot, seal with air fryer lid and cook on Bake mode at 320 degrees F for 20 minutes.
3. Cool down and serve.

Nutrition:
calories 100, fat 1, fiber 1, carbs 2, protein 2

Brownies

Prep time: 10 minutes | **Cooking:** 30 minutes | **Servings:** 8

Ingredients:
- 2 tablespoons cocoa powder
- 2 eggs, whisked
- 4 tablespoons butter, melted
- 1 cup coconut flour
- ¼ teaspoon baking powder
- ½ cup almond milk
- Cooking spray

Directions:
1. Grease the multi level air fryer's pan with the cooking spray.
2. In a bowl, mix the cocoa with the eggs and the other ingredients, whisk well and pour into the pan.
3. Put the pan in your instant pot, seal with air fryer lid, cook on Bake mode at 370 degrees F for 30 minutes, cool the brownies down, slice and serve.

Nutrition:
calories 182, fat 12, fiber 2, carbs 4, protein 6

Cocoa Ghee Cream

Prep time: 10 minutes | **Cooking:** 30 minutes | **Servings:** 4

Ingredients:
- 1 cup heavy cream
- 2 eggs, whisked
- 2 tablespoons cocoa powder
- ½ teaspoon vanilla extract
- 4 tablespoons cocoa powder
- 3 tablespoons ghee, melted
- 2 tablespoons sugar

Directions:
1. In a bowl, mix the cream with the eggs and the other ingredients, whisk and divide into 4 ramekins.
2. Put them the multi level air fryer's pan, put the pan in the instant pot, seal with air fryer lid and cook on Bake mode at 350 degrees F for 30 minutes.
3. Serve the cream cold.

Nutrition:
calories 155, fat 6, fiber 2, carbs 6, protein 4

Coconut Cream

Prep time: 5 minutes | **Cooking:** 15 minutes | **Servings:** 4

Ingredients:
- 2 tablespoons ghee, melted
- 1 cup coconut, shredded
- 1 cup heavy cream
- ½ cup coconut cream
- 3 tablespoons sugar
- 3 eggs
- ½ teaspoon vanilla extract

Directions:
1. In a bowl, mix the ghee with the coconut and the other ingredients, whisk really well and divide into 4 ramekins.
2. Put them in the multi level air fryer's basket.
3. Put the basket in the instant pot, seal with air fryer lid and cook on Bake mode at 320 degrees F for 15 minutes.
4. Serve cold.

Nutrition:
calories 164, fat 4, fiber 2, carbs 5, protein 5

Carrot Cream Cheese Bars

Prep time: 10 minutes | **Cooking:** 20 minutes | **Servings:** 10

Ingredients:
- 2 tablespoons butter, melted
- 4 eggs, whisked
- 2 cups carrots, peeled and grated
- ½ cup coconut cream
- ½ cup cream cheese, soft
- ½ cup almond flour
- 2 teaspoons vanilla extract
- ½ teaspoon baking powder
- 3 tablespoons sugar

Directions:
1. In a bowl, combine the melted butter with the carrots and the other ingredients and whisk well.
2. Pour into the multi level air fryer's pan, put the pan in the instant pot, seal with air fryer lid and cook on Bake mode at 360 degrees F, bake for 20 minutes.
3. Cut into bars and serve cold.

Nutrition:
calories 178, fat 8, fiber 3, carbs 4, protein 5

Pecan Almond Bars

Prep time: 5 minutes | **Cooking:** 20 minutes | **Servings:** 4

Ingredients:
- 3 eggs, whisked
- 1 cup pecans, chopped
- 3 tablespoons sugar
- 4 tablespoons butter, melted
- 1 teaspoon almond extract
- ½ cup coconut flour
- ½ teaspoon baking soda

Directions:

1. In a bowl, mix the eggs with the pecans and the other ingredients and stir well.
2. Spread this on the multi level air fryer's pan lined with parchment paper, put it in the instant pot, seal with air fryer lid and cook on Bake mode at 330 degrees F and bake for 20 minutes.
3. Cut into bars, cool down and serve.

Nutrition:
calories 182, fat 12, fiber 1, carbs 3, protein 6

Chocolate Cream

Prep time: 5 minutes | **Cooking:** 20 minutes | **Servings:** 4

Ingredients:
- 3 eggs, whisked
- ½ cup dark chocolate, melted
- ½ cup heavy cream
- 3 tablespoons butter, melted
- 3 tablespoons sugar

Directions:
1. In a bowl, mix the chocolate with the eggs and the rest of the ingredients, whisk well, divide into ramekins, put them in the multi level air fryer's basket, put the basket in the instant pot, seal with air fryer lid and cook on Bake mode at 360 degrees F for 20 minutes.
2. Serve cold.

Nutrition:
calories 150, fat 2, fiber 2, carbs 4, protein 7

Walnut Bars

Prep time: 5 minutes | **Cooking:** 15 minutes | **Servings:** 12

Ingredients:
- 1 teaspoon almond extract
- 1 cup almond butter, soft
- ½ cup walnuts, chopped
- 3 eggs, whisked
- ¼ cup pecans, chopped
- ½ cup almond flour
- 4 tablespoons sugar

Directions:
1. In a bowl, mix the walnuts with the pecans and the other ingredients and whisk really well.
2. Spread this on the multi level air fryer's pan lined with parchment paper, introduce in the instant pot, seal with the air fryer lid and cook on Bake mode at 370 degrees F for 15 minutes.
3. Cool down, cut into bars and serve.

Nutrition:
calories 130, fat 12, fiber 1, carbs 3, protein 5

Yogurt Cream

Prep time: 5 minutes | **Cooking:** 20 minutes | **Servings:** 4

Ingredients:
- 4 eggs, whisked
- 1 teaspoon vanilla extract
- 1 cup blackberries
- 3 tablespoons sugar
- ½ cup blueberries
- 8 ounces Greek yogurt

Directions:
1. In a blender, mix the eggs with the berries and the other ingredients and pulse well.
2. Pour this into 4 ramekins, put them in the multi level air fryer's basket, put the basket in the instant pot, seal with air fryer lid and cook on Bake mode at 330 degrees F for 20 minutes.
3. Serve cold.

Nutrition:
calories 181, fat 13, fiber 2, carbs 4, protein 5

Coconut Cream Cheese Pudding

Prep time: 10 minutes | **Cooking:** 20 minutes | **Servings:** 6

Ingredients:
- 2 cups cream cheese, soft
- 2 eggs, whisked
- ½ cup heavy cream
- ¼ cup almond flour
- ½ cup coconut cream
- 1 tablespoon vanilla extract
- 4 tablespoons sugar
- 3 tablespoons cocoa powder

Directions:
1. In a bowl mix the cream cheese with the cream and the other ingredients and whisk well.
2. Divide this into 6 ramekins, put them in your multi level air fryer's basket, put the basket in the instant pot, seal with air fryer lid and cook on Bake mode at 350 degrees F for 20 minutes.
3. Serve the puddings cold.

Nutrition:
calories 200, fat 7, fiber 2, carbs 4, protein 6

Rhubarb Almond Cake

Prep time: 10 minutes | **Cooking:** 30 minutes | **Servings:** 6

Ingredients:
- 4 tablespoons butter, melted
- 2 cups almond flour
- 3 eggs, whisked
- 2 teaspoons baking powder
- 4 tablespoons sugar
- 1 cup almond milk
- 1 cup rhubarb, sliced
- ½ teaspoon vanilla extract
- ½ cup heavy cream

Directions:
1. In a bowl, mix the melted butter with the eggs and the other ingredients and whisk well.
2. Pour this into the multi level air fryer's pan lined with parchment paper, put the pan in the instant pot, seal with air fryer lid and cook on Bake mode at 360 degrees F for 30 minutes.
3. Cool the cake down, slice and serve.

Nutrition:
calories 183, fat 4, fiber 3, carbs 4, protein 7

Mango Bowls

Prep time: 5 minutes | **Cooking:** 15 minutes | **Servings:** 4

Ingredients:
- 1 cup mango, peeled and roughly cubed
- ½ teaspoon vanilla extract
- ¼ cup apple juice
- 1 cup plums, pitted and halved
- Zest of 1 lemon, grated
- 2 tablespoons sugar
- Juice of ½ lemon

Directions:
1. In the multi level air fryer's pan, combine the mango with the other ingredients and toss.
2. Put the pan in the instant pot and seal with the air fryer lid.
3. Cook on Bake mode at 360 degrees F for 15 minutes.
4. Divide everything into bowls and serve.

Nutrition:
calories 170, fat 5, fiber 1, carbs 3, protein 5

Rhubarb Coconut Cream

Prep time: 5 minutes | **Cooking:** 20 minutes | **Servings:** 4

Ingredients:
- 2 cups rhubarb, sliced
- ¼ teaspoon vanilla extract
- 2 tablespoons sugar
- 1 tablespoon lemon juice
- ½ cup heavy cream
- 1 tablespoon lemon zest, grated
- ½ cup coconut cream

Directions:
1. In a blender, combine the rhubarb with the other ingredients and pulse well.

2. Divide this into 4 ramekins, put them in the multi level air fryer's basket, put the basket in the instant pot, seal with air fryer lid and cook on Bake mode at 340 degrees F for 20 minutes.
3. Serve the cream cold.

Nutrition:
calories 171, fat 4, fiber 2, carbs 4, protein 4

Lime Almond Cake

Prep time: 10 minutes | **Cooking:** 30 minutes | **Servings:** 4

Ingredients:
- 3 eggs, whisked
- 3 tablespoons butter, melted
- 3 tablespoons sugar
- Juice of 1 lime
- Zest of 1 lime, grated
- ½ cup heavy cream
- ¼ cup almond milk
- 2 cups almond flour
- ½ teaspoon baking powder

Directions:
1. In a bowl, mix the eggs with the melted butter and the other ingredients and whisk well.
2. Pour this into the multi level air fryer's pan lined with parchment paper, put the pan in your instant pot, seal with air fryer lid and cook on Bake mode at 360 degrees F for 30 minutes.
3. Cool the cake down, slice and serve.

Nutrition:
calories 193, fat 5, fiber 1, carbs 4, protein 4

Apple Bowls

Prep time: 5 minutes | **Cooking:** 20 minutes | **Servings:** 4

Ingredients:
- 1 pound apples, cored and cut into wedges
- ½ cup heavy cream
- 3 tablespoons sugar
- 1 tablespoon butter, melted
- 1 tablespoon cinnamon powder
- 1 teaspoon vanilla extract

Directions:
1. In the multi level air fryer's pan, combine the apples with the other ingredients and toss.
2. Put the pan in the instant pot and seal with the air fryer lid.
3. Cook on Bake mode at 360 degrees F for 20 minutes.
4. Divide everything into bowls and serve.

Nutrition:
calories 162, fat 3, fiber 2, carbs 4, protein 5

Mango Compote

Prep time: 10 minutes | **Cooking:** 20 minutes | **Servings:** 4

Ingredients:
- 2 cups mango, peeled and roughly cubed
- 1 cup apple juice
- 3 tablespoons sugar
- Zest and juice of 1 lime

Directions:
1. In the multi level air fryer's pan, combine the mango with the other ingredients and toss.
2. Put the pan in the instant pot and seal with the air fryer lid.
3. Cook on Bake mode at 300 degrees F for 20 minutes.
4. Divide into bowls and serve cold.

Nutrition:
calories 176, fat 2, fiber 1, carbs 3, protein 5

Plums and Cocoa Cream

Prep time: 5 minutes | **Cooking:** 20 minutes | **Servings:** 4

Ingredients:
- 1 cup plums, pitted and chopped
- 1 cup heavy cream
- 1 tablespoon cocoa powder
- 2 tablespoons sugar
- ½ cup coconut cream

Directions:
1. In the multi level air fryer's pan, combine the plums with the other ingredients and toss.
2. Put the pan in the instant pot and seal with the air fryer lid.
3. Cook on Bake mode at 370 degrees F for 20 minutes.
4. Divide into bowls and serve cold.

Nutrition:
calories 200, fat 6, fiber 2, carbs 4, protein 5

Cocoa Bombs

Prep time: 5 minutes | **Cooking:** 10 minutes | **Servings:** 12

Ingredients:
- 2 cups coconut flesh, shredded
- 4 tablespoons butter, melted
- 1 teaspoon vanilla extract
- 1/3 cup sugar
- 3 tablespoons cocoa powder
- ¼ cup heavy cream

Directions:
1. In a bowl, mix the coconut with the melted butter and the other ingredients and whisk well.
2. Shape 12 medium balls out of this mix, place them in your multi level air fryer's basket, put the basket in the instant pot, seal with air fryer lid and cook on Air fry mode at 300 degrees F for 10 minutes.
3. Serve the bombs cold.

Nutrition:
calories 120, fat 12, fiber 1, carbs 2, protein 1

Coconut Berry Cake

Prep time: 10 minutes | **Cooking:** 30 minutes | **Servings:** 4

Ingredients:
- 2 cups raspberries
- ½ cup heavy cream
- 3 eggs, whisked
- 1 cup coconut flour
- 1 teaspoon baking soda
- 4 tablespoons sugar
- ½ teaspoon vanilla extract
- 4 tablespoons butter, melted

Directions:
1. In a bowl, mix the raspberries with the cream and the other ingredients, toss, pour this into the multi level air fryer's pan lined it with parchment paper.
2. Put the pan in the instant pot, seal with the air fryer lid and cook on Bake mode at 360 degrees F for 30 minutes.
3. Leave the cake to cool down, slice and serve.

Nutrition:
calories 193, fat 4, fiber 2, carbs 5, protein 5

Pineapple Coconut Pudding

Prep time: 10 minutes | **Cooking:** 20 minutes | **Serving:** 6

Ingredients:
- 1 cup pineapple, peeled and cubed
- 2 eggs, whisked
- 1 cup coconut milk
- ½ cup coconut cream
- 2 tablespoons sugar
- 1 teaspoon vanilla extract

Directions:
1. In a bowl, mix the pineapple with the eggs and the other ingredients, whisk well and pour into 6 ramekins.
2. Put the ramekins in the multi level air fryer's basket, put the basket in the instant pot, seal with air fryer lid and cook on Bake mode at 350 degrees F for 20 minutes.
3. Serve the pudding cold.

Nutrition: calories 192, fat 8, fiber 2, carbs 5, protein 4

Berry Compote

Prep time: 5 minutes | **Cooking:** 15 minutes | **Servings:** 4

Ingredients:

- ½ cup blueberries
- ½ cup blackberries
- ½ cup strawberries, halved
- 1 cup water
- 4 tablespoons sugar
- Juice of 1 lime
- Zest of 1 lime, grated

Directions:

1. In the multi level air fryer's pan, combine the berries with the other ingredients and toss.
2. Put the pan in the instant pot and seal with the air fryer lid.
3. Cook on Bake mode at 340 degrees F for 15 minutes.
4. Divide into bowls and serve.

Nutrition: calories 173, fat 3, fiber 1, carbs 4, protein 4

Lime Strawberry Compote

Prep time: 10 minutes | **Cooking:** 15 minutes | **Servings:** 4

Ingredients:

- 1 pound strawberries, halved
- 1 cup water
- 3 tablespoons sugar
- ½ teaspoon ginger, ground
- ½ teaspoon vanilla extract
- 1 tablespoon lime juice

Directions:

1. In the multi level air fryer's pan, combine the strawberries with the other ingredients and toss.
2. Put the pan in the instant pot and seal with the air fryer lid.
3. Cook on Bake mode at 350 degrees F for 15 minutes.
4. Divide into bowls and serve.

Nutrition: calories 200, fat 6, fiber 2, carbs 4, protein 6

Pineapple and Coconut Cake

Prep time: 5 minutes | **Cooking:** 35 minutes | **Servings:** 6

Ingredients:

- 2 tablespoons butter, melted
- 1 cup pineapple, peeled and chopped
- 2 eggs, whisked
- 1 cup coconut flour
- ½ cup heavy cream
- 3 tablespoons sugar
- 1 teaspoon vanilla extract

Directions:

1. In a bowl, mix the melted butter with the pineapple and the other ingredients and stir well.
2. Pour this into the multi level air fryer's pan lined with parchment paper, place the pan in the instant pot, seal with the air fryer lid and cook on Bake mode at 350 degrees F for 35 minutes.
3. Cool the cake down, slice and serve.

Nutrition: calories 192, fat 4, fiber 2, carbs 5, protein 7

Chia Pudding

Prep time: 10 minutes | **Cooking:** 25 minutes | **Servings:** 6

Ingredients:

- 1 cup white rice
- 3 tablespoons chia seeds
- 2 cups almond milk
- 3 tablespoons sugar
- 1 teaspoon vanilla extract
- 1 tablespoon cinnamon powder

Directions:

1. In the multi level air fryer's pan, combine the chia seeds with the other ingredients and toss.
2. Put the pan in the instant pot and seal with the air fryer lid.
3. Cook on Bake mode at 340 degrees F for 25 minutes.
4. Divide into bowls and serve.

Nutrition: calories 180, fat 4, fiber 2 carbs 5, protein 7

Plum and Coconut Cream

Prep time: 5 minutes | **Cooking:** 20 minutes | **Servings:** 4

Ingredients:

- 1 cup plums, pitted and chopped
- 1 cup mango, peeled and chopped
- 1 cup coconut cream
- 1 cup heavy cream
- 3 tablespoons sugar
- 2 tablespoons butter, melted

Directions:

1. In a blender, mix the plums with the mango and the other ingredients, pulse, divide into 4 ramekins, put them in the multi level air fryer's basket, put the basket in the instant pot, seal with air fryer lid, and cook on Bake mode at 340 degrees F for 20 minutes.
2. Cool down and serve.

Nutrition: calories 221, fat 4, fiber 1, carbs 3, protein 3

Pineapple Stew

Prep time: 5 minutes | **Cooking:** 8 minutes | **Servings:** 4

Ingredients:

- 1 cup avocado, peeled, pitted and cubed
- 1 cup pineapple, peeled and roughly cubed
- 1 cup water
- 4 tablespoons sugar
- ½ teaspoon vanilla extract
- Juice of 1 lime

Directions:

1. In the multi level air fryer's pan, combine the pineapple with the other ingredients and toss.
2. Put the pan in the instant pot and seal with the air fryer lid.
3. Cook on Bake mode at 320 degrees F for 8 minutes.
4. Divide into bowls and serve.

Nutrition: calories 170, fat 3, fiber 2, carbs 4, protein 3

Dates Bowls

Prep time: 5 minutes | **Cooking:** 20 minutes | **Servings:** 4

Ingredients:

- 1 cup dates, chopped
- ½ pound plums, pitted and halved
- 1 cup coconut cream
- 3 tablespoons sugar
- ½ teaspoon almond extract

Directions:

1. In the multi level air fryer's pan, combine the dates with the other ingredients and toss.
2. Put the pan in the instant pot and seal with the air fryer lid.
3. Cook on Bake mode at 330 degrees F for 20 minutes.
4. Divide into bowls and serve cold.

Nutrition: calories 171, fat 4, fiber 2, carbs 3, protein 6

Rice Bowls

Prep time: 5 minutes | **Cooking:** 25 minutes | **Servings:** 4

Ingredients:

- 1 cup white rice
- 1/3 cup dates, chopped
- 2 cups almond milk
- 3 tablespoons sugar
- 1 cup coconut cream

Directions:
1. In the multi level air fryer's pan, combine the rice with the other ingredients and toss.
2. Put the pan in the instant pot and seal with the air fryer lid.
3. Cook on Bake mode at 340 degrees F for 25 minutes.
4. Divide everything into bowls and serve.

Nutrition:
calories 200, fat 4, fiber 2, carbs 4, protein 6

Dates Butter Bars

Prep time: 5 minutes | **Cooking:** 30 minutes | **Servings:** 8

Ingredients:
- 1 and ½ cups almond flour
- ½ cup dates, chopped
- 4 tablespoons butter, melted
- 2 teaspoons baking soda
- 3 tablespoons sugar
- 1 teaspoon vanilla extract

Directions:
1. In a bowl, mix the flour with the dates and the other ingredients and whisk well.
2. Spread this in the multi level air fryer's pan lined with parchment paper, put the pan in the instant pot, seal with air fryer lid and cook on Bake mode at 370 degrees F for 30 minutes.
3. Cool down, cut into bars and serve.

Nutrition:
calories 172, fat 5, fiber 2, carbs 3, protein 5

Coconut Rice Pudding

Prep time: 5 minutes | **Cooking:** 25 minutes | **Servings:** 4

Ingredients:
- 1 cup white rice
- 1 teaspoon vanilla extract
- Zest of 1 lime, grated
- 2 cups almond milk
- ½ cup coconut cream

Directions:
1. In the multi level air fryer's pan, combine the rice with the other ingredients and toss.
2. Put the pan in the instant pot and seal with the air fryer lid.
3. Cook on Bake mode at 360 degrees F for 25 minutes.
4. Divide everything into bowls and serve.

Nutrition:
calories 211, fat 5, fiber 2, carbs 4, protein 7

Avocado Bowls

Prep time: 10 minutes | **Cooking:** 10 minutes | **Servings:** 4

Ingredients:
- 1 cup coconut cream
- 1 cup avocado, peeled, pitted and roughly cubed
- Juice and zest of ½ lemon
- 2 tablespoons sugar
- 1 teaspoon ginger, ground

Directions:
1. In the multi level air fryer's pan, combine the avocado with the other ingredients and toss.
2. Put the pan in the instant pot and seal with the air fryer lid.
3. Cook on Bake mode at 350 degrees F for 10 minutes.
4. Divide everything into bowls and serve cold.

Nutrition:
calories 121, fat 5, fiber 1, carbs 4, protein 2

Cinnamon Apple Cake

Prep time: 10 minutes | **Cooking:** 25 minutes | **Servings:** 4

Ingredients:
- 1 cup apples, cored, peeled and chopped
- 1 cup heavy cream
- 1 cup almond flour
- 2 tablespoons sugar
- 1 teaspoon cinnamon powder
- 2 eggs, whisked
- ¼ teaspoon vanilla extract
- Cooking spray

Directions:
1. In bowl, combine the apples with the cream and the other ingredients except the cooking spray and whisk really well.
2. Pour into the multi level air fryer's pan greased with cooking spray, put it in the instant pot, seal with air fryer lid and cook on Bake mode at 370 degrees F for 26 minutes.
3. Cool down, slice and serve.

Nutrition:
calories 161, fat 12, fiber 1, carbs 4, protein 7

Cinnamon Cream

Prep time: 5 minutes | **Cooking:** 25 minutes | **Servings:** 4

Ingredients:
- 4 tablespoons butter, melted
- 1 cup heavy cream
- ½ cup coconut cream
- 3 tablespoons sugar
- ¼ cup brewed espresso
- 1 teaspoon cinnamon powder
- 2 eggs, whisked

Directions:
1. In a bowl, mix the melted butter with the cream and the other ingredients and whisk well.
2. Divide into 4 ramekins, put them in the multi level air fryer's basket, put the basket in the instant pot, seal with air fryer lid and cook on Bake mode at 350 degrees F for 25 minutes.
3. Serve cream cold.

Nutrition:
calories 134, fat 12, fiber 2, carbs 4, protein 2

Cheesy Mango Mix

Prep time: 5 minutes | **Cooking:** 20 minutes | **Servings:** 4

Ingredients:
- 1 cup ricotta, soft
- 1 cup mango, peeled and cubed
- 3 tablespoons sugar
- 1 cup heavy cream
- 1 teaspoon vanilla extract

Directions:
1. In the multi level air fryer's pan, combine the mango with the other ingredients and toss.
2. Put the pan in the instant pot and seal with the air fryer lid.
3. Cook on Bake mode at 350 degrees F for 20 minutes.
4. Divide into bowls and serve.

Nutrition:
calories 210, fat 12, fiber 3, carbs 6, protein 9

Cherries and Mango Mix

Prep time: 5 minutes | **Cooking:** 15 minutes | **Servings:** 4

Ingredients:
- 2 cups cherries, pitted and halved
- 2 tablespoons coconut oil, melted
- 1 cup heavy cream
- 2 tablespoons sugar
- 1 cup mango, peeled and cubed
- 1 teaspoon vanilla extract

Directions:
1. In the multi level air fryer's pan, combine the cherries with the

other ingredients and toss.
2. Put the pan in the instant pot and seal with the air fryer lid.
3. Cook on Bake mode at 340 degrees F for 15 minutes.
4. Divide everything into bowls and serve cold.

Nutrition:

calories 162, fat 5, fiber 3, carbs 5, protein 6

Made in the USA
Middletown, DE
07 December 2020